TEACHING URBAN YOUTH

A Source Book for Urban Education

TEACHING
URBAN YOUTH

A Source Book for Urban Education

Editors

PETER G. KONTOS

Senior Staff, Office of Educational Programs
Princeton University

JAMES J. MURPHY

Chairman, Department of Rhetoric
University of California, Davis, California

John Wiley & Sons, Inc.
New York, London, Sydney

*To Cecille
and Cathleen*

Contents

PART FOUR
Essays in Urban Education

PART FIVE
*An Evaluation of Teaching Practices and Teacher
Training*

Appendix

Acknowledgements

Twelve weeks, indeed twelve months is to short a period when one attempts to define, evaluate and develop techniques for strengthening the skills of teachers of urban youth. In order to be at all successful it becomes necessary to develop a program with a spirit of cooperation that will not slow down any aspect of a training program. The Princeton-Trenton Institute had this cooperation and could not have functioned as efficiently had it not been for the able support of the United States Offices of Education, Economic Opportunity and their program and budget directors, a fine and able staff drawn from many parts of the United States, and the strong backing of both the University and the Trenton, New Jersey, Public Schools. Their help in making the Princeton-Trenton Institute a success made this book possible.

Special thanks must go to Parker Coddington, Executive Director of the Princeton University Office of Educational Programs, Professor Heinrich L. Holland, Faculty Director of Summer Studies, for Princeton University, Mrs. Rice Goldstein, Dr. Richard Beck, Superintendent of Trenton Schools, and Dr. Sarah Christie, Deputy Superintendent of Schools in Trenton, whose special efforts made an idea reality.

Much also is indebted to Mrs. Beverly G. Morris, Miss Regina Morris, Miss Bertha Friedberg, Mrs. Mary Struble and Mr. Charles Winthrop for their most able clerical assistance.

TEACHING URBAN YOUTH

A Source Book for Urban Education

PART ONE

The Philosophy of the Princeton-Trenton Institutes

1. The Philosophy of the Princeton-Trenton Institutes

PETER G. KONTOS and JAMES J. MURPHY

In the summer of 1965 and 1966 Princeton University sponsored two six-week Institutes for "Teachers of the Disadvantaged."

Although some minor administrative details were changed for the second year, the basic philosophy remained the same for both sessions. Both the Institutes were a part of Princeton University's continuing efforts to make a contribution toward the educational advancement of high school students who might otherwise have little chance to realize their potential.

There are many definitions of "disadvantaged," but most people now agree that mere economic poverty is only a part of the problem. The psychology of poverty with its desperate hostilities and sullen withdrawals is a fact of life for all too many young Americans. An episode with ten such boys is indicative of the problems.

They sat around a tight circle with an adult counselor. All ten had been silent for several minutes, thinking about the counselor's question. He had asked them what job they would like if they could choose any job—regardless of their qualifications.

Curtis flicked an imaginary piece of lint from his sharply creased trousers. "Well, like man," said Curtis, "if I could do anything, like anything, I would like to be in some kind of destruction business. I mean like tearing things down."

James J. Murphy, Director of the 1965 Princeton-Trenton Institute, was at that time a member of the Princeton University Department of English: he is now Chairman of the Department of Rhetoric at the University of California at Davis.

Peter G. Kontos, Director of the 1966 Princeton-Trenton Institute, served as Coordinating Teacher of Social Studies in the 1965 Institute while Coordinator of Instruction in the Cleveland Public Schools and the Community Action for Youth Program. He is now Director of the Princeton Cooperative Schools Program at Princeton University.

◀ *Photo credit:* **Ken Heyman**

Seven of the boys agreed with Curtis. They wanted to do some kind of tearing down. Two of the boys disagreed. One thought he would like to be a stock boy—"to put things in boxes, to line them up straight." The last boy wanted to be an architect. The others laughed and said, "Yeah, man, you build them and we'll tear them down."

These are representatives of America's teenagers who have been educationally crippled and who represent what is now euphemistically called "disadvantaged youth." These ten boys were part of 1500 others in a high school demonstration program in the Hough area in Cleveland. They were children from one of the highest crime-rate areas in the United States, and also one of the poorest districts nationally. These ten boys had all been adjudicated delinquents. They were at least 16½ years old, but not one had yet completed the eighth grade. The counseling session was the last attempt to save them from becoming drop-outs. They had not been successful in school, nor did they have much hope that they ever would be.

The area of which these boys are products is typical of large cities in the United States. The statistics for these urban pockets of poverty are typical nationally. In the Hough area in Cleveland, for example, 75,000 people are crammed into 2½ square miles. The population of that area rose by 10,000 in an eight-year period, yet not one new building was built. Several were torn down. One-third of the children in school did not have fathers in the home. Hundreds of youngsters over 16 years of age in this small geographical area qualified for aid in the schools' Neighborhood Youth Corps program. This meant that their families had incomes of less than $3000 per year. Seventy-seven percent of the drop-outs from the area's high school were found to be unemployable and unemployed, and 66 percent of the high school graduates from this area also fitted the same category. A feeling of hopelessness had developed. It did not take much to realize that it did not matter whether or not one graduated from high school. The odds were generally against his being employed.

In the area's high school, over seven percent of the children were reading below the fourth-grade level. Over 40 percent of the tenth graders were reading below a seventh-grade level. The average age of the children in the school was a year and a half older than it should have been. Over one-third of all the students failed at least one course every semester. School failures here were the rule rather than the exception. With this environmental framework, it is not difficult to understand the negative and destructive outlook that eight of the ten boys expressed. More remarkable is the fact that one of the boys wanted to be an architect, and another would content himself with stacking boxes in neat rows.

These boys happen to live in Cleveland, but their problems are not unique. Trenton, New Jersey, has a population of 114,000 living in an area of 7.2 square miles. The 1960 census figures reveal a Negro population of about 25 percent (there is reason to believe that this figure is higher today—58 percent of Trenton's school children are Negro), and a family income of $3000 or less for 4600 of the 27,000 families living in Trenton at that time. Poverty and near-poverty were found to be fairly evenly distributed throughout this geographically compact city and thus every one of its 700 public school teachers may be aptly described as a teacher of disadvantaged youth. The degree of educational impoverishment in Trenton is suggested by the finding, again of the 1960 census, that of the 71,000 men and women 25 years of age or more, 17,806 had completed six years of school or less.

The total population of Newark in 1960 was 405,220 and over 19 percent of its families received incomes that year of $3000 or less. In the same year 14.4 percent of Burlington's families were similarly impoverished. Although poverty is not as evenly distributed through these cities as it is in Trenton, those teachers were significant obligations to disadvantaged youth are readily identifiable for purposes of providing special training or support.

As for educational impoverishment, in both Burlington and Newark, as in Trenton, many of the schools' problems are at least the indirect consequence of the cities' large populations of only partially educated adults. In Newark, 53,514 adults (25 years old or more) had completed six years of schooling or less, and in Burlington County over 12 percent of the same age group was similarly deficient in schooling (1960 census data; no education statistics available for the city of Burlington alone). The children of these, in most cases, functionally illiterate adults are students in the cities' elementary and secondary schools today. If these children are to achieve through education a place of worth and consequence in our society, their teachers must be prepared in extraordinary ways to support them. Standard educational strategies have proven as ineffective in breaking the vicious cycle of educational deprivation as have conventional economics in breaking the vicious cycle of material deprivation.

These boys are what educators are now calling products of the psychology of poverty. This condition does not develop full-blown. It begins early in life.

Children raised in inner cities of concrete, asphalt, and steel live in a whirling collage of noise, confusion, and filth. Surrounded by sounds, they do not learn to distinguish between that which is relevant and that which is noise. In school, teachers speak to children who do not hear. The inner-city child's world is colored in shades of gray and black. Adults rarely speak to them about differences in color, or shapes and sizes. The children daily see blank walls and play with household utensils. Toys are luxuries. Their teachers find that concepts such as color, size, and spatial relationships are incomprehensible to them. They do not see the world advantaged children know. Understanding concepts of color and size is an important step toward knowing that written words are a symbolic system. They begin to fail reading on the first day of school. Too many teachers help them to fail.

Many inner-city children, beginning life in deprivation, grow into adults who live only for the present and feel that they are not in control of their lives. Too much of their lives depends on institutions. These agencies structure their futures and have decided their past. The poor therefore live for the present and feel that they can decide little else. Watch the faces of the poor as they stand in line (the poor seem always to be standing in lines) as they wait for unemployment money, relief checks, or food stamps. They are not happy waiting for relief. They are resigned to it and feel that once again someone else has made decisions for them.

The Hostile School

The most widespread and dramatic confrontation between the poor and social institutions takes place in the schools. For many students, the school is just as hostile and frustrating an environment as are their neighborhoods. Fear, ignorance, and deprivation feed on each other; the individual becomes entrapped by lack of skills, lack of education, lack of opportunity, and, finally, lack of hope. For many teachers, an assignment to teach in a slum school is tantamount to an assignment to limbo. The challenge of teaching and the satisfaction of accomplishment are lost in the daily battle to maintain a tenuous and often precarious *status quo*. Lost, too, as a consequence, are their hopes for their students who do so badly need their help and their hope.

Recently the plight of the poor and the state of public education has been reported widely and documented extensively. All manner of organizations, both national and local, are supplying funds and advice. Indeed, concern for the poor has now, in fact, become quite fashionable. But the combined efforts in education of federal, state, and private agencies will have little if any effect on children if their teacher, through whom these resources are funneled, is either ill-equipped or not competent to make use of the new resources. The critical agent for breaking the vicious cycle of poverty that children are victims of is the teacher. But teachers are not being trained to meet the needs of large-city school children. Basically, teacher training institutions are oriented toward an academic, traditional school setting. Teacher training patterns do not emphasize the needs of urban youth and new strategies for their teachers.

Princeton University initiated a summer program in 1964 dealing with 40 high school sophomore boys who seemed capable of leadership, but whose family or neighborhood environment made it unlikely that they would be able to realize their potential. This Princeton Summer Studies Program (PSSP), operated with the help of funds from the Rockefeller Foundation, has continued with 80 more boys during 1965 and 1966. Indicative of the success of the program is the fact that of the first 40 boys in PSSP, 34 are now attending college—several on academic scholarships. This project (now known as the Princeton Cooperative Schools Program), marked the University's first formal entry into the area of secondary education.

Yet it was evident that the University could touch only a small corner of the problem through direct involvement with individual students, no matter how valuable the special approach might be.

Therefore a new kind of approach was begun in 1965, dealing directly with teachers facing the everyday facts of classroom life. Professor James J. Murphy of the Department of English was named director of the new program, and the U.S. Office of Economic Opportunity provided a grant for operation of what came to be known as the Princeton University-Trenton Schools Institute (PTI). Unlike most summer institutes for teachers, PTI concentrated its first efforts on working with one school district to seek the maximum impact.

Working closely with the Trenton Public Schools Administration, the Institute staff developed a training program for 40 Trenton teachers which called for a mixture of the theoretical and practical aspects of the educational process. A morning summer school was established for 150 Trenton ninth- and tenth-graders at Trenton Central High School. Three subjects, English, social studies, and science, were taught by a group of master secondary school teachers. The participating teachers observed and, in many instances, participated in these demonstration classes. Afternoons were devoted to critique sessions with the staff and participating teachers, and a series of lectures by outstanding Princeton authorities in the field of urban education. This was the over-all structure of the Institute and in itself should not generate a great deal of excitement. The heart and flavor of the institute was not in its organization. It developed through an interplay of ideas, staff, participants, and teenagers. Here was a genuine air of charged excitement and innovative fervor.

A constant dialogue was established between staff, participants, and students. Glib or general answers were not acceptable substitutes for the hard realities which teachers had to face in their classrooms. Students suddenly realized the power of a serious question and the joy of learning how to begin to answer it.

A Typical Argument

An example of a participant's pressing for a solid answer occurred when one of the demonstration teachers tried to sidestep with theory a participant's question. The participant asked, "Why didn't you tell your students what a revolution was when they asked you this morning?"

The master teacher said, "You're an art teacher, aren't you?"

"Yes."

"How many of your brush strokes are on your students' canvases?"

"Why, none. It wouldn't be their work if I did that."

"That's why I didn't tell them the answer. It wouldn't be theirs. I want them each to paint their own canvas of ideas. A teacher should stimulate his students to find out for themselves."

The teacher said, "That's great theory. Show me how."

The master teacher went on, lost in philosophical contemplation, ignoring the last sentence. "After all, authorities differ on the nature of a revolution. It wouldn't be fair to the student to let him think that there is only one answer."

"That's fine, but show me how."

"And doesn't a teacher bring to a classroom a very narrow point of view, his own experience? Why not expand the child's experience?"

"Great, but show me how. I mean, do it in your class."

The master teacher knew what the participant meant and had tried to avoid a direct demonstration. He tried to do what he had theorized the next day while the participant observed. What is important, however, was not whether the educational theory could be applied (it was, but only partially; theory in education is much more reasonable than reality), but rather that theory and authority were challenged and tested. The participating teacher had started questioning where earlier he had blindly accepted. This teacher was beginning to think very seriously about his craft—teaching.

Much of what was learned about teaching urban youth was demonstrated in the classroom with the students. Here many of the participating teachers got a new look at what the inner-city Trenton children could do when challenged and encouraged by truly expert teaching. Children who had been considered "unteachable" suddenly were heard to remark after reading and discussing poetry, "Gee, that was fun." Insights not usually associated with many junior high school students became quite common. Verna Dozier of Washington, D.C., who demonstrated the teaching of poetry, reported, "A boy had chosen 'Song to the Men of England.' He had read it well, and with feeling discussed Shelley's call to revolution. When he had finished a girl asked, 'If the country had treated the people so badly, why didn't they go to another country?' The boy returned almost angrily, 'You don't want to leave your country. You just want to make it better.' At another time three or four boys got into an argument about the age of the man in the poem 'Acquainted with the Night.' One young fellow insisted that he was young because 'you'd get yourself together as you grew older,' and a thin lad returned "Down on Willow Street, there're lots of old men walking like this every night. They ain't never made it.' "

Student-Teacher Dialogue

The students also started expressing concern with the kind of teacher they wanted in a self-prescription that made a lot of sense. Lawana Trout, a demonstration teacher of English, at one point encouraged her class to describe what they considered an ideal teacher. She purposely assumed the role of the devil's advocate to spark discussion. Mrs. Trout included some typical excerpts in her description of classes in Part II, Chapter 2.

In a reading class the pupils expressed their disdain for teaching by machine by deciding that some of the answers the machine was giving were wrong. The pupils energetically presented their reasons. Their teacher listened carefully and decided that the pupils were correct. The incident became an occasion for a small celebration as these teenagers successfully asserted their humanity and individuality at least once over machines in a world where mechanization is determining more and more of man's fate.

Children in the science classes were taught a course entitled, "Time,

Space, and Matter." This science course, which was developed by the University, consisted of a series of interrelated sequential investigations, structured toward the student's discovering, through direct observation and inference, something of the nature and history of the physical world around him. Students started asking whether scientific conclusions were interpretations or observations. Interestingly, this same questioning attitude spilled over into the English and social studies classes, as pupils started applying the beginnings of a scientific method to other aspects of their lives.

Greatly encouraged by the success of the 1965 institute, it was decided to extend and build directly upon these experiences. PTI applied for and was awarded a grant from the Office of Education under the National Defense Education Act. Peter G. Kontos of Princeton's Office of Educational Programs was named director. Both institutes were based on the idea that an increase in the competence of a relatively large number of teachers, from a single urban school system, in subject matter and relevant teaching skills can make a significant impact on teaching in that system. The number of participating teachers and students was increased for the 1966 PTI. A close working relationship was also established with the public schools in Newark and Burlington, in addition to the continuing relationship with Trenton. PTI selected 69 teachers from Trenton, Newark, and Burlington, and established a morning summer school for over 200 Trenton youngsters.

The 1966 Institute continued the basic practices begun in 1965: a morning summer high school with teaching based on response-centered inductive methods; a variety of learning experiences for the students, with ample opportunity in the afternoon for the participating teachers to comment and discuss—in short, to work themselves into a response-centered learning situation analogous to that of the summer high school itself. The visiting lecturer-consultants worked in the same vein, encouraging response as a first step to learning. With both students and teachers, it was clear that *attitude* was far more important than *method*. Time and time again, as can be seen in reports throughout this book, new awakenings occurred in classrooms or seminars. The two most common reactions in both Institutes were these:

A *teacher:* "I didn't think these kids could learn that way."

A *student:* "Why can't our other schools be like this?"

There is no one "best" way to teach urban youth. No one has yet written *the* manual for effective teaching. Probably no one ever will. Teaching must be demonstrated, it must be viewed, and a teacher should do both during a relatively short period of time to appreciate and work toward an understanding of the art of teaching. Herein lies the strength and justification of the Institute. It is a laboratory for teaching practices. It is a place where the feel and the indefinables of teaching are shared and expressed as a common creative experience.

This book is presented, then, as an inductive collection of ideas for the reader—a sourcebook for teachers of urban youth.

PART TWO

The English-Social Studies Program

1. Objectives of the English-Social Studies Program

CHARLOTTE K. BROOKS

> "My motto: As I live and learn
> To dig and be dug in return."

These words from a poem by Langston Hughes epitomize the goals of every teacher of English and social studies in the Princeton-Trenton Institutes of 1965 and 1966. To understand and to be fully understood by all—to communicate freely in a democratic society—was emphasized by the six coordinating teachers who worked with students and participating teachers through five weeks of a long, hot, but infinitely rewarding, summer.

No student will "live" in this world unless he can learn to listen, speak, read, and write effectively, and these cummunicative skills must be allied with a real understanding of the history and geography of this and other lands. The threads that run through literature are found in history as well; the language of a people is allied to the geography of the land; the truths and concepts found in one place and in one body of knowledge are found also in other places and at other times.

This report on the English-social studies portion of the Institute will supply no pat answers to questions about the right ways of dealing with disadvantaged youth and their teachers; it will not even insist that the right questions have been asked. It will maintain, however, that some questions must be asked and that answers must be sought.

Whether or not they are right, these are some of the questions I was forced to consider carefully before I could begin to plan this part of the Institute.

Charlotte K. Brooks, supervisor of the English-Social Studies Program for both the 1965 and 1966 Institutes, presents the philosophy of inductive discovery underlying the varied approaches in that program. Mrs. Brooks is Supervising Director of the Department of English for Washington, D.C., public schools.

◀ *Photo credit:* **Ken Heyman**

How can the disadvantaged be identified?

Are we to include the economically and culturally deprived only, or will the culturally different be involved also? How does one differentiate among these groups? Is such differentiation necessary?

What are some of the approaches, methods, and materials that can be useful in an English-social studies program for teachers of disadvantaged youth and for the students themselves?

Before leaving the matter of questions and proceeding to possible answers, it must be stated that an inductive process, the method of inquiry or discovery in which the questioning techniques are of primary importance, became an important factor quite early in the planning and remained throughout one of the major threads connecting the apparently disparate methods used in teaching English and social studies in the Institute. A little later it became equally clear that the same thread connected the total English-social studies program with the Institute's science-mathematics program.

Most of the planning time was spent in a careful consideration of possible answers to the third question. This pragmatic approach was made necessary because of limitations in time, personnel, and material. So little private or federal money has been allocated for English and social studies that it became critical for a decision to be made immediately about what had to be done and how to do it.

My first assumption was that the group of students would not be homogeneous. I have never been fortunate enough to teach—or even to observe—a homogeneous group of any kind. There would be some economically disadvantaged students, I was sure. Among these would be fast, average, and slow learners. There would probably be some middle-class students, I thought, because lack of time precluded careful screening, and the prestige involved with Princeton would engage the interest of some teachers, students, and parents. They might even be convinced that some disadvantage was implicit in their usual failure to associate with the economically or culturally deprived.

A second assumption was that the teachers—for whom the Institute was really intended—would also be a mixed lot. There would be some well prepared and some poorly prepared individuals; there would be some rigidity and some flexibility. I expected little knowledge about what we were going to attempt and, to be honest, this expectation was firmly grounded in my own lack of knowledge about what to expect.

My third and, for the purpose of this report, last assumption was that staff members, coordinating and participating teachers, and high

school students would share a lively and exploratory summer of inquiry and discovery. All of us could certainly learn a great deal from
the science-mathematics part of the curriculum which illogically has
preceded English and social studies in gaining the interest and attention of those federal and private agencies with money to spend on
education. At a meeting in the spring at Princeton I had been given
material concerning this program, and was sure that a similar approach was possible in English and social studies.

These three assumptions influenced the attitude with which I began
to shape the program for the Institute. My own educational philosophy was influential here also. Since there is no place in this report
for an elucidation of a total philosophy, I shall confine myself to
that portion which has some bearing on working with teachers of
the disadvantaged and with the students themselves.

My philosophy? Poverty *alone* has little or nothing to do with cultural deprivation, except as it prevents access to books, plays, music,
art, and the leisure to engage in cultural pursuits. Many economically
impoverished persons have always taken full advantage of public
libraries, free concerts, and other such activities. Differences in race,
religion, and national origin *alone* do not result in cultural deprivation.
Negroes, American Indians, immigrants who do not, or whose parents
do not, speak English, persons from rural areas who must learn to
live in cities, speakers of urban or rural dialect, and people from
the so-called "lower classes" who have values and ideas that are not
middle class—not one of these is necessarily culturally deprived. Each
one comes from a different culture and, unfortunately for America,
he quickly becomes disadvantaged when he is not accepted by whatever the prevailing culture of the region happens to be.

Is this splitting hairs? Perhaps, but if methods, materials, and personnel are to be developed for the disadvantaged, these factors must
be considered. Any American from New Jersey might well be culturally different in England and in Mississippi—and thus
disadvantaged.

Implicit in my assumptions that teachers and students would be
heterogeneous groups was the feeling that some would be disadvantaged in the sense indicated in the portion of my philosophy just
cited. A program, then, must be planned that would provide for differences in backgrounds, goals, values, and education of teachers and
students, and that would permit the kind of summer envisioned in
the third assumption, that is, a lively and exploratory summer of
inquiry and discovery.

What would be most helpful for such teachers and students? Each one must be accepted and treated as a worthwhile human being with a contribution to make and each must be aided in the discovery of the nature of those concepts so often glibly mouthed or passed over in English and social studies. Questions must be asked and answers must be sought—and perhaps not found. What is the nature of language? Is one dialect better than another? How does a poem mean? Is there a difference between listening and hearing? What is justice? Is freedom defined in the same way by everyone?

Could we have one curriculum for everyone involved? No such curriculum in English or social studies was immediately available for the ninth and tenth grades we would be reaching in 1966. Listening, reading, writing, speaking, literature, and many aspects of social studies must be included.

Why not concentrate upon reading skills alone? Too many people equate disadvantaged students with slow or mentally retarded ones. We might lose some students with such an emphasis. On the other hand, some consideration must be given to these essential skills, since it is true that poor reading is sometimes a result as well as a cause of disadvantage. A new and content-oriented approach might help, with consultants carefully selected to push the "all teachers are teachers of reading" point of view.

What about standard speech and usage? This is one of the biggest problems in working with the disadvantaged, especially with those who are culturally different in the ways discussed earlier. Often the "different" language alienates and confuses the teacher. Drill in grammar and speech does not help when the basic approach is a rejecting one. A teacher with a knowledge of linguistics would help here where a consideration of the nature of language, its history and geography, and its dialects would certainly engage the interest of students—and perhaps of teachers. Consultants and material in the resource room might trigger additional study, and perhaps new attitudes.

Personnel and material would be critical. How could selections be made in such a short time? It became necessary to select persons who shared a common philosophy, although methods and materials might differ, and it was essential that, after selection, these persons be used most effectively. Accordingly, on the basis of the assumptions, philosophy, and the many questions that had been raised, I could make decisions about areas and persons.

Since the 1965 Institute schedule was slightly different from that of 1966—although the objectives were the same—it is probably best to describe it first. The six coordinating teachers for 1965 were chosen early in the spring.

Although general subject areas were outlined, at no time were these staff members told what to teach. Our dialogue began in March with correspondence, telephone conversations, and two meetings. Tentative plans were made, and very early I began to see that a compromise had to be made if our program were to fit into the pattern of the already determined science-mathematics plan. We had no one curriculum, already studied and used by the teachers who were to work in the Institute. We had no time to decide upon a curriculum nor had we a place to prepare, practice, and polish it. Accordingly, although we preferred teaming permanently with the science-mathematics staff, retaining the same participating teachers and students for the duration of the Institute, I decided to try rotation.

The rationale for rotation was relatively simple. Given the assumptions, philosophy, and the kind of program needed, it was necessary to devise the best way of insuring the exposure of every student and teacher to a number of possible approaches to the teaching of English and social studies to disadvantaged youth. Although continuity is important in teaching, and rapport must be developed over a period of time, in this special situation a decision had to be made quickly.

Since without an agreed upon curriculum there would not necessarily be continuity even if each group of students and participating teachers remained with one coordinating teacher, and since each was operating within a special sphere, rotation among the teachers seemed feasible. Also, since each group of students and participating teachers would remain together, and a degree of continuity and rapport could thus be provided, the compromise seemed reasonable. The group would be together in the science-mathematics program for the duration of the Institute, and this would provide not only stability but also a chance to study the effect of the obviously desirable team stability as opposed to our reluctantly accepted compromise of rotation. Finally, the plan began to seem, under the circumstances, a positive approach to engaging all participants in an exploration of the best ways of learning together.

Each of the five coordinating teachers accepted the major responsibility for at least one specific aspect of the English-social studies curriculum. The 40 participating teachers and approximately 150 students were divided into five teams on each of the two levels: ninth and tenth grade. Each coordinating teacher worked with a team for one week, changing at the end of that time to another group of teachers and students.

The nature and history of language was the curricular area of Mrs.

Lawana T. Trout, who helped students to see themselves as well as their language while they studied loaded words and propaganda.

Miss Verna Dozier had teachers and students looking directly at poetry to find for themselves truth and beauty.

The reading program planned by Mrs. Thelma H. Johnson involved a laboratory approach and ways of dealing with heterogeneous groups.

Daily journals were kept by students under the guidance of Miss Angeline Anderson, who concentrated upon compositional skills. Reading and personal experiences were used as motivation for written composition.

Mr. Peter Kontos sent his students to original sources to seek answers to questions about freedom and justice. In this social studies class, role-playing became a way to help students understand history and themselves.

The question about approaches and methods partly resolved, Mr. Howard Cranford was asked to order all materials needed by each coordinating teacher. In addition, he secured many books and other equipment and supplies for participating teachers and students. His report contains complete listings, but it is important to note here that every teacher received four professional books on the first day of the Institute, and had easy access to hundreds of others for six weeks. Some students ended the summer school with no fewer than ten books, given to them as a planned part of the program.

Most of the books provided for teachers and students were paperbacks, for these small books are easily handled in quantity. Disadvantaged students in a summer program should not, we felt, be loaded down with (and possibly discouraged by) huge anthologies, history texts, grammar handbooks, and similar books. The economically disadvantaged were thus provided with reading material they needed and wanted; the culturally deprived were given a start—hopefully—toward an interest in books and learning; the slow learners and poor readers were given practice with material that would whet their appetites for improvement; and perhaps some households and neighborhoods now had many books where formerly there were few or none.

Consultants were selected carefully to complement and extend the program. Usually they visited classes at Trenton, participated in the critique sessions based upon the morning demonstrations, and lectured to all teachers in the afternoon. Some were willing to demonstrate and to serve as resource persons for study groups.

Other important aspects of the Institute include the functioning together of the science-mathematics staff and the English-social studies staff, and visits from publishers and other persons who are developing material for the disadvantaged.

The 1966 Institute program differed only in detail, not philosophy.

Again in 1966, as they did in the initial venture of 1965, the English and social studies courses used the discovery and inductive methods to elicit answers from students at eighth-, ninth-, and tenth-grade levels and to encourage their involvement in learning. A great deal of discussion went on, and there were role-playing, pantomime, drama, debating, and even finger painting. In one class blindfolded students attempted to discuss their feelings and to write, and tried to identify objects they could not see. In another classroom the communicative arts and American history were fused in an integrated approach that involved study of newspapers, card-playing, and listening to and discussing "If I Were President, Oh Yeah!" by Timmie Rogers.

Elsewhere, exemplary practices included free and uninhibited discussion of life situations, made graphic by blackboard sketches, and a concern with real democracy in the classroom. Students in still another class were seeing and discussing prejudice as shown in cartoons, newspapers, poetry, novels, and biographies.

Individual reports submitted by coordinating teachers will detail what was done in each class, but the heart of the matter in every room was the student as an individual. Although each teacher, through correspondence before the opening day, had selected and submitted an idea, an outline of planned work, and a list of materials, each was flexible enough to adjust the plans to the requirements of students and teachers in the summer program.

David Sohn, in eighth-grade English, employed the visual approach, using a variety of films and pictures to involve the students in a wonderful sensory world of color, metaphor, and imagination. Students viewed intently, became deeply involved, discussed with heightened perception, and wrote with growing fluency.

Peter Carlin's eighth-grade social studies class concentrated upon techniques developed in Cleveland in the Pathfinder program. Students explored, found motivations for their actions, and gained insight into their personal lives.

In ninth-grade English, John Gallagher and the teachers who worked with him selected courage as a theme about which students and teachers built learning experiences. The many facets of courage were explored, and listening, speaking, reading, and writing skills were taught within this context.

Ninth-grade social studies, taught by Phyllis Jackson, concentrated upon a geography program that drew ideas from students instead of pouring in facts; it engaged students and motivated them to learn. The unit "thread" was a list of the five elements common to all societies: survival, the family, religion, conflict, and striving for immortality. In this summer program survival was the theme, and films, readings, pictures, and other media were used to elicit from students conclusions about this idea.

Lawana Trout, who taught in the 1965 program, returned this year to teach the tenth-grade English class. Three students from last summer's program were in her class. Involving language, literature, and composition, one of her most effective units was prejudice—a tension-packed, provocative theme which effectively engaged the intellectual and emotional energies of students and teachers, and led to free and unhampered discussion of the effects of prejudice upon the hater and the hated.

A study of the report of Evelyn Harper, who taught the tenth-grade social studies class, will show that she was often able to integrate her efforts with those of Lawana Trout. Emphasizing the communications aspects of social studies, she used newspapers to help pupils perceive the world in which they live.

An excerpt from a poem by Gwendolyn Brooks might be the most appropriate conclusion for this overview.

"But in the crowding darkness not a word did they say."

In the darkness of that world inhabited by the disadvantaged, there must be some light. There is danger in refusing to face that dark world, to enter it, and to cope with the educational problems there. In the long, hot summer of discontent and disorder, consideration given to the problems of teaching the disadvantaged is surely one of the best ways to begin a dialogue with that world.

With communication established between the dark world of the disadvantaged and the bright world of the educated, with a commitment on both sides to understand and the intention to be understood, there is hope. Teachers of English and social studies developed in the summer of 1966 new ways of looking at language, literature, and composition; teaching the arts and skills of listening, speaking, reading, and writing; and finding common themes in history, geography, literature, and language.

And "they"—the students in the English and social studies classes—said and wrote many words in the growing brightness of their new world.

2. *Involvement through Slanted Language*

LAWANA TROUT

LANGUAGE

"I will look into the face of each child that I teach and measure my worth as a teacher by what I can give to that child."

This line expresses my hope for my contribution to the Institute. I wanted to create a learning atmosphere that evolved from my experiences with each child and with the entire class. I wanted each student to feel that I was interested in him as a person outside of school and as a participant in my English class.

"This Institute is for the *teachers,* not for the students" never convinced me. I know that if I focused on the students, the teachers would learn what I had to teach them. While watching me question students in sequential structures, the teachers could learn about inductive teaching. While watching me encourage students to answer and to listen to each other, to argue with each other, and to respect each one's contribution, the teachers could learn how to create a student-centered discussion. While seeing me role-play various types of teachers to elicit student reactions to these types, the teachers could assess the influence of their personality and techniques on their classes. While analyzing my creation of a classroom atmosphere that was sometimes radically different from theirs, the teacher could observe how my approach to students controlled their performance and attitude.

My method was inductive; my subject matter was language. My

Mrs. Lawana Trout, National Teacher of the Year in 1964, played a prominent role in the English-social studies programs of both the 1965 and 1966 Institutes. In 1965 she concentrated on securing student response through the subject of Language and Propaganda, then turned to the Protest Movement in 1966 to spark classroom involvement. Now a member of the Department of English at Central State College, Edmond, Oklahoma, she has published a number of articles including "My Laboratory of Life," an essay published by NEA and translated by the U.S.I.A. for foreign publication.

primary objective was to convince the teachers that they need not be the filter for all knowledge in the classroom. In the traditional classroom, the teacher dispenses knowledge and selects limited views of the content. Discussion is teacher-centered; questions come from him, not the students. Answers are often for the teacher rather than for the student.

In contrast to this type of classroom, I wished to show the advantage of using many sources (records, magazines, newspapers, etc.), and of using discussion that was student-centered. Their comments shaped my lessons. Perhaps I should inject the thought that their reactions did not control or determine my lesson. I had some broad concepts outlined for the lesson; student comments and questions filled in the blanks. When possible, I "directed" myself out of the learning picture and allowed the students to focus on themselves.

Institute Classes

The following classes are representative of those I used during the 1965 Institute. Many students have no concept of language history; language is limited to what they are now speaking. I hoped to develop two major ideas: first, that language has a history and that history is characterized by changes, and second, that they already know a great deal about the history of their language.

The lesson was taught in four sections. First I played the record "A Thousand Years of English Pronunciation." Students guessed what language was being played and we discussed the reasons for their guesses. They followed scripts as they listened to selections from *Beowulf* through the 1611 version of the Bible. They listed changes (sound, alphabet, spelling, etc.) that they observed in the development of the language.

Second, I gave students a copy of a language tree and after giving them time to study it, I asked for comments. At the end of the discussion, I asked for any relationships they saw between the tree and the record.

Third, I gave students blank maps of Europe. We imagined we were Celts living in Britain 50 years before Christ. By writing dates and people on the maps, we traced the invasions and conquests, each time noting the effect on language. We noted relationships between the maps, the tree, and the record.

Then I gave the students a mimeographed page of quotes from Shakespeare. I posed the question, "If this is the only record you had of language in the 1600's, what would you know about the language of that time?" In their discussion the students noted the differences between Shakespeare's language and ours—that there were no grammar rules for English during his time and no dictionaries for the English language. They made these observations; I did not give the facts.

Throughout the discussion, we used examples from their slang and from modern language to contrast modern and historical English. The discussion moved to the language of the future—if it will change and how it will change. We imagined we were studying English 1000 years from today. Students guessed the changes that would probably take place and they discussed possible characteristics of the future language.

The student reactions were positive in most instances. It was not successful when I had some who had too much difficulty in reading the materials and in following the movement of the lesson. In general the students were fascinated by the record and the idea of change in language. Some students asked to take scripts home with them so they could make copies of Old English. Unfortunately I could not give them copies. The lesson was more successful with the older students; perhaps one reason was that they had had world history.

Teacher reactions varied from great enthusiasm to mild interest. Two or three negative ones felt the material was too difficult.

Advertising

Students were asked to write advertisements. They had imaginary jobs in a firm which added money to their checks when their ad raised sales. They were allowed to choose pictures of products to sell (cars, records, Hondas, etc.) or to make up their own products. They were encouraged to "sell" to their classmates and teachers and to do quick illustrations if they liked. Then they were asked, "What did you sell? What did you assume about people when you wrote the ad?" Through discussion of these points, we drew conclusions about the psychology of advertising and advertising techniques.

Then we applied these conclusions to examples of advertising. Students noted that certain words were "loaded" and slanted to appeal to particular groups. They divided into groups and worked with the participating teachers in analyzing ads in various types of magazines.

Student participation was excellent during this lesson. They "acted out" their commercials with humor and zest. Some were serious in their efforts to sell. Others did humorous and satirical ones. Some worked in teams and divided the speaking roles when they made their presentation to the class. Some wrote clever slogans and verses.

Students were asked to list other people who used loaded words. As they contributed names, they were encouraged to explain their choice. Parents and teachers were the most popular discussion topics. The discussion on school and teachers often took the full period. Students gave examples of loaded words including: *sit down, shut up, get out, failure, detention, very good, education, learning,* etc. Students talked about their reactions to the words and whether the words accomplished the teacher's purpose.

Typical excerpts from the lesson follow. (I often role-played the opposite of their comments to spark the discussion.)

Students: We want a teacher who cares about us and tries to understand us.

Teacher: What do you mean I should get to know you? I have over 175 kids a day . . . papers to grade, tests to make out. . . . How can I get to know you?

Students: But you're not a good teacher if you don't *try* to know us. You have to be interested in us as people. You need to know about our abilities. Everyone doesn't learn the same way.

Teacher: Oh—How can I find out about your abilities? I guess I can look at your test results. Do you think that is a good idea?

Students: NO . . . because the tests don't always tell what we know. Sometimes we're scared on tests and sometimes we don't understand the questions. You can tell about us by watching us.

Teacher: Say that I was your teacher at the beginning of the year . . . you've told me that you react to teachers very quickly and decide what you'll do for them . . . I come in and say, "I've heard about you, and I want you to understand that there will be no getting by with anything in my class. I can get just as mean as you can. There will be no trouble from any of you."

Students: I *hate* you already! (exact words). I wouldn't ever do anything for you because you are not giving us a fair chance.

Students: We'd just try to run you off and show you we were not going to do your work. We'd try to think of ways to get back at you.

Teacher: Well, what do you want in class? I guess you want to just play all the time.

Students: We want a teacher who does something different. You get tired doing the same old things day after day. All the classes are the same.

Students: We like to discuss and give our ideas.

Teacher: Your ideas . . . you're here to learn from *me*. I'm the one who is educated. I went to college. I've read books. If you talk, we'll never get through all my material.

Students: We learn more when we can try out our ideas and opinions. We read and think too. You'll never know what we read and think if you don't listen to us.

Students: The way some teachers teach . . . they don't even need to be here. If they put their talks on tapes, they could just play them. They teach like machines.

The discussion moved to what they *did* like in teachers and we described a model classroom, a model teacher, and a model student. We also talked about different types of students, the purposes of school, and the conditions that promoted maximum learning. I should emphasize that this was not a "gripe session" for what is wrong with teachers. I wanted to give them the opportunity to air their views, make their suggestions, and gain insight into teacher, student, and classroom psychology. I was surprised at the open, frank comments that poured out because I did not know them well, and they were obviously not accustomed to this type of discussion. But their remarks were spontaneous and sincere.

Time was given to discussion of students' use of loaded words, their slang expressions, unfavorable names, etc. Every class mentioned *urban renewal, poverty,* and *slum* as words that were extremely loaded to them.

They were asked to look at pictures in *Stop, Look and Write,* and to give negative and positive impressions for the same picture. They sometimes developed these into paragraphs. One of the most popular pictures was that of an old Negro man sitting in a theatre that was completely deserted. Sample negative: "An old dirty bum . . . a lazy man . . . a worthless old man." Sample positive: "A lonely old man thinking about his family. He has left them to look for work." "A kind old man worrying about the racial problem." "An old man who is sad because people won't respect him."

Propaganda

Mimeographed copies of propaganda techniques were distributed. As we discussed them, we related them to Trenton problems. [For example, if you had a project to improve Trenton, what would you choose—recreation park, youth center, etc.? Why do you need it? Who would you want to give a testimonial? What would you have him say? What are the loaded words in Trenton?] Students were given background information and then asked to create their own propaganda (civil rights, reporting on incidents from several points of view).

Propaganda and war were topics. Students read and discussed *Springboards* on Nazism. A large reprint of Picasso's "Guernica" was put at the front of the room and students discussed it. I also gave them a picture of Teddy Roosevelt charging up a hill. This was a painting that glorified war. While commenting on the two opposing views of war, the students observed that art can be used for propaganda as well as words.

Esquire and Scope Issues

The July 1965 issue of *Esquire* was used for Teenage Day. Students were invited to bring records. This edition has interviews with teenagers and articles on their world. We discussed the article dealing with their language. The *Scope* issue focused on teenage writing, art, sculpture, and photography.

Evaluation

In view of the many problems facing the Institute in the beginning, I think it was an outstanding success. Coordinating and participating teachers were not positive of their roles in the Institute (at least the English coordinating teachers were not), and the first two or three weeks were frustrating because of these confused interpretations. However, since the Institute was "a first," these problems could not have been anticipated and solved.

I think we favorably influenced a great number of "middle-ground" teachers. We strengthened those who agreed with our philosophy from the beginning. I'm sure we failed to change the "die-hards," but they must now face the fact that the students' performance changed as the classroom approach changed. Some English teachers were eager to try our materials, and they also discussed ideas they wanted to develop into units.

The teachers seemed to become more receptive to the aims of the program after the third week. They advanced more constructive criticisms and they began to talk about how some of the techniques demonstrated could be used in their classes. The resource room, which had an occasional visitor at the beginning of the Institute, became filled with teachers collecting and previewing materials.

One of the strongest assets of the Institute was a teacher's opportunity to see the inductive method emphasized in all classes. They seemed surprised and impressed by the fact that science and English teachers were using the same classroom techniques.

I feel that the English program could have been more effective had the teachers stayed with the students for the six weeks. The rotation placed tremendous handicaps on effective inductive teaching. We did not know how to adjust the difficulty level because we had no time to learn about our students. However, I noticed that many spoke to me and came by to see me after they left my classes. I think this type of warmth was a result of the friendly atmosphere which all the teachers radiated in and out of class. There was little time to develop concepts. However, I understand that rotation was unavoidable in this Institute, and there were some advantages to the participating teachers seeing different approaches.

I am convinced that the program was a positive educational experience for the students. They eagerly voiced their approval of classes and teachers several times. It is interesting that many "failures" and "problems" (so labeled by the Trenton teachers) became our "stars." For example, Trenton teachers made comments similar to, "I had him all year and he never said two words. He talked in your class several times today." "I am amazed she didn't give you any trouble." (This student was a favorite of one of the visiting teachers.) "I was surprised at how much the kids knew about that topic." I suspect the students responded more positively because the change was in the classroom atmosphere rather than in them. Teachers also noted surprise at "how sensitive" the students were. For example, when the class analyzed descriptive sentences and advertisements, the teachers seemed amazed at the students' ability to manipulate colorful words. They had obviously underestimated and misjudged the students' ability and performance.

On the other hand, they were surprised to find that the students were deficient in some areas. The teachers had assumed that the students knew material which they did not know. For example, they were surprised that the students had great difficulty with concepts of time and place. Students could not locate countries on a blank map and they could not handle history in relation to time. They discussed the idea that perhaps the disadvantaged have problems in these areas because they do not have travel experience.

The following was distributed to students early in the unit.

PROPAGANDA DEVICES

Name-Calling

This is a device to make us form a judgment without examining the evidence on which it is based. The propagandist appeals to hate and fear. He does this by giving "bad names" to those individuals, groups, nations, races, policies, practices, beliefs, and ideas he would have us condemn and reject. Today's bad names include: Fascist, dictator, Red, Communist, alien, trouble-maker, rabble-rouser, constitution wrecker, etc. Use of "bad names" without presentation of their essential meaning, without their pertinent implications, comprises the most common of all propaganda devices.

Glittering Generalities

The propagandist identifies his program with virtue by the use of "virtue words." He appeals to our emotions of love, generosity, and brotherhood. He uses words like truth, freedom, honor, social justice, liberty, public service, the right to work, loyalty, the American way, progress, democracy, and constitution defender. These words suggest shining ideals. Hence the propagandist, by identifying his individual group, nation, race, policy, practice, or belief with such ideals, seeks to win us to his cause.

Transfer

This is the device by which the propagandist carries over the authority, sanctions, and prestige of something we respect and revere to something he would have us accept. If the propagandist succeeds in getting the church or nation to approve a campaign in behalf of some program, he thereby transfers its authority, sanctions, and prestige to the program. Thus we may accept something which we might otherwise reject.

Symbols are constantly used. The cross represents the Christian church. The flag represents the nation. Cartoons like Uncle Sam represent a consensus of opinion. These symbols stir emotions. A cartoonist, by having Uncle Sam disapprove a budget of aid for the underprivileged, would have us feel that the whole United States disapproves aid costs. By drawing an Uncle Sam who approves the same budget, the cartoonist would have us believe the American people approve it. Thus the transfer device is used both for and against causes and ideas.

Testimonial

This is a device to make us accept anything from a patent medicine or a cosmetic to a program of national policy. In this device the propagandist makes use of testimonials. When a well-known socialite or a Hollywood star says, "I use Blank . . . ," the reader imagines she will become equally glamorous if she uses the same product. When a labor leader publicly endorses the President's foreign policy, readers instinctively believe that the whole powerful economic group known as "labor" will also support the policy—therefore it must be a good one. This device also works in reverse. Counter testimonials are employed in social, economic, and political issues.

Card-Stacking

"Card-stacking" is a device by which the propagandist employs all the arts of deception to win support for himself, his group, nation, race, policy, practice, belief, or ideal. He stacks the cards against the truth. He uses underemphasis and overemphasis to dodge issues and evade facts. He resorts to lies, censorship, and distortions. He omits facts. He offers false testimony. He creates a smoke screen of clamor by raising a new issue when he wants an embarrassing matter forgotten. By this method, a mediocre candidate, through the build-up, is made to appear an intellectual titan; an ordinary prize fighter, a probable world champion; a worthless patent medicine, a beneficent cure. By means of this device, propagandists would convince us that a ruthless war of aggression is a crusade for righteousness.

The Band Wagon

The "band wagon" is a device to make us follow the crowd, to accept the propagandist's program en masse. Here his theme is: "Everybody's doing it." Because he wants us to "follow the crowd" in masses, he directs his appeal to groups held together by common ties of nationality, religion, race, environment, sex, or vocation. All the artifices of flattery are used to harness the fears and hatreds, prejudices and biases, convictions and ideals common to the group; thus emotion is made to push and pull the group on the band wagon.

Slanting in Newspapers

Instructions to the Teacher

Select newspapers from various sections of the country which also represent various political views. Distribute one to each student (if possible a different paper to each student). Ask them to skim to note differences and similarities in the papers. Then ask them to find one article concerning one event (if possible) and to compare ways of "reporting the facts." What can you note about this newspaper from this one article? What are the general views of this newspaper regarding political issues? Allow the students time to browse through the papers making comments as they compare editorials, headlines, pictures, position of stories, etc. Ask them to list techniques of slanting they can identify and to give examples.

Provide help for the student in identifying and analyzing slanted news. (For thorough coverage see Chapter 30, *Scholastic Journalism*, English and Hach, Iowa State College Press, Ames, Iowa.)

I. *Factors that may cause newspapers to slant news*
   A. Politics
      1. Know whether the newspaper follows the beliefs of a political party or is independent.
      2. Know which of the following classifications best characterizes it: radical, conservative, liberal, or extremely conservative.
   B. Religion
      1. Know if the paper is affiliated with a particular religious faith, as, for example, the *Christian Science Monitor*.
      2. Know some of the differences between the Protestant, Catholic, and Hebrew faiths in order to detect evidence of religious emphasis. For example, the attitude of the papers may vary on divorce and perhaps public education.

C. Race and Nationality
1. The U.S. has a number of foreign language newspapers and attitudes of these papers may vary considerably on many questions of public interest.
2. The attitudes of Negro newspapers may vary from those of so-called "white" publishers. Public housing is one example.
D. Labor
1. Know the paper's attitude toward labor and capital.
2. Understand the special occupational interests of your local paper.
E. The Human Factor
1. Since newspaper men have certain beliefs and attitudes and they have been conditioned by environment, background, and education, they may be unknowingly prejudiced in handling a story of a certain type.
2. Perfect objectivity is a goal never completely realized.
II. *Common methods of editorial emphasis*
A. Overwriting or Underwriting a News Story
1. A few newspapers may fail to write a story fully, on purpose, but still publish part of the story in an attempt to vindicate themselves of the charge of failing to publish all the news.
2. Newspapers may overwrite stories that conform to their policies or that deal with themselves.
3. Many people judge the importance of a story by its length, whereas, in reality, the length may have very little to do with its importance.
B. Creating a News Story
1. Newspapers occasionally create news stories by sponsoring campaigns of various kinds or by crusading against civic evils or for civic improvements. Most of these are legitimate news.
2. Some create stories that work a disservice to the public.
C. Publishing only Those Facts which the Newspaper Wants the Public to Know
1. A newspaper may state that it publishes the truth, but there is a difference in only half the truth and a full explanation.
2. By publishing only those facts which the paper wants the reader to know, it can distort a story out of proportion to its true news value.
D. Failing to Select the Right Feature, either Intentionally or Unintentionally
1. There is sometimes a difference of opinion in what the feature story should be.

2. A few newspapers intentionally distort the news by playing up the wrong features. If a reader is not discriminating, he can receive the wrong slant on a story.

E. Displaying a Story Too Prominently or Not Prominently Enough
   1. News may be distorted by the position and headlines given to the story.
   2. Position on the front and inside pages is important.

F. Using Words that Mislead the Reader
   1. Relying on the connotative and denotative power of words.

G. Failing to Reveal Sources of Information
   1. Sources should be stated openly.
   2. Expressions such as "according to an undisclosed source" and "according to a usually reliable source," should not be accepted without further verification of facts.

Preview of Program before Start of the Institute

Lawana Trout—Summer Schedule

I. Students will have an opportunity to study and discuss propaganda, feelings, and ideas about racial problems. Through writing ads and analyzing propaganda in newspapers (editorial cartoons, articles, editorials, etc.), students will realize that certain words have certain feelings. They will become aware of techniques of persuasion. For example, they will slant one ad several ways: for teenagers, for rich women over 40, for poor people, and for other groups. Participating teachers will examine the local newspapers with their groups for propaganda. We will emphasize that propaganda is not necessarily bad or good.

Next, we will discuss other places that "feeling" words are used: classroom, home, court, and others. At least one class period will be spent with the teacher role-playing various types of teachers (permissive, unconcerned, dogmatic, etc.), and the students will react to this type of learning situation.

II. Through studying the rise of Hitler and his concentration camps, we will note what can happen when people are controlled by persuasion and propaganda. Springboard publications on Nazism will be used. Other material will include "Night and Fog" (concentration camp film), "The Twisted Cross" (a film on Hitler's rise to power), and the film "The Diary of Anne Frank." Students will read selections from the books *Night and Fog* and *The Diary of Anne Frank*.

III. We will explore some attitudes and problems involving minority groups. Through literary selections, we will focus on the current protest movement. Students will read parts of *Nigger, Go Tell It on the Mountain, The Fire Next Time, To Kill a Mockingbird,* and *Why We Can't Wait.* Students will also collect their own materials for a project. They will debate the role-play. For example, they will debate the topic of violence vs. nonviolence from the viewpoints of Martin L. King, James Baldwin, and Malcom X. They will read selections written by students their age concerning sit-ins, marches, etc., and they will write reactions. They will perform parts of "In White America." The film "A Raisin in the Sun" will be shown and scenes from the play will be acted out.

We will look at publications of the John Birch Society, KKK, the Citizens' Rights Committee, and various forms of hate literature. For example, each student will examine a copy of a Citizens' Rights Committee newspaper which is against Negroes and Jews.

After these experiences, the students should become aware of many views toward complex racial problems. They may be more discriminating when they read propaganda and slanted materials, and they should develop deeper insight into how they themselves feel about these problems.

> I have a dream that one day every valley shall be exalted, every hill and mountain shall be made low, the rough places will be made plains, and the crooked places will be made straight, and the glory of the Lord shall be revealed, and all flesh shall see it together.
>
> Martin L. King

TEACHING THE PROTEST MOVEMENT IN 1966

"I hate you!"
"Like man, I'm tellin' you . . . there ain't no land of the free and home of the brave and we gotta move."
"Nigger . . ."

Anyone walking by my classroom door might have been stunned as he overheard these student reactions. President Kennedy told us, "The nation that makes peaceful revolution impossible makes violent revolution inevitable." I wanted to evoke a peaceful revolution in my classroom—a revolution in thinking, a revolution in feeling, a revolution in teaching. Students examined some of the complex and chaotic events of the protest movement. They read and wrote propaganda. They studied and practiced techniques of persuasion. By observing the con man, the hate monger, the advertiser, and the polished politician, they recognized that words are feelings. They reacted to poems, plays, and films that told the story of the black-white struggle. They wrote scripts and performed them. They wrote arguments and debated them. They compiled a Protest Notebook that included compositions, poems, paintings, pictures, daily reactions, articles, and personal insights.

Introduction to the Unit

The unit was opened with calm material. To my students I was a white southern stranger who spoke with a soft accent. I respected them and avoided creating hostility with controversial material.

Since advertising plays a prominent role in students' lives, it was a familiar vehicle for making students aware of the "feeling" of words. For quick stimulation I asked them to choose from a collection of pictures something they wished to sell (Hondas, cigarettes, record albums, cars). They wrote several types of ads: serious, satirical, or humorous for radio, television, magazines, or newspapers. They "sold" their products to the class.

We played with personal slanting by comparing two columns that included items like

Finest quality filet mignon	First-class piece of dead cow
She is deeply interested in her husbands affairs.	She has her husband under her thumb.

Students were asked to rank lists of words.

Example: lush, heavy drinker, pathological drinker, drunkard, alcoholic, sponge, old soak, person with a drinking problem.

They did conjugations similar to Bertrand Russell's conjugation of irregular verbs:

I am sparkling. You talk too much.	He is drunk.
I am beautiful. You have good features.	She isn't bad-looking if you like that type.

They slanted one ad to reach several different groups: teenagers (jive talk), poor people, middle-aged women, young men.

In one exercise we started with a neutral word and slanted it positively and negatively: car (antique—wreck), (teenager—young adult). The class gave other words which we slanted like "urban renewal," "poverty program," and "disadvantaged."

We also wrote slanted descriptions of people and pictures. Students selected a picture or a person and wrote neutral, positive, and negative views. One commented, "You can *make* people and things be anything you want to by the words you use." This observation was applied to situations that happen outside the classroom.

Next we moved to propaganda. They offered definitions of propaganda and noted that "advertisers sell products and the propagandists sell ideas." Local newspapers were examined for propaganda and from our observations we formulated a list of propaganda techniques: name-calling, transfer, testimonial, and others. In anticipation of the following lessons on the protest movement, we looked at articles relating to it.

Students examined over 100 simple editorial cartoons. Each student explained his cartoons to the class and we listed observations about what makes a cartoon: symbolism is often used, captions and situations often depend on the reader's familiarity with past events, etc. Some questions included, "If you were going to show *hate* (love, peace, anger, fear) in a cartoon, what would you use? (Answers: confederate flag, slave, Uncle Tom, the government.) What would you use to show good and bad? (The cross for good and for bad, I'd crucify somebody on it.)

Our study of propaganda was not limited to words and pictures; we also looked at it in films and paintings. We showed "The Twisted Cross" which expresses Hitler's power. A three-foot print of Picasso's "Guernica" was put before the class and students wrote one word as a reaction to the painting. They gave "confusion, frustration, fear, struggle," and when one shy girl said "loneliness," the class roared with laughter. She stoutly defended, "Those people are in trouble and are afraid; fear makes people lonely." No one laughed. They noted that this painting could be called antiwar propaganda.

The Protest Movement

It was time to introduce the protest movement. Students had been made aware of the power of words in persuading and in conveying feelings. During these lessons I had had an opportunity to create an emotional climate that was open and warm. I had cultivated a oneness in the class group, but students were free to disagree with anyone's ideas—including the teacher's. Perhaps I should note that this permissiveness was in regard to the material being studied. There was firm discipline of the class behavior.

The approach to the opening lesson went like this:

"Have you been taught anything about the protest movement?"
"No."
"Do you think it should be taught?"
"Yes."
"Why?"
"Because it is us."
"Because adults are always tellin' us we are the future, but they don't get us ready for it. They never talk to us about civil rights. They just bury it."
"That's right. They never listen to what we think."
"Why should we as teachers listen? All you do is cause trouble, knifing and fighting each other."
"Yeah . . . and we'll probably keep doin' that as long as you think about us that way. . ."
"Hey, you gonna let us talk about *The Man* as well as about us?"

Students gave a lively case for studying the movement. None spoke against it. I agreed to study it as an experiment, and periodically we stopped to evaluate what they thought about our study, how it should be changed, and if it should be taught in the regular school year.

Our study was divided into two simple parts: (1) What are some of the problems of the protest movement? (2) What are some possible solutions to these problems?

The following accounts give sketches of representative lessons.

I Wonder Why

Students moved their chairs into a close group to share *I WONDER WHY* with the teacher. In this sensitive picture book a Negro child tells us, "I like rain. I like snowflakes . . ." and ends with "I wonder why nobody likes me." Following the book, we listened to Joan Baez sing "Birmingham Sunday." Students were asked to write on the topic of prejudice. (Why are people prejudiced, my thoughts on prejudice, etc.). This lesson was effective. Jerome, who had always watched me with hard veiled eyes, met my gaze during the song about the death of the little girls. The raw pain was bare before me in his dark look. After that the veil was gone.

Nigger

Since this word is offensive and explosive for many people, I planned its use carefully. One day when I asked for words to show hate in a cartoon, a student replied, "You would use . . . no, I don't think *you* would, but some people would use 'nigger.'" I wrote the word on the board and we discussed it briefly. When students said the word, I repeated it. By the day we were ready to study *Nigger,* they were ready to accept it. I opened this lesson by looking directly at a student that I knew very well (a volunteer from last year's class who was not eligible for the program, but who came to my class every day) and saying, "How do you feel when I say *Nigger* to you?" He laughed. I said it to another student and he laughed. I repeated it in general to the class and they laughed. "Why did you *laugh?*" "Because we know you didn't mean it?" "How do you *know* I didn't?" We discussed other questions. Is this word used only by whites to insult you? Do Negroes also use it? How? Can it be a good word? When? Have you had any experiences with this word? One boy told of a fight he had had with a white boy at the close of last year's institute over the word. Several others volunteered stories. What are some possible reactions when you are called this? (fighting, walking away, giving a "cool" answer). What are some "cool" answers? The boy who had had the fight said he'd walk away next time because he didn't want to pay more court costs.

Why do you think Gregory titled his book *Nigger?* Who will this book sell to? We read Gregory's line, "Dear Momma—Wherever you are, if ever you hear the word "nigger" again, remember they are advertising my book."

I had torn apart Gregory's *From the Back of the Bus* and *What's Happening* (two joke books), and each student was given a joke to tell the class. In our discussion, they told that he was fighting civil-rights issues in the same way they reacted to my name-calling . . . with humor.

Students had prepared roles from *Nigger* to read and they performed for the class. One part dealt with prejudice in the classroom and I asked if this were realistic. How does a teacher show prejudice? "I once had a sixth-grade teacher who was always screamin' and yellin' at us . . . 'You dirty little colored kids are ruinin' our school . . .'" and the student began to act like the teacher. In their enthusiasm others joined in, some defending and others crucifying teachers. Later in the lesson, I role-played several types of teachers and the students reacted. Armed with a strong stare and a belligerent voice I threatened, "I know all about you. I've heard about how tough you are. I want you to understand that you'll get away with *nothing* in here. I can be just as mean as you can." "I Hate You!" exploded one boy. Observing this Negro class were 12 white teachers. When I saw students reacting this freely, I know rapport had been established.

Go Tell It on the Mountain

Students read portions of the book for background situations and then role-played the scenes. For example, the son came home gashed from a fight and his father, who preached white hatred, screamed, "It was white folks, some of them white folks *you* like so much, that tried to cut your brother's throat." This scene was contrasted with one from *Nigger* in which Gregory is bleeding in the gutter and a white woman helps him and takes him to the hospital. By this time we had identified prejudice problems in the areas of housing, voting, and education. In addition to the book scenes, they role-played a housing problem: a Negro family trying to move into a white neighborhood. The real estate dealer, the Negro family, and representatives from Negro and white communities had a meeting. They also did a school problem: parents trying to enroll their Negro child in a white school. Characters included the principal and students with various conflicting viewpoints. Scenes were taped and played for discussion.

A Raisin in the Sun

"A Raisin in the Sun" was the film which involved them totally. They were given the book to read if they wished, and most of them did read the play. Part of one discussion revolved around who they felt the money belonged to, and what should have been done with the money. They argued violently about whether Ruth should have the baby or an abortion. We also discussed the self-image of the characters that is revealed in their lines. How did this image affect the character's actions? What are some Negro images today? How do these images affect a Negro's actions? How do they create problems for the Negro? What do you think happened after the family moved to their new home?

Expressions with Paint

At first glance, an observer might have thought that students were having a good time smearing finger paint around on their pages, and part of the time they were. However, other things were taking place. A girl scratched her nails down the page—fingers tense, face tight . . . "This is *hate*," she said. After discussing expression through color and forms, and after looking at books of paintings, students were asked to express some of their feelings about civil rights.

Malcolm X, Martin Luther King, White Nationalism

Students were exploding like firecrackers all over the room. The fevered pitch of their emotions seared through their pleading, persuading, and plotting. Juvenile spokesmen for Martin L. King, Malcolm X, and white nationalists presented their cases to a tense audience.

In previous lessons they had been evaluating possible solutions to civil-rights problems and they had investigated basic principles of several groups: KKK, John Birch Society, Black Muslims, Black Power, and the nonviolence movement. They read Baldwin, King, Malcolm X, Carmichael, Foreman, Wilkins, and others. They compared the constitution of the Ku Klux Klan with the stated beliefs of the Black Muslims and they explored the multiple definitions of black power. They analyzed the publications of the John Birch Society that related to civil rights. They reacted to the Citizens' Rights committee newspaper, *The White Man's Viewpoint*. They collected quotes, records, interviews, pictures, cartoons, and speeches. They took notes as they listened to speeches by Malcolm X and Martin L. King. From these notes, they refuted the main arguments and discussed effective ways to answer an argument. They conducted interviews and did a television program for the other class members. They investigated two riots in depth: Harlem 1964 and Watts 1966. They held a trial based on the testimonies in *Mississippi Black Paper*.

These activities climaxed in the final debate that opened with each group (Muslims, black power, and nonviolence) presenting its principles. Then the class was open for discussion and argument. We were living President Kennedy's peaceful revolution. Each faction had filled the room with its propaganda: signs, slogans, pictures, and projects.

In addition to these lessons, we read from *Our Faces, Our Words*, *The Negro Protest*, and *The Fire Next Time*. We prepared for choral reading poems by Langston Hughes, Richard Wright, and James Weldon Johnson. The best reaction came from Gwendolyn Brooks' poem:

We Real Cool

The Pool Players
Seven at the Golden Shovel.

We real cool. We
Left School. We
Lurk late. We
Strike straight. We
Sing sin. We
Thin gin. We
Jazz June. We
Die soon.

Students also did scenes from *In White America*.

Reactions

Teachers

"Do you really think you're teaching *English?*

"I knew you were asking for trouble the day you said 'Nigger' to that boy, but I was wrong. Two nights ago, I was telling three Negro boys that I taught last year about your class. I told them about what you had said and they approved, much to my surprise. Then we discussed the word and I realized that I had been prejudiced about that and many other things. I won't ever have trouble with the word again. Thank you."

"These students are not being honest with you. They really resent your harping on their problems. It is a mistake to teach this."

"Anyone who would teach this stuff is crazy!"

"The experiences of the Negro pupil in Mrs. Trout's program were patently valuable to him. Festering spots of shame, frustration, hatred, and hopelessness were lanced by probing and cleansed by honest discussion. There can be no doubt that the Negro pupil enrolled in this program has emerged a better person and a potentially more effective citizen."

"It may work for you . . . but how can I teach it with wild, disrespectful kids, bum administrators, and illiterate parents?"

"But . . . aren't you afraid the students will get *emotional* about all this if you allow the discussion in your classrooms? How can you dare expose these problems to juveniles?"

"The use of group dynamics, especially in the units taught by Mrs. Trout, exceed in value courses given in college on the use of techniques of group action. My observance of the excellent relationship of pupil-to-teacher and the rapport with the teacher in the examination of ideas of a controversial nature made me aware that subject matter heretofore avoided might be used in my classroom."

"Man, you've got guts! This is great. I'm going to try it too!"

"There was never any doubt that Mrs. Trout was in full control, the children were learning, and what's more, wanted to learn. It was a delight and a pleasure to watch her."

"I have seen the disadvantaged from many views: lectures, films, books, and teacher discussions. But I have never seen these students reacting to their problems under the direction of a sensitive teacher. The protest movement was a strong and powerful way to show us what they feel. The students gave me more insight than all the other combined sources. This is the way to prepare teachers to cope with these problems."

Most typical remark all summer: "You're going to teach *What?*"

Evaluation

There were three major weaknesses in my work this summer. First, there was no time to explore the historical aspects of the problems. Also, we emphasized the literary aspects since we were an English class. In our limited time, we focused on the present. Consequently, students missed a perception of sequence, and cause and effect relationships. They did not have a view of change and development in the movement. I am convinced that the teacher should begin with the present, but the past gives support to the study.

Since the Institute was aimed at exposing teachers to multiple approaches and materials, I was not always able to develop projects in depth. This was detrimental to the students. I moved faster at times when I desired.

One serious shortcoming of the study was that it did not directly probe the students' neighborhood environment. Although we shared emotional and intellectual experiences, the study lacked physical dimension. We brought the movement to the classroom, but we did not follow it home. Questions about the students' neighborhood might have been raised: What are some of the problems? What is being done to meet these problems? Some possible topics for investigation include:

Business (credit stores, neighborhood stores)
Crime (gangs, their hangouts, etc.), students review police records
Libraries
Churches
Recreation (playgrounds, parks, what do people do?)
Population statistics
Housing
Agencies (social workers, summer programs, federal and local
   projects)

Students may concentrate their study on only a small area, like
one block, and share their findings. They may be asked to conduct
interviews, make charts, graphs, and surveys. They can read books
dealing with these topics. Group work is possible. Had time and
my knowledge of Trenton permitted, my next area of study would
have corrected this weakness in my program.

Should the Protest Movement Be Taught?

It is difficult to find a magazine without an article on civil rights.
It is rare to hear a newscast without an account of new violence.
It is impossible to read any newspaper without a report of the black-
white struggle. How can we *not* teach the movement in the schools?
Where else can students be exposed to all sides and be left free
to choose their own ways?
The summer of 1966 records its hot spots: Chicago, Brooklyn, Balti-
more, and Cleveland. This summer we too staged a demonstration.
Sometimes our conflict was an invisible one and it never reached
the headlines, but many of us shall remember the inner war we
fought. There were no bricks and Molotov cocktails; there was freedom to speak and to listen.

> Like Martin L. King, Langston Hughes also spoke of a dream.
> What happens to a dream deferred? Does it dry up like a raisin
>   in the sun
> Or fester like a sore and then run?
> Does it stink like rotten meat
> Or crust and sugar over like a syrupy sweet
> Does it sag like a heavy load,
> Or does it explode?

If we have strong, sensitive teachers to lead classroom revolutions,
perhaps fewer dreams will fester, run, and explode.

3. Reading, Writing, and Seeing: The Visual Approach to Stimulating Reading and Composition

DAVID A. SOHN

At their best, films communicate valid and significant human experiences which illuminate our common humanity and which we should want to share with our students. At their worst (and they share this fault with all media), they present a dehumanizing view of man against which the best defense is trained intelligence and aesthetic judgment. The power of the moving image to manipulate, to editorialize, and to form values and attitudes makes it imperative in this age of film and television that the audience be equipped with the competence needed to understand the rhetoric of the projected image.

> Rev. John M. Culkin, S.J.,
> "Film Study in the High School"

The basic word in my course was *See*. When Hart Leavitt and I wrote the book *Stop, Look and Write*, we described our purpose: "What this book proposes to do is provide a method whereby both students and adults can learn something about the art and power of observation. You might call the method, 'A Beginner's Course in How to See.' " To "notice," to "perceive," to "see" in the best possible way, one needs to practice looking for such things as similarities, differences, emotions, gestures, colors, details, and conflicts. They are all part of the technique of the art of observation. Archibald Mac-Leish, the poet, has cited the goal: it is to learn to see feelingly.

Using *Stop, Look and Write* and *The Family of Man* throughout the course as springboards for discussion and observation provided

---

David A. Sohn used motion pictures in the 1966 Institute to spark a lively sense of "seeing" that led many students to enthusiastic reading and writing about the world around them. Mr. Sohn is a member of the English Department of Middlesex Junior High School, Darien, Connecticut.

texts of photographs that the student could observe again and again. A wide variety of films, however, was the major medium for stimulating reading, writing, and discussion.

The film "Rainshower" (Churchill Films) was one of the first films screened. It is a specific film about the progress of a rainshower and its effects on animals and people. The only dialogue in the film is at the beginning, where it is explained that a photographer started out one day to see what he could see. It was about to rain, and these were the things he saw. The color photography was particularly striking as the students followed the progress of the storm from the country to the city. Shots of animals doused by the rain, a spider drenched by water, a boy chasing the animals to the barn for cover, work stopping in the city, and many others prompted discussion and gave the students a vivid example of how the camera can tell a story without words.

Following this introduction, which was concerned with beauty and specific imagery, we pursued the theme of *Horror*, both real and imagined. Through an error, we received a feature film based on "The Tell-Tale Heart" (but certainly a radical departure from Poe's original) instead of the color short subject with the same title. This film, nevertheless, motivated the students to read the story "The Tell-Tale Heart" in *Great Tales of Horror*, by Edgar Allan Poe. "The Cask of Amontillado" was also shown to stimulate reading. Students were encouraged to read other stories by Poe in the same volume, but they were not required to do so. Several read "The Masque of the Red Death" and "Hop-Frog." Poe's imagined horror was then related to the horror of the real world.

A large reproduction of Picasso's "Guernica" was pasted on the board in front of the class. We discussed what it might mean—how it depicted the horror of war. We then saw the short film "Guernica," in which sections of Picasso's picture are juxtaposed with scenes of the bombed village of Guernica and the horrors of the Spanish Civil War. Next we saw "Night and Fog," the Resnais documentary on the Nazi concentration camps. Contrasts between the empty camps after the war and the film clips and still photographs taken by the Nazis during the war revealed the extreme horror of persecution, starvation, and death in these murder factories clearly and vividly to the students. These films "out-Poed" Poe, certainly, and offered the chance for a discussion that differentiated "real horror" from "imagined horror." Before showing "Night and Fog," we examined the picture of the Warsaw Ghetto prisoners being herded out of hiding by the Nazis. "Night and Fog" is a powerful, realistic film that involved the students. Several asked, "How could something like this happen?"

Moving from the theme of *Horror* to the theme of *Fantasy*, we showed "The Red Balloon" and "Moonbird." "The Red Balloon" was another film that told a story without dialogue. It was possible to bring out such elements in this story as conflict, symbolism, and narrative line. The fantasy, of course, lies in the fact that the balloon takes on human characteristics as it becomes attached to the boy and is finally destroyed by a gang of boys at the end of the film. "Moonbird" was a short film about two boys who dig a hole to catch the moonbird. It is an excellent fantasy. I followed these with a reading of the first few paragraphs of Theodore Thomas' "Test" (from *Ten Top Stories*), which is about an automobile accident, to encourage the students to read it over the week-end.

In regard to the first units, the participating teachers commented in various ways. "I felt 'The Red Balloon' was a good opener for the summer school session. I think it surprised the students to see something new in English, and it nicely tested their powers of observation. The showing of Poe's films was indeed a success. They encouraged a reading of Poe, and the discussions that followed were filled with details that showed an alertness and interest on the part of the students."

Another wrote, "I found this to be an interesting week for several reasons: first, the holding power of the film was vividly demonstrated when *the entire class* gave up its break to see a film through to the end ('The Tell-Tale Heart'). Second, the use of the film to stimulate reading was amply displayed. From a completely 'cold' start on Tuesday, most of the class read several Poe tales by Friday, and I believe all of them will read Monday's assignment ('Test,' by Theodore Thomas.)"

Still another wrote, "When Mr. Sohn asked, ten or so said they'd read 'The Tell-Tale Heart.' Several mentioned they'd read other stories. In a class this size that I taught last year, not more than five read the stories—even though they had the threat of a daily quiz as 'motivation.'"

A fourth commented, "It may be a minor point, but I was impressed by the fact that everyone brought his book on the second day. No mention was made of bringing books—and this was a constant battle in my school. Who can blame the student for not wanting to weight himself down with several huge tomes? Small paperbacks, such as the ones we gave out, are much less imposing and troublesome."

The second week, we showed the following films: "The Pearl";

"New York, New York"; "Corral"; "Morning on the Lievre"; "Diary of Anne Frank"; "White Mane"; and "Dream of Wild Horses." The aim of this week's lessons were to:

1. Interest students in reading by developing interest through seeing films—"The Pearl" and "The Diary of Anne Frank."
2. Develop a sense of seeing details—*Stop, Look and Write.*
3. Develop a sense of interpretation of values—"The Pearl."
4. Understand the term *conflict* and determine the conflict(s) in a story—"White Mane."
5. Recognize film as an art form—"New York, New York" (abstract art) and "Morning on the Lievre" (a series of beautiful scenes and poetry combined).
6. Draw conclusions and develop judgments—"The Pearl."
7. Understand how mood is developed—"The Diary of Anne Frank."
8. See relationships (similarities and contrasts)—"The Diary of Anne Frank" and "Night and Fog."

Before I showed "The Pearl," I passed out the paperback novel and suggested that the students might like to read it. One teacher observed, "Jasper doesn't do homework, but he became involved with *The Pearl* and it was a wonderful thing to watch. Oblivious to the before-class hustle and bustle, Jasper sat reading the book. All during the movies, he read it. Mr. Sohn passed out *The Family of Man,* and Jasper kept reading. Finally he became interested in the pictures, so he kept his place with his finger in *The Pearl,* and glanced at *The Family of Man.* Soon he was back to reading *The Pearl.* He glanced up occasionally to see the movie 'The Diary of Anne Frank,' but most of his attention remained with *The Pearl.* The next morning I asked him, "How do you like that book *The Pearl?*" He answered, 'Oh, it's all right.' "

While teaching *The Pearl,* the word "parable" was introduced in connection with the film. Pages 10 and 17 of *Stop, Look and Write* were used to emphasize seeing details, and the "seeing" theme was related to the film "New York, New York," which is a film of distorted images shot through trick lenses—everyday scenes during a day in New York City. "Morning on the Lievre" is a more literal treatment visually of a trip down the Lievre river in Quebec—a visual translation of a poem by a Canadian poet.

"Corral" and "White mane" told simple stories and contained the elements of a good tale. "Corral" is a short film about the roping and saddling of a wild horse in Canada. It contains no dialogue.

"White Mane" is a beautiful story about a French boy's love of a horse. It compared nicely with "The Red Balloon," for both concerned a young boy's love for something beautiful that in the end is destroyed by the evil in men's hearts.

"Dream of Wild Horses" is a surrealistic no-dialogue film in slow motion of wild horses playing, then running through fire. One teacher called it "a strangely haunting study of odd colors and motion." It is, in effect, a visual poem.

One conclusion made by the students was that "The Red Balloon" could not have been as effective in black and white, whereas "The Diary of Anne Frank" was better in black and white because most of the film takes place in one room. The effect of this variable on the impact of a film is an important one to discuss.

After seeing "The Diary of Anne Frank," students were given the opportunity to borrow and read the book if they wished to do so. At least seven students read the book. This film put the "horror" so vividly shown in "Night and Fog" into specific terms as the students saw the effect of the Nazi terror on one family. As one teacher commented, "For all its horror, 'Night and Fog' stays somewhat abstract, 'The Diary of Anne Frank' makes it real."

"Animal Farm" was shown to combined classes. The book was then given to students who felt they might like to read it. Many of them did so. "I was surprised at how well 'Animal Farm' came over," wrote one teacher. "I had seen it before on TV and was not particularly impressed." The animated film was done in color, whereas the TV version had been seen in black and white. This film related nicely to the theme of tyranny and oppression that we had discussed.

"The Big Fair" was used to teach the concepts of "comparisons," "contrasts," and "theme." This is a short film that develops the theme, "The playthings of youth can become the weapons of maturity." Teacher reactions were interesting:

"Ah, the word *theme* finally emerges!" commented a teacher, "Although it was presented in a very broad sense at first, as the whole series of comparisons was presented in 'The Big Fair,' it later emerged quite clearly."

"After watching 'The Big Fair,' the students were able to list comparisons," said another.

"Pat, for instance, would barely manage to mumble something when called on at the beginning of the course. Now she is an eager volunteer, waving her hand on almost every question," one reported.

"The Great Adventure" was one of several films made by the Swedish director Arne Sucksdorf. "'The Great Adventure' gave rise to a whole host of ideas including conflicts of various sorts, some values, pursuit, a cycle of life in the forest, of the animals, of man, and of boyhood, to list a few," commented a teacher. A link of similarities was developed with this film and "The Red Balloon," "White Mane," and "The Diary of Anne Frank." The other films of Sucksdorf, "Shadows on the Snow," "A Summer Tale," and "A Divided World" were brief ones that developed the contrasts between the world of nature and the world of civilization. Such films can be related to reading Jack London, Mary O'Hara, John Steinbeck, and others.

"The Golden Age of Comedy" illustrated the nature of humor and the art of communicating through purely visual language. The elements of surprise and cruelty in much visual comedy were discussed.

"Hand in Hand" is a film about the nature of prejudice. It is about two English children, one a Catholic, the other a Jew. As they investigate their respective religions, they come to realize that they do not differ fundamentally in purpose, but that the adult world imposes prejudice on the young.

Four of the films which most involved the students were shown toward the end of the course. "A Raisin in the Sun," "On the Waterfront," "Nobody Waved Goodbye," and "The Wild Ones" proved to be outstanding in their power to stimulate thought and discussion. Unfortunately we did not have the books for "A Raisin in the Sun" or "On the Waterfront," although several students asked for them day after day. As one teacher put it, "Anyone in the audience must know by now just how powerful a device films can be. Any doubters should have seen the reaction 'A Raisin in the Sun,' 'On the Waterfront,' etc." The gripping power of these films was a joy to watch.

Through the courtesy of Brandon Films, we were able to show "Nobody Waved Goodbye," a Canadian film about a teenager who is unable to communicate with his family and so rebels, causing his eventual embroilment in a great deal of trouble. It was a remarkable film because of the reality of the problems and the honesty with which it was made. The students identified readily with the main character, Peter. One teacher commented, "By far the best thing we saw this week was the Canadian film 'Nobody Waved Goodbye,' a study of a 'misunderstood' teenager who has no contact with and cannot communicate with the adult world. He has no values, no goals, no ambitions, and no understanding. This film could easily lead to a study of *Catcher in the Rye*, *A Separate Peace*, and perhaps *David Copperfield* and 'Henry IV, Part One.'"

We also saw "Bartleby," the remarkable film made by George Bluestone at the University of Washington. This version of the Melville story was excellent for discussing "character." It also related well to the theme of rebellion. One teacher wrote a comparison of the two films, "Bartleby and Peter (of 'Nobody Waved Goodby') are two individuals who, motivated into rebellion, react completely differently. Bartleby, a would-be free spirit who lacks spirit, withdraws from society. In a sense he is another Ghandi, for he makes use of passive resistance to gain his end which, in this case, it really does. Peter, on the other hand, stands up and fights against the forces which would restrain him from the freedom he seeks. These two films can, I believe, be used in developing a lesson on civil rights. A parallel can be drawn between Bartleby, a believer in nonviolence, and Peter, who strikes out to gain his ends. Also, they can be used in discussing the recent tower killings (in Texas) by Charles Whitman, for it can be argued that his actions are indicative of his discontent with society."

"The Wild Ones" could also be used in this unit, for it shows the rebellion of motorcycle gangs and the problems of law and justice versus mob violence and chaos in society. The students were given copies of *Mid-Century*, the paperback anthology that contains "Cyclists' Raid" by Frank Rooney, the short story on which "The Wild Ones" was based. Coincidentally *The Hunterdon County Democrat*, published in Flemington, New Jersey, ran a story only a few days before the screening of "The Wild Ones" which reported that a group of 50 to 60 cyclists had invaded a nearby tavern and terrorized the customers. The news story, which sported the headline "Chain Gang Motorcyclists Invade County and Keep Police Jumping," virtually paralleled "The Wild Ones" except that the result was not as violent, for the Flemington police did come to the rescue. The story did show, however, that it could happen here, even in New Jersey.

The film "Runner," a short Canadian film, showed the experiences of a track star. It is an excellent study of motion and rhythm. It was used to lead the students to read *See How They Run,* a story about a long distance runner in *Ten Top Stories*. One teacher suggested that the film could also be related to the film "The Loneliness of the Long Distance Runner."

Perhaps the films done by Norman McLaren for the National Film Board of Canada should be treated as a group. During the course, we viewed "Serenal," "Horizontal Lines," "Rhythmetic," "Short and Suite," and "A Little Phantasy on a Nineteenth Century Painting." The films were among the most imaginative shown to the students, and perhaps among the most imaginative ever made. "Serenal" is a conglomeration of moving colors that seem to tell a story. An extremely op projective film students see many different things in it. It runs only four minutes, but is a powerful stimulus for writing. "Horizontal Lines" is a film that shows lines multiplying to the accompaniment of Pete Seeger's banjo. One line eventually spawns a great number of others, then there is a scrambling, and finally a recession to only one line again. The film seemingly is simple and foolish to some when they first see it, but when it is viewed again, one realizes that it contains the elements of a story that has conflict and builds to a climax, then to the denouement. The other films are just as imaginative, and just as usable for teaching the elements of fiction and for stimulating writing.

"A Short Vision" is a brief animated film about a thing that flies over a town, drops a bomb, and destroys the world. It is tremendously effective in its unexpected shock effect as the mood develops and the bomb drops. This film was used to motivate the students to read *Hiroshima,* by John Hersey, which was passed out to them after they saw the film. Before the film, students examined pictures of destruction and war in *Stop, Look and Write* and *The Family of Man.* One picture in *The Family of Man* was a photo of a girl who had survived the bombing of Hiroshima and had suffered severe burns.

The film "1800 Days" was made for Westinghouse by Hugh and Suzanne Johnston. In four minutes this remarkable film compressed the salient events of a five-year period. It is excellent for teaching time concepts and precise observation.

Student Reactions

The students were positive about the course. The visual approach was a new experience to all of them. The following comments are representative of their reactions:

"I've seen many movies these weeks, and they have made me want to read more. The selection of books and movies was very good. I think I have improved in writing and thinking. I will always remember these six weeks."

"I have really enjoyed myself most of all in English. It is sometimes interesting and sometimes dull, but I have never had an English class like this. I wish that the regular English classes in school were like this."

"During this summer course, I became more interested in English. I wish we could have movies in our own English class in school. I feel that it encouraged me to read books and stories. If we were lucky enough to have it this way in school, we could have a movie one day a week and discuss it the rest of the week. It was so nice to have all the books. They were interesting and I enjoyed them. I had a wonderful summer and I really enjoyed English."

"I have seen movies that have urged me to read the book. So I did and then compared the two. I also wrote compositions on the movies and books. We all wrote them and got different ideas. To me this English is the most interesting course I have ever had or heard of."

". . . It's a great way to get some of these children (Including Me!!!) to open up books and read them. You really didn't come right out and tell us that you were trying to increase our will to read, but I found out that's exactly what you were doing, and I'll never forget your methods or the enjoyment I got out of this class."

Teacher Reactions

The following excerpts from the final papers of the participating teachers will give some idea of their feeling about what we did during the course:

"I would have to conclude that what we saw in regard to using the film to stimulate writing was new and fresh, that the students find it interesting and enjoyable, that it's fun to teach this way, and best of all, that it works. It can promote a great deal of writing. No one could ask any more of a method."

"I should say one other thing about the use of films, and that is that I learned that properly selected and used films have a universal appeal and a tremendous capacity to grip and move an audience. I was a dying fox, but I was also a mad killer clutching a bloody, throbbing heart, a horse plunging in a fiery surf, a red balloon deflating pomposity, a man anguished to learn that riches can bring terrible grief rather than anticipated joy, an imprisoned girl with a soaring spirit and a free mind, a cowboy, an autumn leaf floating toward winter on the Lievre, a brutal boxer, a boy in love with an otter, a pie-in-the-face comedian, and a dot frantically looking for a place to rest. I'm saying that I didn't just watch a lot of pictures. I was involved. I am not exceptional. What happened to me happened to everyone there. We were all involved. Therein may lie salvation for English teachers, who constantly fret about the same dilemma: 'How can we get our students involved?'"

"This is my first experience with a new medium for teaching, and

I found it to be extremely effective. I am most impressed. The use of films has the advantage of conveying ideas to the student more quickly and effectively than a textbook. It has the further advantage of being able to convey a whole range of ideas and themes in a shorter time period than I imagined. It bypasses the problem of having a teacher force a student to read a book, and it alleviates the added problems for a teacher of: (1) wondering whether the student has read the books, and (2) wondering if he understood what he has read. The observation of a film gets a point directly to a student in the surest and quickest way possible."

"Showing a novel or short story in film form to a group of disadvantaged youth is a great equalizer. It gives this type of student something to talk about both to the students in his own group and even students in a so-called higher class. In a way, it can be said that a book to be read is unfair to certain youth, whereas a film to be seen is fair to all youth . . ."

"Maybe some traditional teachers will conclude that Mr. Sohn is opposed to reading. On the contrary, Mr. Sohn has done a great deal to bring about a desire on the part of the student to do more reading. In Mr. Sohn's room there is an abundance of paperback books of the best type. Students are given these books and they are encouraged to read them. No student is ever forced to read. He reads because he wants to read or because he knows the choice is his. There is no fear of failure or punishment of any kind."

"Are the students in Mr. Sohn's class reading? A goodly number of them are. Whenever Mr. Sohn asks a question about a comparison between the book and the film, the response has been surprising to at least one person. As a participating teacher, I was somewhat amazed at the amount of reading that took place on a voluntary basis. One student in particular said that he had read three books. Even if this student told a half-truth, he still has accomplished a great deal."

"If I could utilize any of the techniques I have encountered here, I would employ the Look, See and Write method. I would show lots of movies with the intention of stimulating reading and writing. I would employ the saturation technique with books. Fader's library borrowing technique was an excellent mechanical device: give the child two books; every time he wants a different book, he trades one in."

"Mr. Sohn's technique has made me aware that children, even those who are classified as 'slow,' can handle profound ideas. Movies are an excellent way to present these profundities. 'The Great Adventure,' for example, dealt with many of these weighty issues: the short life of grief and joy in the forest (and in society, perhaps?); no one can catch and hold a dream alive for long; the inevitable pain in growing up; the conflict between man and nature, man and boy, etc. Fader said in his book, semiliterate children do not need semi-literate books. Many aspects of this Institute have combined to tell me not to underestimate the capabilities of these children, not to treat them with condescension. They can cope with the great moral issues. They will, in fact, become deeply involved with great issues such as civil rights, Naziism, prejudice, etc. Since an English class should relate with life in the outside world, I plan to stop avoiding these issues. I plan to bring my classes out of that foreign, Victorian world of Silas Marner and into the world of the midtwentieth century."

Conclusion

The students reacted enthusiastically to the course. Many were moved to read the books we provided. Many became more aware of such relationships as comparisons and contrasts. The uses of positive reinforcement and the consequent lack of pressure had beneficial results. In such a short time writing fluency could not be developed. Writing must be taught and developed in class with these students. Assigned homework in writing simply does not work. Time limitations prohibited doing a great deal of "in-class" writing, but those compositions that were written frequently showed a great deal of imagination and potential.

The films were shared with the afternoon program on film-making, and many participating teachers were exposed to the films in evening screenings.

The participating teachers in my course read four books: *How Children Fail* by John Holt, *Summerhill* by A. S. Neill, *Revolution in Teaching* by DeGrazia and Sohn, and *Teacher* by Sylvia Ashton-Warner. The general reaction to the readings was favorable. They felt that many of the ideas in these books were provocative.

I had the feeling at the end of the course that a great deal of enthusiasm was generated for the visual approach to learning from both the students and the participating teachers, and such interest, of course, was my objective. It should be interesting to see *if* and *how* these visual techniques will be applied in the actual school situations.

The following is the prospectus handed out to participating teachers before beginning the courses.

THE VISUAL APPROACH TO STIMULATING READING AND WRITING

Various types of visual stimuli will be used to motivate the student to read and write. The course will be based on the paperback text *STOP, LOOK AND WRITE*, with other types of media related to it. For example, a number of films will be shown to the student for a variety of purposes—such as "The Pearl," which will be shown to the student to motivate him to read the novel; "White Mane," which will be used to stimulate writing and motion; and "On the Waterfront," which will be used both as a springboard for writing and an illustration of the motion picture as a work of art.

In regard to writing, there are three objectives: to teach the student to observe carefully and to interpret his observations imaginatively; to teach the student to think in terms of metaphor and imagery; and to help the student to develop fluency in his writing.

To stimulate reading, books and collections of short stories related to motion pictures and filmstrips will be available. Most of the time, the student will be encouraged to read the printed work, but not required to do so. It is hoped that he will want to read further and will develop a desire to read more. Paperbacks will be used exclusively. Students will do one individual project related to the visual approach.

More positive attitudes toward reading and writing are outcomes that we wish to achieve. Reinforcement theory will be emphasized as part of commenting on student work (no negative comments but accentuation of the positive). We also hope that teachers may find new ideas and methods to use with their classes.

4. Communicating—Is It English or Social Studies?

EVELYN R. HARPER

"Although we are in a social studies course, I am learning English."

Student comment

Our objective, planned around a thematic approach, "Communicating Effectively in a Democratic Society Is Imperative," was to create dynamic and challenging programs for each student so that he might become enthusiastic in effecting the following:

1. Change in self-concept
2. Reinforcement of communication skills
3. Feeling of success
4. Rise in aspirational level
5. Stretched mind: An enlargement of concepts and insights
6. Multiplicity of rich, happy, and rewarding experiences in speaking, writing, role-playing, creating, reading, listening, sharing, perceiving, evaluating, and problem-solving
7. Better understanding of sequences of events, groups of simultaneous events, cause-to-effect and effect-to-cause relationships
8. Cognizance of the individual rights and responsibilities in a free society
9. Desire to discover the truth about social situations by wide, well-selected reading
10. Understanding of the importance of reading and satisfying recreational and intellectual curiosity through reading
11. Ability to discriminate between fact and opinion
12. Reinforcement of study skills

Evelyn R. Harper, 1966 Kansas Teacher of the Year, secured enthusiastic student response in 1966 through multilevel uses of familiar communication devices like films, newspapers, and records. Mrs. Harper is Reading Consultant at Atchison High School, Atchison, Kansas.

Our objectives were ambitious for a five-week Institute. We wanted to acquaint our students with a wide body of materials relative to democratic human relations which would help them to develop the foregoing objectives, and reinforce positive attitudes, ideals, values, loyalties, and appreciations, within a meaningful and purposeful content. We wanted them to learn and think clearly and precisely about what they were reading or information gained through communication media, as well as to speak, write, and listen more effectively. Consequently, the five participating teachers and I agreed at the beginning that in addition to preparing the content and accumulating all available materials possible, each must bring his very special skills, both in human understanding and teaching techniques, into the classroom.

It is generally understood among educators that the teacher's skill and personal attributes are among the most important elements needed in helping an individual to learn, whether he is considered disadvantaged or advantaged. Foremost among those special attributes and skills is a genuine understanding of students, a sincere desire to help them, an ability to make the students feel wanted by putting them at ease, and the capacity to aid students in discovering and measuring their individual capacities, abilities, interests, and possibilities as a help in directing their individual pattern for further training, learning, and contributions, along with a willingness to persist in the task. We tenaciously and happily held to this view throughout the five weeks, which made the objectives functional and attainable.

A good relationship existed between the students and participating teachers. The students, whose range of ability and background was as wide as that in a typical sophomore high school class—from 4.8 to 12.5 in reading; from 75 to above 125 in IQ—were assigned in groups of five to each participating teacher. As one student remarked, "I like Mr. Pontani. He is my special teacher." All participating teachers were very special to their five students. They made home visits, kept records and attendance, taught, assisted with problems and in fun activities, gave guidance and genuine personal concern, which culminated in a good student-teacher rapport. Of course, the students and participating teachers were very special to me.

On a brief interest inventory that we devised, the students indicated by majority checks that they enjoyed collecting stamps and pennies, reading mysteries, sports, television, playing rock and roll and jazz records, listening to the radio, dancing, reading comic books, attending movies, playing cards, and were concerned with the youth problems and civil rights. In addition to numerous mysteries listed as their favorite books, the following were given: *Tom Sawyer, Black Like Me, Patch of Blue, The Cool World, School Life for Teenagers, Black Beauty, Heidi, To Kill a Mockingbird, Teen-Age Tales, Gone With the Wind, The Good Earth,* and *Hot Rod.*

We asked, "Suppose you were going to write a book for others your age. What would the title be?" The responses included: *How to Find a Job at 13, 14, 15 Years Old, How Can Teenagers Get Along with People, Book on Happenings, Freedom for People, The Cool World of Teenagers, Hurts, Rights for Minorities, Problems Teenagers Face, Getting Along with Parents, Fight, Work, Love, Play,* and *Future Life.*

Again, these replies pointed up their concerns which were valuable in structuring a program in social studies, as were the reading scores gained from administering the *Gates Reading Survey, Form 3,* and additional information secured from students' permanent school records.

Before securing the foregoing information, due to the time element, we began playing it by ear, collecting books, mostly paperbacks, records, posters, films, poems, magazines, newspapers, pictures, machines, games, gadgets, and stories, as well as planning trips and making original source materials so as to enhance responsiveness and vitality from students relative to the personal-social problems. We arranged furniture in a semicircle, creating a more informal, friendly atmosphere. The bulletin board was made attractive with book jackets and reviews. A bright multicolored tree made from contact paper was placed on the front blackboard. Upon entering the room the first day, Linda exclaimed, "What happened to this room? It's different! I like it fixed this way!"

Most of the students seemed to respond well to the tree, the room decorations, and seating arrangements. They were especially happy about writing their names on a favorite-colored leaf and adding it to the friendship tree, which was symbolic of joining a circle of friends. The participating teachers reported that they, too, liked the idea as an "ice-breaker." At first, one teacher questioned the feasibility of its use in a high school classroom of 35 or 40 disadvantaged youth. Later he relented, however, and stated that he was going to try it, for the friendship tree might work. We felt that this was good. And Goethe's quotation came to mind, "Daring ideas are like a chessman moved forward; they may be beaten, but they may start a winning game." This quotation came to mind many times during the summer.

The preplanning had paid off. We established rapport with students in a relatively short time and created a friendly give-and-take atmosphere of respect and challenge, conducive to learning and teaching.

The area of concentration, "Communicating in a Democratic Society," was a fusion of the communicative arts and American history projected in an integrated approach. Using the inductive method, instruction was for the most part centered around the social studies content. The participating teachers and I combined resources and competencies and did team teaching. We used the reading-skill approach: (1) Built background concepts with carefully planned meaningful illustrative materials (related and correlated); (2) emphasized vocabulary study and growth; (3) set purpose; (4) SQ3R (survey, question, read, review, recite); (5) culminating activities for evaluation and reinforcement; and (6) self-testing.

Experience-broadening activities, such as role-playing, debates, group dynamics, games, trips, films, books, card-playing, discussions, magazines, newspapers, and other illustrative materials played a major part in the inductive method of teaching and learning. They were teaching techniques used for building up the student's responsiveness, both to the vitality of social studies and to the effectiveness of the communicative arts in achieving vitality. The important thing was to introduce the students to social studies actively, not passively, by leading them to "make it on the spot" out of materials derived from their experience; providing an opportunity in the process for each student to develop the habit of reacting to a situation, a sensitivity to social situations, a way of assessing and relating to school situations, culminating in questions of values and standards that had to be answered. The start was from something known, and something was always known.

Newspapers were wonderful springboards for teaching social studies. *The Evening Times,* a Trenton newspaper, furnished us daily (without cost) a large quantity of newspapers for classroom use. By correlating and using this intrinsically interesting here-and-now source of current happenings, many of the unfamiliar concepts became familiar and the remote became concrete for a large number of students. This was exciting and gratifying, for achievement and success build confidence.

The first week was spent exploring the postulate that competency in social studies rested on a foundation of effective communication skills. Communication skills and social studies were defined and correlated. The newspaper, one medium of communication, was chosen, among others, as desirable for study and improvement by the class. The initial discussions and considerations were in small groups, with each participating teacher acting as a consultant for one group. After group discussions, students reassembled, and shared and refined the information. New words from *The Evening Times* were added to the students' vocabulary-study list in their Princeton University notebooks.

Role-playing by students of the word "cool," as used in Langston Hughes' poem "My Motto," compared with its usage in Warren Miller's book *The Cool World,* pointed up a few important generalizations which were formulated by the students and teachers and placed on the board and in notebooks: (1) Words have many meanings. (2) A person cannot comprehend, react to, or be influenced by the ideas of an author unless he can identify the printed words used to convey these ideas. (3) To communicate successfully, in any task, a person must understand the necessary concepts, possess vocabulary knowledge, and have the ability to handle the language relationships involved. (4) Effective reading is vital to personal development, economic efficiency, and civic responsibility in a democratic society.

Following the discussion on reading and the concept that instruction in study skills often contributes to increasing efficiency in reading and ultimately to the person's security, a lesson was held using the SQ3R technique. The question was asked, "How many have used the SQ3R formula before?" The answers were negative. SQ3R was translated to mean: S—survey (look over title, overview, section headings to determine purpose and scope,) Q—question (formulate questions to be answered by reading), R—review (call to mind what is known about the subject, fundamental information on which to build), R—reading, and R—recitation (answering all questions, either orally or in writing). Together, we read the selection "U.S. Teen-Agers—The Golden Confusing Years," *Readers Digest,* July 1966. The discussion became so heated that prepared debates ensued. The students responded very well to the formula. In their themes, they related their plans to make use of it in their studies.

Dr. John Furbay's recorded lecture "Let's Join the Human Race," was played as a listening experience and a culminating activity of reinforcement of effective communicative ideas. Dr. Furbay, internationally known lecturer, reiterates that effective communication tends to eliminate prejudices, hatreds, ignorance, and many other limitations that breed differences and misunderstandings in the world today. "All peoples and races of the world are more alike than different," he emphasizes consistently. The class listened and related well. Original skits, paragraphs, conversation, pantomimes, debates, and role-playing were their lively forms of reaction and clarification of concepts. Fred said, "I don't like talking records. I like swinging records. I like this one. I understand it."

For the remaining weeks, consideration was given to the catalytic units of the developmental theme, "Communicating Effectively in a Democratic Society Is Imperative": "The Newspaper as a Means of Communication," "The Function of the Press in a Democracy," and "The Responsibility for Individual Rights in a Free Society." The following brief outlines may point up a few approaches we found successful by using the inductive method.

I. The Newspaper as a Means of Communication

A. *Teacher Prepared*

1. *Objectives*
   a. To help students understand the main features of a newspaper
   b. To teach students how to use the newspaper and how to interpret it
   c. To understand the importance of the press in a democratic society
   d. To reinforce the communication and social studies skills
   e. To think critically
   f. To enhance the enjoyment in reading the newspaper daily
2. *Resources*
   a. *The New York Times,* Office of Educational Activities, New York City (free materials)
      ———*A Basic Text for Problems of Democracy Courses*
      ———"How to Get the Most Out of Your Newspaper"
      ———"Public Opinion: Its Role in a Democracy"
      ———"The American Newspaper"
      ———"Vitalizing the Curriculum with *The New York Times*"
   b. Reigner, Charles G., *English for Business Use,* the H. M. Rowe Company, 1964
   c. *The Evening Times* (a copy for each student)
   d. An assortment of daily newspapers
   e. Scott, Foresman and Company chart, "Propaganda Devices that Can Mislead You" (free)
   f. Bulletin board display of *The New York Times* supplement, "The American Newspaper"

B. *Built Background and Stimulated Interest*

a. A current news story—The massacre of eight student nurses in Chicago created intense reactions that a debate incurred.

Mary: "I'd shoot the murderer on sight!"

Scotty: "Why?"

Mary: "Because he's crazy, like crazy, man!"

Scotty: "I disagree! He's due a fair trial!"
This discussion gained momentum with others taking sides.

Teacher: "Yes, you may. You may use all of the available materials."
The interest in the debate was high. (The focus was on the Bill of Rights, Constitution of the United States, dictionary, newspapers, and presentation structure, which provided old and new concepts and skills, but also information and lead questions for the newspaper study.)

b. Introductory Quiz on Newspaper Reading
   (1) How many newspapers do you read daily?
   (2) How many different major fields are treated in the average daily newspaper?
   (3) Do you read newspapers from areas other than your home town area, and compare contents?
   (4) Do you read for information, recreation, both?
   (5) Do you look at all of the pages of the newspaper or do you just read certain chosen parts?
   (6) Have you ever gone on a guided tour of a newspaper plant?
   (7) Do you on occasion read some new (to you) portion of the newspaper?
   (8) Could you explain how the news is gathered and selected for publication in a good newspaper?
   (9) How many columns does a newspaper contain?
   (10) Are you a "Headline Reader," "Front Page Reader," "One Subject Reader," "Sports and Comics Reader?"
   (11) How many columns does a page of the newspaper contain?
   (12) Do you sincerely believe you get all that you should out of the daily newspaper in the time available?
      Inquisitiveness prompted students to scrutinize the newspapers for both the correct answers to the quiz and for self-evaluation, using the questions written on the blackboard: (1) What is my favorite newspaper? Why? (2) Which parts of the newspaper are my favorites? Why? (3) What is the physical make-up of my favorite newspaper? Is it a good paper?

Students were requested to bring in their newspaper the following day, if it were different from the *The Evening Times*. Favorite papers were analyzed in terms of the foregoing questions and answers.

C. Developed Vocabulary Continuously

1. *Daily News* is a *tabloid.* What is a *tabloid?* (Example)
2. How does it differ from a standard newspaper?

D. Brief Outline of Content

1. Getting Acquainted with the Newspaper
    a. Physical Make-up of the Newspaper
        (1) Size of sheet
        (2) Number of pages
        (3) Masthead
        (4) Second section
        (5) Etc.
2. Main Parts of the Newspaper
    a. News Index and summary
    b. The headline
    c. The masthead
    d. The editorial
    e. The columnist
    f. The cartoon
    g. Departments
    h. Foreign news
    i. National news
    j. Letters to the editor
    k. Local news
    l. The human interest story
    m. Society news
    n. Sports
    o. Book reviews
    p. Obituary
    q. Food, family, furnishings
    r. Weather report
    s. The dateline
    t. News services
    u. Foreign news service
    v. Special features

(Pupils were asked to analyze their favorite paper after presentation and discussion.)
3. What Is News?
    a. Definition
    b. Types
        (1) Local   (2) Foreign   (3) National   (4) Etc.
4. The Newspaper's Place in the Community
5. Uses of the Daily Newspaper in Daily Life
6. The Function of The Press in a Democracy
7. Types of Readers and Their Motives for Reading
8. Propaganda Devices that Can Mislead You
    a. Name-calling
    b. Glittering generalities
    c. Transfer
    d. Testimonial

e. Plain folks   g. Card-stacking
f. Band wagon
9. Examples of Good and Bad Reporting
10. Critical Reading (Cause and Effect, Effect and Cause), etc.

As an outgrowth of this unit and the desire of the students to visit *The Evening Times* of Trenton, we visited the plant and took a guided tour which was very informative and interesting.

As a result of the visit to *The Evening Times,* a short composition was written about the trip. A critical evaluation followed. A thank you note was sent to the editor of the paper.

A brief discussion was held on the "Main Parts of a Composition" before students attempted to write (developed with students).

1. Main Parts of a Composition
   a. Beginning (introduction)
   b. Middle (development)
   c. End (conclusion)
2. 3 B's
   a. Be brief
   b. Be interesting
   c. Be seated (when talking)
3. Qualities of a good composition
   a. Long enough to cover subject
   b. Short enough to be interesting

An Original Composition

MY TRIP TO *THE EVENING TIMES*
By Linda Hicks

After having a lesson on the subject of newspapers and learning many different terms, our social studies class went on a guided tour of the Trenton *Times'* plant. Students walked from their homes to make the tour and returned to school by automobiles in time for the third hour class.

The trip proved to be very effective for when we began to visit the different departments, the class's complete attention was on the speaker. Also, the students seemed to be very interested in the variety of machines. They showed this interest when they got back to school.

The whole tour was a complete success and was given the

final touch by Mrs. Harper, who treated the class after the tour. We had delicious food in the Trenton *Times'* cafeteria.

The successfulness was also shown the next day when we had an interesting discussion on the new terms and information about the Trenton *Times.* Students have a better understanding of newspapers and will be better readers.

Interesting prepared oral reports were given on the subject, "How My Newspaper Reading Has Improved."

Before a thank you letter was written to the editor of *The Evening Times,* the following lesson was taught.

THE BUSINESS LETTER

Purpose of the Lesson

To culminate our series of lessons on the newspaper, propaganda, and visit to *The Evening Times.* To write a business letter to the editor of *The Evening Times,* thanking him for allowing us to take the tour, expressing our appreciation for free newspapers which we received daily throughout the summer, extolling the value of the newspaper in our lives. To learn the proper form and content of a meaningful business letter.

Objectives. 1. To learn how to express oneself in a business letter.

2. To purposefully tie-up the various sections of the unit on the newspaper.

3. To practice group thinking in the creation of the letter.

4. To bring committee work into focus by pooling the sum of comments expressed in the committees.

5. To point out the accessibility of newspapers, and the influence newspapers have on us and we on the newspapers.

Skills. 1. Achieving individual contributions in a group setting.

2. Proper technical form of the business letter.

3. Actual individual writing of the letter.

4. Writing one letter, representing the group, to the editor of *The Evening Times.*

Resources. 1. The cooperating teachers.

2. Reigner, Charles G., *English for Better Use,* the H. N. Rowe Company, Chicago, 1964.

Development. 1. Discuss the various parts of the business letter and show on the board just what they look like.

2. Have students write the form of the business letter in their notebooks.

3. Show illustrations of accepted business form.

4. Committees work up a business letter to the editor.

5. Pool resources and results to write one complete letter.

6. Final writing of the letter, typed, by two of the students.

The culminating activity was the writing of the letter.

The interest of the students gained momentum on the subject of civil liberties, with increased concern about the Chicago murder trial, newspaper study, and current events, and ultimately prompted the next unit, "Development of Individual Rights in a Free Society." The following outline is indicative of the approach.

Development of Responsibility for Individual Rights in a Free Society

CENTRAL THEME. Maintenance of a system of individual rights in a free society is determined by the best possible relationship that can be achieved between individual liberty and society's need for order.

MAJOR CONCEPT. Respect for the fundamental worth, dignity, and privacy of the individual is of the essence in our society and underlies all the specific guarantees in the Bill of Rights.

Objectives

Attitudes. 1. Appreciating our American heritage.

2. Recognizing the dignity and worth of every individual.

3. Recognizing the values of imagination, perseverance, sacrifice, and hard work.

4. Being sensitive to one's individual responsibility to improve and preserve our heritage.

5. Changing one's self-concept.

Skills. 1. Evaluating the worth and appropriateness of specialized sources of information.

2. Sharing information with others by means of oral and written reports, panel discussions, role-playing, games, and other special activities.

3. Reinforcing study skills.

4. Projecting a feeling of success.

Resources. Record: "If I Were President—Oh Yeah!" by Timmie Rogers.

Film: "The Diary of Anne Frank," a 20th Century-Fox production.

Film: "A Raisin in the Sun," Columbia Motion Pictures.

Record: "A Time to Live," New Jersey Petroleum Company, Trenton.

Record: "Count Down," Dr. John Furbay, Columbia Record Productions.

Field Trips: Cultural Center, New Jersey State Library and archives; Island Beach; United Nations; Metropolitan Museum of Art; and American Natural History Museum.

Other Resources. Abramowitz, Jack, *American History Study Lessons,* Unit 9, Follett Publishing Company, Chicago, 1963.

Bragdon, Henry Wilkerson et al., *Frame of Government,* Macmillan Co., New York, 1962.

New Jersey State Division on Civil Rights, poster and pamphlet.

Report of the Williamstown Workshop—A Program to Improve.

Bill of Rights Teaching in High Schools, Civil Educational Foundation, Inc., New York, 1962.

Bacon, Francis L., *A Graphic Story of Our Democracy,* Denoyer-Geppert Company, Chicago, 1966.

Chart to integrate with *A Graphic Story of Our Democracy.*

Reviewing American History, Amsco School Publications, Inc., New York.

Wilder, Howard B. et al., *This Is America's Story,* Houghton Mifflin Company, Boston, 1964.

Development

The record "If I Were President—Oh Yeah!" by Timmie Rogers was played for the class, which was most enjoyable for the students. They related well and expressed themselves freely about the differences between the "rights" guaranteed by the law and the reality of the law. Through humor and satire many of the "institutions" of our society were examined in the record and discussed and role-played by the students—voting rights, literacy tests, freedom, civil rights, a Negro as president of the United States, etc. This record proved a novel and stimulating method of getting students really involved in activities and concerns relative to expressing, developing, and reinforcing concepts of human rights and citizenship responsibilities.

Two films, "The Diary of Anne Frank" and "A Raisin in the Sun," also were very valuable. These were shown in English classes, following the Timmie Rogers record. Developmental inquiries on the Anne Frank film follow.

(1) Students were asked to give their opinion of the picture. (Responses were written on the blackboard.)

(2) *Question:* Could something like that ever happen in the United States? (Santayana's quote, "Those who forget the past are condemned to repent it," was correlated and developed with the concept.)

(3) *Question:* What protection does the citizen have in the United States to protect him against totalitarianism? (A definition of *totalitarianism* was formulated with the students.)

(4) The instructor summarized with Lord Acton's quote, "Absolute rule rules absolutely." (This led to a discussion of the meaning of democracy.)

(5) The students were requested to read the first two paragraphs of the Declaration of Independence, using "Sweet Land of Liberty." *Question:* Is this democracy? (The vast problems and implications depicted in the film "A Raisin in the Sun" were interjected at this point for evaluation, classification under cause and effect, and correlation.)

(6) The teacher drew a tree on the blackboard which was labeled, "The Growth of Human Rights." The branches showed the problems: Discrimination in education, housing, jobs, etc., and the attempted solutions—the federal civil rights laws of 1957, 1960, 1964, and the New Jersey civil rights law. Explanations of the provisions of each law were given, and the problems each attempts to deal with were briefly given and discussed with the class.

(7) The idea of the equality of man, the right to happiness, etc., were discussed. (Majority rule/minority rights. Concessions and agreements were used.)

(8) *Question:* How are the concepts so aptly outlined in the Declaration of Independence, the Bill of Rights, and the Constitution of the United States guaranteed to U.S. citizens? (Students defined individual freedoms and rights as shown on Chart D. (The instructor reviewed all basic concepts, outlining on the blackboard.)

Culminating Activities

One subject, "What Living in a Democratic Country Means to Me," was developed with the writing of a theme and a skit.

Dr. Jack Abramowitz's Unit 9, *American History Study Lessons,* was used to develop the "Origins of the Civil Rights Movement and the Causes of Bias and Prejudice in American Race Relations." The

unit is so very well structured with built-in techniques that it is not
was used to develop the "Origins of the Civil Rights Movement and
necessary to present it. The unit was effective in the learning-teaching
situation.

As noted throughout this report, systematic instruction in study
skills was given; activities involving all of the communication arts
and skills were consistently stressed; and multilevel materials were
used. The reading test, Gates Reading Survey, Form 3 (Teachers
College, Columbia University, New York City), was evaluated with
each student to determine his assets and liabilities in reading competency. The importance of reading skills was discussed. It was emphasized to the students that these test results were only one estima-
tion and that they should check with their counselors, and English
and reading teachers in the fall for further guidance. A change in
the fourth-hour scheduling, however, was disappointing because it
limited individual reading instruction after the first two weeks to
a very few lessons.

Special reading materials used both for individual and class instruction included the following. *Controlled Reader* (Educational Developmental Laboratories, Inc., Huntington, New York): "I Do Strange
Things in My Sleep," "How I Learned to Love My Dad," "Stalked
by a Grizzly," and "Mary Reed—Pirate"; *Study Skills Library,*
GG(EDL): "Practice in Making Inferences," "Practice in Recognizing
Fact and Opinion," "Practice in Classifying," "Practice in Summariz-
ing," "Practice in Finding Main Ideas"; New Rochester Occupational
Reading Series; *The Job Ahead,* (SRA); *Readers Digest,* June, July,
1966, *Educational Editions,* a variety of teacher-made materials, and
a variety of paperback books. *The Evening Times* was used both
for social studies and all communicative-arts skills.

The techniques and materials discussed in this report have stressed
the intensive use of the best possible teacher attributes and skills,
well-defined goals, student action, multiplicity of concrete materials
and activities, and a carefully structured program that is flexible and
vitalized enough to permit each student to achieve to the maximum
development of his ability; accepting the opportunity to do so; beginning at his current status and continuing in the direction most suitable
for him at his own rate. These emphases are essential in helping
the culturally disadvantaged fulfill his potential.

Students and participating teachers reported that the program was
successful in fulfilling the purposes set at the beginning of the summer
studies. In addition to outward manifestations of the new learning,
students commented frequently about its effectiveness.

Some Student Reactions

1. "Teachers are so friendly and interesting in summer school. They make you like school. Why can't teachers be as friendly and interesting during the rest of the year?"

2. "I have never been to the ocean before. It looks just like the picture. Gee, I am seeing and learning a lot on these trips." (*Ed. Note:* It is interesting that at the age of 16 this child had never been to the ocean, only 35 miles from Trenton.)

3. "I had to think about a lot of things this summer I never thought before. I understand better, I suppose."

4. "I liked the movies, paperback books, and the trips, and the way we talk about them.

5. "As a card shark, I liked the cards 'cause I had fun and learn words to."

6. "We have started taking *The Evening Times* after I told my mother that I like to read it now."

7. "It's fun to act out social studies, Mrs. Harper. I learn more that way."

8. "Visiting a museum was more interesting than I thought. I am going back and take my little sisters and brothers."

9. "I did not like social studies, but it has been so easy this summer that I like it, especially the debates, trips, and games."

10. "Although we are in a social studies course, I am learning English."

11. "I enjoyed the summer school very much. It was fun, and what's more, it was educational, which will help me next year."

12. "The PTI gave students a chance to meet some very fascinating people and a chance to help express himself amongst others of his own level."

13. "I think that the Trenton-Princeton Summer Institute is much better than the regular school year. I mean that you learn more in a few weeks that you come here than you do in a whole year in regular school."

14. "I like the newspaper and civil-rights discussions."

15. "I liked the way the class proceeded. I did everything you asked as you are kind and understanding. You answered all of my questions. I wish I had you for my real teacher all of the time."

16. "A person is a person in your class which is different in regular school. A fellow does not have a chance."

17. "The summer program was interesting. It enriched my knowledge on certain matters. I enjoyed racism and the constitution and the funny record most."

18. "I enjoyed the teachers I had, summer school, the many trips, and talking about many interesting topics."

19. "I liked the way I learn words about many problems that I can talk about better like understanding problems and civil rights."

20. "I hope that Princeton Institute will sponsor this program again next year, because I will make it my business to be here."

5. Survival as a Key to Student Involvement

PHYLLIS JACKSON

Now that the urban poor have been discovered, such terms as "experimentation" and "innovation" have become catchwords of urban education. Projects and experiments multiply, yet visible change in the operation and quality of inner-city schools remains imperceptible. And that lack of visible change will continue unless the training of the classroom teacher—the real agent of educational change—improves.

With this, then, as a premise, we logically proceed to the question of how this may be accomplished. There are several answers and several approaches. Ideally, one would start at the core of the problem, namely, with formal teacher education. But what of the teacher who has already passed through the academic halls and has been ill-prepared to face the problems of teaching in the inner-city school? What of the educator who has passed through the pedagogy courses more hampered than helped, and is completely unaware that he is unprepared to face these problems at the outset? His experiences, his trials and tribulations in the classroom awaken him to this. Then what shall he do? How shall he prepare? With this as our problem we look for the agent of change, the "retooling" center, that will better prepare the teacher to meet the monumental task of everyday teaching in his own special situation. The Princeton-Trenton Institute, from its very inception, was created to fulfil his needs, to meet his acute and ever-growing problem.

The teacher-dominated, text-oriented, student-recitation type of classroom simply has not met the needs of inner-city youngsters. This is a fact and where it is denied, there is hypocrisy. And who are,

Phyllis Jackson, from Cardoza High School in Washington, D.C., uses a "survival" theme from India and the American West to lead students in the 1966 Institute into examining their own neighborhoods. Miss Jackson's experiences in the Peace Corps form a background for her interest in this area.

in fact, functional illiterates? Students not working up to capacity. How else do we explain the high-potential but low-performance student? We are producing high school graduates who are destined for mental institutions and welfare rolls; who are, in fact, to become statistics to be subsidized by me. Who will deny the role of the schools in their failure? Who will deny the role of the teacher in their failure? Who will deny all this?

Such a classroom environment as just described ultimately alienates students and confirms in their minds that what happens in the schools is divorced from reality. It is the student that we are to be concerned with, and if the student reacts badly to the text-oriented, teacher-dominated, student-recitation situations, we are then obliged to produce the materials and methods that the students will respond to. It is a clear case. If the students come to learn and we are not teaching them with the present curricula, then the curricula must go. And if that is the case, the students are push-outs, not drop-outs. They are the future. Who will defend the democracies, whether in rhetoric or war? Certainly not these former students.

Therefore we need a program which has an approach which maximizes interaction between teacher and student, that draws out ideas from youngsters rather than pours in facts, that will engage children, capture their imaginations, minds and hearts, and motivate them to learn. What follows is a question. How will we do this? By using good materials.

The geography course was based upon three assumptions about classroom materials:

1. Much of the curriculum material in use now deadens interest and hastens dropping out.
2. Materials emphasizing relevance, people, and controversy will pay off in student motivation.
3. Materials that include racial and cultural diversity may encourage students to think better of themselves.

The emphasis in the geography course was upon demonstrating how a single theme—survival—could be used throughout the course. The idea of survival was introduced by a reading entitled "The Mountain Men." The reading gave several instances and evidence of changes that man had to undergo in order to survive on the North American continent, namely, in the Rockies. The students were asked to enumerate the changes and to suggest why these men underwent them. The students enjoyed this reading tremendously and with it we had the makings of rapport right from the beginning. We took the reading further and asked if moving into different neighborhoods changed the ways in which they as teenagers behaved. We were able to establish relevance by discussing the idea of the whole concept of environmental influence upon behavior. Students fell into two camps. One, if you move into a tough, rough neighorhood, you have to be rough and tough also or people will not respect you. The second camp decided that you have to have respect, but after you had gained it, you did not have to behave like the rest of the group.

The next episode in survival was built around a wonderful film made in 1922 by Flaherty entitled "Nanook of the North." The students responded very well to this film and to Nanook and his plight in the quest for food for the survival of his family. The students were asked to consider how this "wonderman" survived in the upper reaches of the Hudson Bay with so little that was material or manufactured. Before the students viewed the film they were handed a paper with a statement which they were asked to elaborate upon after the film had been shown. The statement was—As you view this film, be able to explain the following: "It is not what a man has or how much he has, but what he does with what he has." The students were asked to keep the statement in mind as they viewed the film. The resulting papers were very effective.

In class discussion the next day we were able to bring in the Biblical parable of talents and to discuss the merits of capitalizing upon what we have, again making the materials relevant. Students admired the way of life of Nanook of the North and felt that each man had his worth when he did as much as he could, no matter what his situation. The students were then asked if they thought they could survive under similar conditions. The remarks were interesting. The students began by saying that they could not. The discussion then turned to something very interesting for educators. One boy challenged the group by declaring that he could, provided he had been taught early enough to master the skills needed in that particular environment. He said, "I could do that same 'junk' if I knew I had to and 'they' taught me early enough from the beginning." The statement is significant because for educators the "they" becomes "we" and it becomes a challenge that we as educators must respond to. The students came around and felt that they could exist and produce in any society, provided they were taught how.

Although time did not allow, in the normal course of study we would have looked at survival throughout the world. The student would have been allowed to view survival in an industrialized society, in a ghetto in particular. At Cardozo, the students are given a reading called "A Spanish Harlem 'Fortress,'" taken from *The New York Times Magazine,* January 3, 1965. The students are presented with a view of life taken by Richard Hammer from an 18-year-old Puerto Rican boy who is completely hostile to society. The problem the students are confronted with is whether or not this youngster can actually survive with his attitudes toward society which are so negative. The usual answers are "No," he cannot, and he must change and adapt in order to meet the demands of society.

At Princeton, with the idea of survival fixed firmly in the minds of the students, we went to India. We were in monsoon Asia, but we looked first at the question of how man survives in India. We explored the monsoons and Indian society.

The readings on India combine an attempt to have students arrive at a concept common to all societies, and to develop key skills in an interesting and relevant context.

The unit on India, as a part of monsoon Asia, was introduced by a set of transparencies "Monsoons and Indian Society." (These transparencies were prepared by the "Febton-Wallbank World History Program" and are available at Educational Audio-Visual located in Plainville, New York.) These educational materials introduce the students to a hypothesis and the students are encouraged to evaluate it. The students learn to read charts and graphs in order to gather the necessary information to test the hypothesis. The transparencies are structured in such a way that they allow the student to define monsoons through graphic illustrations. Instead of the student receiving a "spoon-fed" definition of a concept crucial to understanding monsoon Asia—and survival in monsoon Asia—they cannot proceed until their definition of the monsoons is their own and fixed in their minds.

These transparencies also acquaint students with the topography of the Indian subcontinent and demonstrate that the rainfall is seasonal and the distribution varies. Students are encouraged to suggest conditions which seasonal rainfall brings about for survival. The students easily came up with several suggestions. They had read charts, graphs and maps; they had been asked to draw conclusions and then define them, so they were well prepared to tackle the Indian problem and offer several valid remedies. They were able to state their recommendations in the form of a hypothesis because they had been groomed for this. Each student was asked to give reasons for his hypothesis and was able to do so.

Two readings on rice were included because the production of this crop is so intertwined with survival. We at Cardozo are attempting to produce a completed unit on rice. There is an excellent film on rice put out by McGraw-Hill that can further elaborate upon this unit, since in the area of monsoon Asia, it is the "prince of grains." Rice feeds more than half the world's population.

Survival, as a theme for the students, was successful. As we left this topic, it was explained to the students that survival is an element common to all societies. The students were then asked to name any other elements which they felt were common to all societies. They were able to identify two: the family (which in most cases they termed "people") and religion. With these two other elements named, the students were then ready to go on to other aspects common to man and investigate them.

GEOGRAPHY

How Does Geography Affect Man?

We are going to be studying many foreign lands. When we study India and China, we will be anxious to find out how geographic locations affect the ways in which man lives and has lived. But for a start, we will read a selection about own West.

As you read the following selection, keep in mind the ways in which environment changed the living habits of these early Americans. Also try to list ways that geography would influence how men live throughout the world.

"The Mountain Men"*

To stay alive, the Mountain men must adjust themselves completely to the wilderness world about them. Enemies were everywhere. Some were Indians; the Blackfeet were sworn enemies of all whites. Others were wild animals. Grizzly bears—great savage beasts as tall as a man, with raking claws that cut to the bone—roamed the Rockies in such numbers that one Mountain man counted 220 in one day. Constant vigilance was needed to stay alive in such a land.

To exist in this savage environment, the Mountain men must slip backwards in the scale of civilization until their wilderness skills matched those of their red-skinned opponents. Some descended to a level of savagery below that of their foes. Edward Rose was such

---

* *Source:* Ray Allen Billington, *The Far Western Frontier* (1830–1860)

a man. He joined the Crow Tribe and abandoned civilization entirely. A fellow trapper saw Rose lead his tribesmen to victory against a Blackfeet war party in 1834, then whip his followers into a bloody frenzy as they hacked off the hands of the wounded enemy warriors, pierced their bodies, and plucked out their eyes. Equally touched by this turning back to savagery was Charles Gardner, who borrowed the nickname of "Phil" from his native Philadelphia. Sent out on a journey with a lone Indian companion, he was given up for lost after howling winter gales swept the countryside. To his friends' surprise, Phil appeared after several days, but without the Indian. As he unpacked his mule, they saw him pull out a shriveled human leg, which he threw to the ground with: "There, now, I won't have to eat you anymore," he said as he threw it down.

What excellent fighters they were! They fought as did the Indians, taking advantage of the brush and rock cover as they faced their enemies, shooting with unerring accuracy. After one battle, a group of trappers fell to arguing who had killed one Indian chief. One trapper insisted that they would find his bullet in the left eye; when the body was pulled from the creek where it had fallen, the bullet was exactly in that spot. Like red men, they scalped their victims when the fight was over. Like the red men, they ended all battles in hand-to-hand combat where they used their knives and tomahawks with deadly skill.

"I have held my hand in an ant-hill until it was covered with ants, then greedily licked them off. I have taken the soles of my mocassins, crisped them in the fire, and eaten them. In our extremity, the large black crickets which are found in the country were considered fair game. We used to take a kettle of hot water, catch the crickets, and throw them in, and when they stopped kicking, eat them."

Like the red men, too, they grew accustomed to alternate periods of feast and famine. During months when the buffalo left the mountains, the mountaineers grew thin and gaunt; in the spring when the herds returned, they grew fat and sleek once more. For when the first cow was killed in the spring they were assured a feast fit for a king. About a fire of buffalo chips (manure) they propped row upon row of choice "hump ribs." While these sizzled, the Mountain men often drank some of the buffalo's blood, which reminded them of warm milk. Then the liver was eaten raw, flavored with the contents of the gall bladder. If the cow buffalo was pregnant, they were able to have one of their best dishes: the raw leg of unborn calves. This did not agree with the stomach of easterners, but it made the faces of Mountain men shine with grease and gladness.

The Mountain men not only borrowed their eating habits but their language from the Indians. . . . They gestured frequently and meaningfully as they spoke for they were adept in sign language that was the Indians' means of communication. From the Indians, too, they borrowed words: a man was a "child" or a "hos" or a "coon." A hungry person was "wolfish" and needed to fill his "meatbags"; a celebration was a "big dance"; to run was to "make tracks." Nor could Mountain men utter more than a few words without saying the "wah" or "ugh" or "heap" of the red men.

If the speech of the Mountain men showed the influence of their environment, so did their mental attitude. Their philosophy of life was based on the uncertainty of survival: men could only live in the wilderness by becoming used to hardships and misfortune. Death was so commonplace in a land where danger lurked at every turn, there was no mourning for the dead in the mountains; when a trapper heard that a man had been killed that was a friend, he would only shrug his shoulders and say: "Poor fellow! Out of luck."

6. The Writing of Students with Nothing to Say

ANGELINE E. ANDERSON

It is said that the competent teacher can do wonders even without a text. The challenge of instructing teachers of culturally deprived children and at the same time offering the children something worthwhile made this summer an unusual one. According to the plan of the English program, I was to cover the area of composition and insert a bit of English as a second language. Could the ogre of written composition be taught inductively to these teachers? How could youngsters who had nothing to say be encouraged to write?

Since the participating teams and pupils moved from one English teacher to another each Wednesday, I felt it was imperative for the children to have a sense of security, perhaps a father or mother image, through their participating teacher whom they referred to as *our sponsor* or *our group teacher*. The same group of Trenton teachers remained with their particular team of children throughout the Princeton-Trenton Institute and could develop a good rapport with their charges. This was important for both teachers and pupils.

At every opportunity the group teacher was given an important position with the pupils. He or she checked the notebook daily, gave permission for checking out and returning books, sat with the group in discussions, master-minded the bull sessions on the values questionnaire, took charge of field trip slips, and the daily attendance record. At times this individual also presented some particular material or operated equipment for the good of the whole class. The group teacher in this way became a respected guide, not a piece of scenery. Subtle suggestions were made as to the possible methods of encouraging writing on the part of the pupils. The mechanics were not marked

Angeline Anderson came to the 1965 Institute from Calvin Coolidge High School in Washington, D.C. Her policy of "read, write, discuss" in teaching composition overcame the resistance of many students who felt they had nothing to say on paper.

by the group teacher. The children were to be encouraged to think, to express themselves, and to write, not to feel inhibited by correction of errors.

Composition was taught in various ways, both oral and written. Reading the works of others furnished models to imitate and also material for discussion and creative writing. Role-playing was developed both by reading plays and using imagination on material stimulated by interest. What was of interest? Our own Trenton, a historical city; Princeton, a Big-Three university affiliated with this Institute; field trips in the environment; and people like ourselves and others— these were the source materials used.

Because of the short time each group had, we developed a section of a notebook under the heading of our choice: "My Record" or "My Journal" (one wrote "My General"). No child suggested and none accepted the adult suggestion of "My Diary." Each day the date was written (in ink) as it appeared on the board.

A stimulating environment is conducive to learning. So with the help of the group teachers, a bulletin board of composition material criteria was posted. This was a mistake. Down it came, to be replaced by colorful book jackets of stories about the United States and a literary map of our country. Paperbacks from the Scholastic unit, biographies, plays, short stories on baseball, science fiction, teenagers, mysteries, and particularly by Edgar Allan Poe were spread around the room on the ledge of the blackboard within easy reach of all. A book on Nat King Cole (*Sepia* memorial issue) was very popular.

One day as the pupils and group teachers came into the room they were caught in a literary lure by books. It was highly contagious. The first students arrived early and started reading. Their heads were buried in books. These could be borrowed by signing out with the sponsor. Another bulletin board was covered with illustrations showing the power of words of Shakespeare, Poe, and Browning. There were also pictures of young people dreaming at a school desk or performing a science experiment, and the children could put themselves in that person's place. This could have used for composition.

On the blackboard itself were questions on stories, suggestions for work, and the agenda for the day. Dictionaries were conveniently placed on low open shelves between book-ends for those who neglected to bring them. Copies of other books such as *Tales of New Jersey* and books with illustrative covers were scattered around the room for easy browsing. One boy commented, "You must have a hundred dollars worth of books in this room." They had a thirst for knowledge from books—and "forbid them not." The furniture (movable, thank goodness) was arranged according to the size of the class in a circular, semicircular, or "u-shaped" pattern so that all occupants of the room were visible to each other at all times and could be reached for assistance or distribution of materials. During group work with sponsors, each nest of desks and chairs was moved beyond hearing distance of the others. This informal atmosphere was very helpful in encouraging expression. In fact, when we enacted the "Happy Journey from Trenton to Camden," we put four desks together to simulate the family car.

The books around the room aroused the curiosity of the group upon entering the room and so the first order of business was an introduction to the books. We found that many of the people in the books had problems to overcome or particular character traits that helped them succeed in life. From this we turned to the listing of traits. When the students tried writing of a trait they needed or admired, very little appeared on the paper, but when they thought for a moment and found someone whom they admired, the words flew onto the paper.

"Richard has courtesy. He is a well-dressed boy. I mean he keeps himself clean. He is not loud and wild like lots of kids."

"My friend has cheerfulness toward life." The sponsor commented, "Very good. Are you talking about yourself? I think 'Yes.'" The student replied with a large "No."

"Jesus Christ had traits of all that is good, dying for all of us that we might live. These are the reasons I admire and love him."

"She does not get angry."

"This girl is very friendly and puts people at ease. She is helpful to newcomers at school or anywhere. She has a beautiful singing voice but it doesn't change her attitude. I admire her so because she has the trait that I wish I had because I'm quite shy and don't make friends easily."

"My parents are my ideal because they are honest, reliable, dependable, and trustworthy."

"I admire my friend because I wish I could make new friends as fast as she can."

"I know a young man who always does his very best on his job ever since he got started. He never goes to sleep on the job. I admire a person who does the opposite of what I do. A person like him will get far in this world."

"Everything in this world is hard, you must work hard for anything you want and sometimes you still don't get it."

"Many years of my life have passed but I'm still young (16). Each and every year on December 25th an ideal of mine comes down the chimney to greet me with joy of the holiday season. This lovable one is Santa Claus. Although there isn't a Santa Claus, I'm sorry to say, Mom and Dad do a wonderful job. My parents have the finest traits because they are *mine*. If it were not for my parents I would just be some old bum roaming around the streets day after day. I'd have no happy home to go to."

"This boy has an air of calmness about him."

The next step was to check on our own personal code. (See the code questionnaire at the end of this chapter.) Omitting names from the papers allowed us to give "honest" answers rather than the expected ones. The youngsters were very concerned about this. Later the forms were collected and a tabulation revealed the following pattern:

Question	Group 1				Group 2				Group 3				Group 4			
No.	a	b	c	d	a	b	c	d	a	b	c	d	a	b	c	d
1	5	1	1	2	5	–	2	4	3	–	–	3	10	1	4	2
2	6	3	–	–	4	6	1	–	5	1	–	–	7	9	1	–
3	–	8	–	–	–	7	1	3	–	6	1	3	–	15	2	–
4	–	4	–	5	–	1	1	9	–	1	1	4	2	3	2	10
5	7	2	–	–	9	1	1	–	5	–	1	–	16	–	1	–
6	2	5	2	–	5	4	2	–	2	2	–	2	5	7	3	2
7	7	–	2	–	8	–	1	2	5	1	–	–	13	3	–	1
8	1	1	7	–	1	1	9	–	–	1	5	–	2	1	14	–
9	–	9	–	–	1	10	–	–	1	5	–	–	2	13	1	1
10	3	2	2	1	2	62	3	–	–	4	2	–	7	8	1	1

Using blank forms, the groups held their discussions.

After being assigned a number which corresponded with that on a *Personal Code* book of the Scholastic unit basic set, we each received our copy and read silently the story of "Night Man." After discussion we wrote our opinion of the character and what we would have done in his position. "Turley seemed like the average teenager wanting to be independent and wanting a girl to call his own." (This seemed to be the consensus of the students.)

After reading "The Prize Winner" about a girl's problem of code we listed the traits of the characters and wrote comparisons or contrasts of Turley and Kay.

Since the fourth item on the questionnaire involved a certain problem, we read "The Snob" and followed this with further group discussion.

Since a trip was scheduled for Trenton we discussed the slogan, "Trenton Makes—The World Takes," and here we became involved in certain language patterns of speech of the culturally deprived. We used the booklets supplied by the local telephone company on the State of New Jersey and after free reading wrote on a factual topic.

A field trip to Philadelphia was another source of composition. An outline was developed as a post-mortem of the trip in one class, and this operation should never have been performed. The atmosphere was hostile. Another approach was tried. The play "Happy Journey to Trenton and Camden," was enacted by the class with the setting in the middle of the arena of desks and after discussion of this play and trips in general we went to a written evaluation of the Philadelphia trip in a very pleasant atmosphere.

Diary writing was shown by *Anne Frank, Diary of a Young Girl*. This was distributed to all after an introduction and a reading assignment made as homework. The next day we discussed personal code and the relationships in the family. Because the diary mentions under the entry of Saturday, June 20, 1942, that "In 1938 after the pogroms, my two uncles (my mother's brothers) escaped to the USA" we assumed that one of the uncles came to New Jersey and described him as he is today, 28 years later. One student wrote, "Anne Frank's uncle is about six feet tall. He is married and has a daughter about 17 years old. He is now in St. Francis Hospital. He is not a heavy-set man." This was written by a girl who does volunteer work in a hospital. Revealing?

"The Diary of a Modest Go-Getter" by Robert Benchley showed a humorous form of the story of Paul Revere's ride. This was supplemented by *John Ransom's Diary*, with an introduction by Bruce Catton. If time had allowed we would probably have revised some historical happenings in the area ourselves.

One of the field trips planned was a visit to the Music Circus to see "Oliver." A summary of the story by Charles Dickens was read in class and the songs from the original Broadway musical were played on the record player to acquaint the pupils with the story and to make them aware of the license taken in changing from book to musical. The wording of the summary was awkward so the pupils, using dictionaries, tried to rephrase the wording to everyday, clear language. The opaque projector was used to demonstrate certain parts of the composition as revised. One of the students' papers was used for this lesson. This device was for the benefit of the sponsors as well as the pupils. We had quite a discussion over *gruel,* some claiming it was soup! This led to a discussion of foods and the regional names for items such as soft drinks, cottage cheese, buns, and doughnuts.

Reading the story of Althea Gibson presented in the *Experimental Reader,* we wrote of the traits necessary for champions. Then we compared her to other greats such as Thomas Jefferson from *Personal Code* and George W. Carver in *Beyond Fame or Fortune* by Lawrence Elliott. We also had a brief quiz on Carver before writing an opinion on the man and his struggle to be helpful to himself and humanity. We followed the policy of "read, write, and discuss."

Participating teachers were given "Points to Consider in Correcting Themes" (purpose, content, organization, style or flavor, and mechanics) as a guide for themselves but were warned not to correct mechanics of the children's work. They were to write words of encouragement to the youngsters. "I do think I could have been helped more if the teacher had put a comment of some kind on my work," said one youngster in regard to his sponsor.

One day, instead of writing the current year, we dated the entry 20 years in the future to see what we would be doing if our dreams and ambitions came true. This combined imagination and desires, and was much enjoyed by the students. We figured our ages, our occupations, our attainments, and nobody was at a loss for words. One lad envisioned himself married with several children, one of whom bore his first name, and had a bit of dialogue regarding the mother's hair coloring (I saw the mother at our program and it was true). Another spoke of a ranch-style house with "lots of surrounding ground—ten acres," and owning three cars—a Cadillac, sports car, and everyday car. Still another wanted to teach, and to found a home for mentally retarded. A future air force nurse had a split-level, eight-room house on a hill. Several expressed a desire for houses in California.

We closed with a discussion of our reaction to President Kennedy's untimely death and comparing it to President Lincoln's. Then we read lines from "The Lonesome Train" with a class chorus, light voices of girls, heavy voices of boys, a teacher narrator, and volunteer soloists, and ended with the word *Freedom.*

Prior to this each pupil received stationery, stamp, and pen to send a personal letter of opinion of the work. Many were general in comment saying they liked the preview of Trenton High School, the opportunity to meet some of its teachers, the variety of teachers from many parts of the country, the field trips, the informal atmosphere in the classroom, the class participation in small groups, the individual attention of teachers, the stories in *Personal Code,* the people involved in personal struggles, the fun of using many ways of learning, and many stressed the joy of reading and the desire to have more time to read books.

Here are quotations from these letters, sent directly to the teacher:

"I feel that my summer was put to good use and I will go into the 11th grade with more knowledge from short visits in each classroom than I did in all my sophomore year, honestly."

"This summer institute was very different from regular school."

"It was wise to have students and teachers both participating in the classes."

"On the whole the summer institution was interesting as far as the English program was concerned."

"I especially enjoyed the paperback books, but I think there should have been more time for reading books."

"I am very glad you asked us to write a letter to you. I wish all our teachers had asked us to. This week has been very enjoyable because you made us want to learn in a very special way. This summer has been very interesting and I hope next summer I can come again."

"I liked reading stories and poems aloud the best. I am glad you were my teacher for a week. Thanks for the books and everything else."

"I hope there will be more summer schools like this in the future."

"Well, I haven't been in this class really long enough to tell you how I like it, but having five teachers in the class at one time you can get a lot done."

"I enjoyed reading different stories in the room. I wish we had more time to read. I would like to have books to read all the time, I enjoy reading very much."

"I enjoyed meeting people my own age and meeting some that I shall be going to school with this fall."

"I think you picked some nice books for us to work with."

"Thanks for letting us take books home to read."

"I'm sorry we could not have you as a regular teacher for the summer. Each day I would tell my mother about the different activities we did in class. I learned many new things in paragraph writing with your help."

"I liked the way you are helping us in the pronunciation of our everyday words."

"I thought it would be fun to be part of a university program."

"The first week of the program was fun. We had a chance to write out our thoughts of what we had read. I plan to return next summer and hope to see you there. I never knew summer school was so much fun."

"My English classes have been the most enjoyable because we expressed ourselves more in writing and group discussions. I plan to read the whole story of Althea Gibson as soon as I can get to the library."

"I'm not too good when it comes to writing so this letter will be short. Usually I don't like to read aloud in front of people but you made me feel comfortable and as though I could read as well as anyone else."

"The English and science made you think on your own, and nowadays there is not too much of that in the classrooms since they are so crowded."

"I wish our regular classrooms were as interesting as these summer classes."

"I liked the free milk, books, tablets, and science kits. Class went quickly." (Signed: your giggling student.)

"It was nice for the teachers to sacrifice their summer to teach us. It is a good experience for both teacher and student."

"There is only one thing I dislike but no one change this but me so I guess it's best for me to keep it to myself. I hope my teachers were not sorry to have me as a student."

"Somehow I must agree with a fellow classmate who thinks you are a guidance teacher. I agree because of the emphasis you put on personal code. I enjoyed every minute of it."

"The various areas of composition were very enriching. I had not enjoyed composition writing before our sessions began, but thanks to you a new door to composition has been opened."

Overheard: "She starts class on time."

In introducing the book on *Sunrise at Campobello,* I asked whose picture was on the cover. Receiving no answer, I asked, "Does anyone have a picture of Roosevelt in his or her pocket?" Still no answer. "Does anyone have a dime?"

Response came, "Oh, is that who that guy is? I've wondered who he was. Who's the lady on the other dime?"

Materials Used in Teaching Composition

Books

Personal Code—Scholastic kit with basic text and supplementary paperbacks
Assorted paperbacks of interest to teenagers
Webster's Dictionary (paperback)
Anne Frank, Diary of a Young Girl
Tales of New Jersey—donated by New Jersey Telephone Company
Supplementary books by telephone company regarding telephone and Edison and Bell
Experimental Reader by Warren Halliburton

Miscellaneous

"A Modest Go-Getter's Account of Paul Revere's Ride," Robert Benchley
Summary of Charles Dickens' *Oliver Twist*
"Oliver!"—record of Broadway musical's original score
"Beyond Fame or Fortune"—reprint of article in May 1965 *Reader's Digest*
Book jackets of stimulating books
Post cards of Washington, D.C.
Literary map of United States
Picture book of scenes for development reading
Pictures to stimulate writing and thinking, from magazines
Memorial edition of life of Nat King Cole
Record player
Opaque projector
Historical map of New Jersey

PERSONAL VALUES QUESTIONNAIRE

Directions

Ten situations are described below. Each of them involves a young person confronted with a problem of personal code. Read each situation carefully. For each of these situations, choose the action which *most nearly* represents what you would do in a like situation. Print the letter of your choice in the blank provided to the left of each situation.

1.———You are taking a test in school and you notice one of your friends copying your answers. You would (a) wait until class is over and then discuss the matter with your friend, suggesting that he refrain from doing it again, (b) report the incident to the teacher, (c) ignore the situation, (d) get up and move to another part of the room.

2.———Having bought some candy in the drugstore, you step outside and find that you have been given too much change. You would (a) return the extra change, (b) pocket the extra change, (c) give the extra change to a charity drive, (d) give the money to a friend and ask him to return it for you.

3.———You have a library book which has pictures you need for your history report. You want them badly. You would (a) tear out the pages and pay the library for the book, telling the librarian that you lost the book, (b) return the book and ask the librarian where you might find similar pictures, (c) tear out the pages, return the book, and say nothing, (d) turn in your history report without any pictures.

4.———You are walking down the street with a new friend whom you wish to impress. You meet the woman who helps your mother with the cleaning. In her strong foreign accent, she greets you. You would (a) pretend you don't see her and keep going, (b) stop, introduce your friend to her, explaining that she is a maid in your home, (c) say "hi" quickly and keep going, (d) stop, introduce your friend, and have a short friendly conversation with the maid.

5.———Because the mathematics assignments are getting more difficult all the time, you find that your father is really doing all the problems while trying to help you with your homework. You are actually falling further and further behind in the course. You would (a) go to your teacher and explain that you do not understand the problems and assignments, (b) ask your father to stop giving you help, (c) ask to be changed to an easier math class.

6.———Your friend beckons you to her locker. She whispers to you, "I just heard that Sally was seen with Mike on Saturday night. You know she's supposed to be going steady with

Jack. All the girls are talking about it." You would (a) listen to your friend and say nothing further about it to anyone else, (b) tell your friend that you think it is simply gossip and that your friend should not say anything about it, (c) suggest that you and your friend go to Sally and tell her what is being said, (d) immediately tell Jack what you have heard.

7.———You want to attend the baseball game next Friday night, but your mother explains that she must take care of your sick grandmother that evening. She asks you to stay home with your younger brother. You will (a) stay home with your brother as your mother asks, (b) plan to go to the baseball game, suggesting that your mother hire a baby sitter, (c) plan to go to the baseball game, promising to return as soon as it is over, (d) agree to stay home if your mother will pay you a baby sitter's wages.

8.———On Halloween night several of your friends ask you to accompany them on a window-soaping jaunt. After soaping several car and store windows, your friends decide to steal hubcaps from some nearby cars. You would (a) accompany them without question, (b) try to talk them out of the idea, leaving the group if you fail, (c) try to talk them out of the idea, accompanying them if you fail, (d) make an anonymous telephone call and report the plan to the police.

9.———You have done baby sitting for several families who do not object to your having friends in. A new family employs you with strict instructions not to have any visitors. Shortly after they leave for the evening, several of your friends come to the door. You would (a) ask them in as you usually do, (b) tell them they must leave, (c) ask them to invite more friends in for a party as you have decided that you won't work for this family any more since you have to baby-sit alone.

10.———You are on a picnic with some people who were graduated from high school last year. One boy opens a box and takes out several cans of beer which he begins to pass around. Your parents strongly disapprove of drinking. You would (a) refuse the beer, indicating your disapproval, (b) refuse the beer, explaining that you simply do not like it, (c) accept the beer and drink it, (d) accept the beer and secretly pour it out.

Directions

In each of the sentences below, underline the *Subject* with one line and the *Attitude* with two lines.

Example. My friends are charming companions.

1. Youngsters like pets.
2. Many of my studies are fascinating.
3. Reading teaches many interesting things.
4. Women of wealth like to shop in expensive places.
5. Watching the seasons change is a never-to-be-forgotten experience.
6. A hot day in the city is something to remember.
7. A summer vacation is a wonderful experience.
8. Radio and television announcers often encounter embarrassing situations.
9. Old people are difficult.
10. Boys have unusual manners.
11. Camping can be exciting.
12. Man's existence is fraught with unknown dangers.
13. Many opportunities are open to people who have a broad background.
14. Work can be good for people.
15. Sometimes writing can be profitable.
16. Children are sometimes amusing.
17. It is unwise to believe everything you hear.
18. Colors sometimes suggest controversial ideologies.
19. People's eyes reveal their personalities.
20. An emotional response to problems is useless.

7. Revolution and Justice: Role-Playing in Social Studies

PETER G. KONTOS

One of the Trenton teachers was concerned, after he had observed my 1965 class, with the fact that I had refused to define the word revolution when asked to do so by the students. I had instead asked them what they thought it meant. I asked him, an art teacher, if there were many of his brush strokes on the canvases of his students. He answered that he didn't put his brush to their work, and that if he did, the canvases would not truly be the pupils' works of art but, rather, extensions of his own ideas. I told him that I tried to avoid the same pitfall in teaching history.

This conversation typifies much of what we were about—explaining and demonstrating the inductive method. The pupils were "discovering" the answer to a problem by using their experience and reasoning abilities. Each was painting his own canvas. It is the method that Dr. Charles Keller of the John Hay Fellows Program calls "drawing it out instead of pouring it on." It is the method that was used in the social studies classes in the Princeton-Trenton Institute.

Basically, the curriculum and techniques used were chosen to serve as a showcase for the inductive method of teaching. The curriculum in social studies revolved around two themes which lent themselves well to two in-depth studies using the discovery method—the idea of revolution and the concept of justice. Three techniques—role-playing, discussion, and composition—complemented the inductive inquiry

Peter G. Kontos, onetime Coordinator of Instruction in the Cleveland Public Schools Community Action for Youth program, and an editor of the *Springboards* reading series, attracted much attention for his work in role-playing teaching methods during the 1965 Institute. He became Director of the 1966 Institute and is now a senior staff member of the Princeton University Office of Educational Programs, and Director of the Princeton Cooperative Schools Program.

and allowed some concentration on the development of basic skills necessary for the study of history.

Role-playing was used as a motivational device in order to stimulate interest and to involve the pupil in class participation. This device sparks pupils' interest almost immediately because it creates an attitude of controversy and conflict. The student becomes involved in class discussion because he is comfortable in a situation in which he is not penalized for making mistakes. If the student is wrong, it is the character of the role being played that is wrong, not the student who is playing the role.

A class discussion in which the pupil is urged to participate, rather than a teacher's lecture, provides an arena for testing a pupil's conceptions against other pupils' arguments and for the testing by the teacher of the credibility of pupil responses.

Composition called for a final restatement of the students' historical position in a logical and organized argument and, at the same time, it encouraged the correct use of basic communication skills.

Each of the techniques used in a sequence would complement and reinforce the others. It was not essential, however, to begin with role-playing and to follow in sequence with discussion and composition. The three techniques could be used interchangeably.

The classroom investigation of revolution was scheduled for a four-day period. The fifth day was usually reserved for a trip or other miscellaneous activity which, as it turned out, might or might not be related to the social studies curriculum. The pupils began the first day by taking a quiz which was not graded or collected. The quiz was based on five misconceptions of revolution discussed by Carl G. Gustavson in the chapter on revolution from his book *A Preface to History*. The students were asked to identify as true or false the following statements:

1. A revolution is caused by the misery of the people.
2. One of the principal reasons for a revolution is the tyranny and brutality of the government.
3. The transfer of power occurs when people storm the citadels of the government in the course of a civil war.
4. In a revolution, the people rise spontaneously and take power.
5. The result of a revolution is to gain greater freedom for the people.

After taking the quiz, the students were asked to defend or attack the validity of the statements. Most of the pupils felt that these statements were fairly accurate generalities regarding revolution. The

teacher then made the statement that he thought that all of the statements might be false. The reason for this conclusion was not given
by the teacher at this time, even though the pupils pressed him for
his reasons. Instead, the teacher said that the statements would be
re-examined at the end of the four days to see if the pupils had
changed their minds.

It was important to emphasize at this point that the pupils' arguments were just as valid as were the teacher's, and that perhaps
the teacher did not have the correct answers. The teacher suggested
that perhaps they could get closer to a better analysis of the statements if they studied the idea of revolution in depth. The pupils
were then asked how they would plan a revolution if the teenagers
of Trenton decided to take over that city. Through the inductive
method the pupils realized that one of the elements necessary to
the planning of a revolution was a knowledge of how other revolutions
had occurred, and that by examining past revolutions they might
be aided in planning their "revolution." They also discussed methods
of gathering data and types of historical testimony by distinguishing
between primary and secondary evidence.

The class decided on the American Revolution and the civil-rights
movement as their case studies. These were selected because they
were both relevant to the pupils' own experiences, and because the
class felt that there would be ample resource material available for
their analysis. The class assignment was to find and read as much as
possible on the cause of the American Revolution for class discussion
the next day. Possible sources for this investigation were discussed.

On the second day a role-playing situation was structured. A summit meeting was to be held between American colonists and the British government, supposedly just before the outbreak of hostilities
in 1775. The students were asked to try to resolve the differences
between these two factions. The class was divided into two groups.
One of the groups was designated American colonists, the other,
representatives of the British government. Both groups were given
copies of the Declaration of Independence (although it was pointed
out that it had not yet been written), Patrick Henry's "Liberty or
Death" speech, and a selection from Thomas Paine's pamphlet *The
Crisis*. The students were also encouraged to use and share another
resource material they had found as part of their homework
assignment.

Each group met separately during the first half of the class period
and planned its presentation, trying to interpret the historical positions
of the group it represented. During the second half of the class period,

the students held their "summit meeting" and argued from the point of view either of the colonists or the British. Their homework assignment was to write a composition presenting the view of the opposition and a restatement of their own position.

On the third day the compositions were discussed and a decision was usually reached as to whether there was any relationship between the principles and causes of the American Revolution and the present civil-rights movement. The entire class listened to a recording of Dr. Martin Luther King's speech "I Have a Dream." Another role-playing situation was then structured. The group that had played the American colonists were asked to play a host of roles representing various attitudes of segregationists. The group that had represented the British point of view were cast in the roles of civil-rights workers. The time was established as the present and the place as Mississippi. The two groups were to meet and discuss their differences in another mock "summit meeting."

The civil-rights group was given a *Springboards* reading selection entitled "Civil Rights" and selected testimony drawn from *Mississippi Black Paper*, which was compiled by the Misseduc Foundation, Inc. The segregationists were also given a copy of the same *Springboard* lesson and selected articles from *Life* magazine which quoted attitudes of Ku Klux Klan members and other segregationists. The pupils were encouraged to find additional sources. The groups met individually for the remainder of the period to organize their arguments and to explore possible sources of additional information.

On the fourth day the role-playing situation was allotted the first 20 minutes of the period. The class discussion after the role-playing compared the American Revolution with the civil-rights movement. The students were then asked to re-examine the original statements regarding revolution and to write a composition defending or attacking the original statements by Gustavson.

The investigation of the concept of justice was also planned to cover a four-day period. Selections from Edwin Fenton's *32 Problems in World History*, the essay "We Are Not Superstitious" by Stephen Vincent Benet, and the entire film, "The Ox-Bow Incident" were the curriculum materials for the study of justice.

The Fenton materials were introduced on the first day. They consisted of selections from Hammurabi's Code of Law and from the Old Testament. These readings expressed the "revenge theory" of justice. The teacher played the role of Hammurabi during the course of the first period and defended Hammurabi's point of view to the students, who played the roles of senate investigators. The class in the discussion which followed decided that punishment alone was not an acceptable form of justice. During the entire course of the four-day period, the pupils were encouraged to keep a written journal defining their conception of justice.

On the second day the students read the Benet essay which described the Salem witch trials. The pupils again assumed roles and passed judgment on the teenagers in history who had instigated the witch hunts. They found, however, that they used punishment and revenge as justice. A situation was created in which the teenagers had revolted against the adults in society and were now faced with the task of establishing a new society. In their discussions they arrived at the conclusion that, in order to have justice, they must first establish, like Plato, a "just state." The state that the teenagers felt would work best closely resembled the American democratic society.

The pupils viewed "The Ox-Bow Incident" on the following day and, on the fourth day, discussed safeguards against the breakdown of justice in a democratic society.

The pupils studying the concept of justice were exposed to the historical skills of using and evaluating primary and secondary evidence. They also learned to withhold historical judgment until they had weighed the factors which had contributed to the actions and decisions of past societies and individuals. They were, however, neither encouraged nor discouraged in interpreting history according to contemporary moral standards. Making moral judgments became an individual concern to each pupil, as it is and should be with the trained professional historian.

This was generally the plan and activity of the classroom demonstrations. There were, of course, slight variations in some of the classes. Larry Cuban, of the Washington, D.C., Cardoza project, for example, taught two of the classes for one day and discussed the causes of the American Civil War. There were also differences in the individual makeup of each of the classes, and the various interests of the pupils caused some of the ideas to be more fully developed than others. One class, for example, might express more interest in the ideas of freedom and its application to revolution than would the other classes.

It was interesting to note that a few of the teachers had never known that the role-playing method existed, and they completely rejected its use in a classroom situation. By the end of the session, though, many teachers and some of the few skeptics were discussing ways by which to improve and implement the role-playing technique in their own classes in Trenton.

A few other incidents merit recording. Early in the Institute a teacher volunteered to teach part of the class period. His topic was to be a comparison of the French and American Revolutions. This portion of the class turned out to be a lecture, in which the teacher spoke for 18 of the 20 minutes allotted. The teacher asked questions, but the pupils simply did not respond. Halfway through the questioning period, the teacher said, "I just don't know how to get you kids to answer." His admission and recognition of this problem was a beginning. He began to question some of his methods. He returned at the end of the Institute and asked for and received world history materials which were problem-centered and which required more pupil participation than did the traditional textbook.

During the final week of the Institute, two of the teachers assumed roles which would have made a traditional teacher uncomfortable and perhaps vulnerable. A situation was structured in which the teenagers had taken over America and had called on the two teachers to defend the ideas and attitudes of the adult world. The teachers in this session allowed the teenagers to question openly the values and traditions of adult society. I think they would not have felt as secure in a similar situation at the beginning of the Institute. Another teacher was overheard early in the Institute to say, "Nothing can be done with these students." But later he said, "Before anything can be done, it is the teacher's responsibility to know all that he can about his students." This remark represents a striking shift in attitude.

The pupils were a joy. It was remarkable and thoroughly enjoyable to witness a transformation in their thinking. They became more inquisitive; they were no longer satisfied with a pat or glib answers from their peers and, possibly most important, they relied more upon and were more confident in their own abilities than had been the case during the first week of classes. Two incidents are illustrative of this change. The first occurred when, during the third week of classes, the pupils began to define the words *patrician* and *plebeian* by the way they were used in the readings rather than by asking me for the definitions or simply skipping over the words as they had done during the early weeks of classes.

The second incident occurred when one of the students was challenged by another to define the word *freedom*. Her definitions proved weak and unconvincing. Challenged again to provide a definition, she replied, "Well, maybe I don't know now, but I've got all week-end to find out." On the following Monday she produced a well-written, well-documented essay on the meaning of freedom. I had neither assigned nor prompted her to write this essay. Instead, the stimulation had been provided by another pupil.

I think that I shall never forget these students. It would be difficult to forget a group of students represented by a girl who said to me after the first week, "Thank you. You are the first teacher that ever told me I did something good."

Much of what was done this summer can never be described fully, even if the most minute records were kept; for teaching, I feel, is an art form. Any description of a work of art, whether the work be good or bad, can never really do that piece of art justice. Nor has anyone yet written *the* manual for effective teaching. I suspect that no one ever will. Teaching must be demonstrated, it must be viewed, and a teacher should do both, during a relatively short period of time, to appreciate and work toward an understanding of the art of teaching. Herein lies the strength and justification of the Institute. It became a living laboratory for teaching practices. It became a place where the feel and the indefinables of teaching were shared and expressed as a common creative experience.

8. An Unashamed Adventure in Poetry

VERNA DOZIER

The Plan: What Was Intended

I wrote the following memorandum before I left Washington in June to give to Charlotte Brooks the day before the institute opened:

I am unashamedly going to offer an adventure in poetry to these young people. I shall share with them some of my favorite poems, suggest ways of appreciating poetry, and give them the opportunity to explore on their own and tell us about delights they find.

The use of the word "unashamedly" marks a philosophy and a method. Advice I have long treasured is that if you have two pennies, with one buy bread for the body, with the other buy violets for the soul. Poems are the violets. John Keats said,

Beauty is truth, truth beauty,—that is all
Ye know on earth, and all ye need to know.

Poetry is its own justification. Those who love it know that. I think everyone should have an opportunity to learn to love it.

When I told a fellow teacher about what I planned to do this summer, her response was to tell me of another teacher who, hearing of a former student in a death cell, observed, "And I tried to teach him about the sonnet." I smiled and said, "She may have given him the one glimpse he had that there was also wonder and order and beauty in life."

All the teacher can do is provide the opportunity. She shares what

---

Verna Dozier, whose educational background includes Bennington College, Syracuse University, and Union Theological Seminary, brought poetic experience to students in the 1965 Institute. Her students' reactions to liked and disliked poetry—including "The Biggest Failure"—were used in adapting classroom activities to their own level of experience. Miss Dozier is a member of the faculty of Ballou High School in Washington, D.C.

is meaningful to her. She plants a seed. She is content to leave the harvest in other hands, well aware that all seeds come to harvest. That fact does not lessen the commitment of the sower.

The Process: What Was Done

The first three weeks the poetry units were four-day sessions. The first day was motivation, the second development, the third application, and the fourth presentation or test. The last two weeks each group had five days, and it was planned that the third day be given over to a record. The use of the record proved such a fiasco, however, that the third day the following week was given over to a study of longer poems.

The first day of the unit was motivation. The objective was to make poetry as appealing to the students as it was to me. To that end I selected poems I liked, poems that were short, and poems that had a relevancy for them—not hackneyed moralities or beatnik sophistication about switch blades and hot rods but great and good poetry about the human condition: love, death, loneliness, family life, city life, hopes, and fears. I tried to read each poem to help them share in what for me was a meaningful experience. During each first period we would do some choral reading. At least six poems would be used, four mimeographed ones each passed out just before it was read and one from each text to be used that week. By the end of the third week, the students were building up an interest in poetry, and the fourth group of students on their evaluations so clamored for opportunity to choose the poems to be discussed that the fifth week the first day was a process of "you choose one and I'll choose one." I felt that the selection of short poems as a stimultion had been justified when a pupil wrote as his suggestion for improving the course: "They ought to write longer poems."

The second day there was much choral reading and a few tentative efforts at individual reading. Also on the second day an effort was made to call attention to "how a poem means" to quote John Ciardi. I did very little with meter except to illustrate that poets made their lines gallop or plod for specific purposes. To put it awkwardly, I am considerably uncommitted to the necessity of being able to scan as a requirement for the appreciation of poetry. I consider myself living evidence to the contrary. I did, however, call attention to the poet's art in the structure of his poem: stanza, verse, rhyme, punctuation; and we paid much attention to the use of metaphore and exactness of language.

The third day of the fourth week was given over to the record which will be discussed later under the heading "The Biggest Failure." The third day the fifth week was given over to long poems which the students selected: "The Highwayman" and "The Raven."

The fourth day (third day of the four-day weeks) was the students' day for exploring on their own. They went off into separate rooms with a participating teacher, no more than five students to a room. Each student had about a half-hour by himself to leaf through two books of poetry and find a poem that in some way said something to him. Then he studied it as we had studied the poems the days before. (We had reviewed our method before we separated.) Then he talked it over with his participating teacher. Sure of his poem now, he retired to his corner of the room and practiced reading it aloud. When he felt he had the reading under control, he tried it out on the participating teacher. Having won the teacher's approval, he was ready to share it with the class and that sharing was the activity for the fifth day—presentation or test day.

On presentation day each student stood up and read his poem while the others followed in their books. Then each student discussed the poem as he understood it and answered questions put to him by his classmates or the teachers. Many students chose poems they had been introduced to in earlier courses. I had no objection to this criterion for selection. A poem is to be lived with for a lifetime.

Textbooks Used

Poetry I, Richard Corbin, editor, New York: The Macmillan Company, 1962.

Poetry II, R. Stanley Perterson, editor, New York: The Macmillan Company, 1962.

Types of Literature, Edward N. Gordon, senior editor, New York: Ginn and Company, 1964.

Evaluation

On the last day of each series of lessons, the students and teachers were asked to evaluate the courses. Each one was given a white slip and asked to identify the evaluator only by the letter S if he were a student and T if he were a teacher.

On the board, with letter identification, I wrote the kinds of things we did.

A. Listened to teacher read poems she liked.
B. Listened to each other read poems we liked.
C. Discussed poems together.
D. Examined poems carefully together.
E. Explored poetry alone.
F. Read poetry aloud together.
G. Read poetry aloud alone.

(For the third week a participating teacher had suggested I let the students write about the poem before they talked about it. I did so, and for this week the list had an H—"Wrote about poems." This item drew a negative vote from a teacher and from a pupil. On the fifth week the H was "Listened to records."

Then I asked the class to write by number 1 the letter of the activity they enjoyed most, found most helpful, wished there had been more of, would like to do again. If there was none, they wrote none.

By number 2 they were to write the letter of the activity which they enjoyed least, found least helpful, wished there had been less of, never want to do again.

By number 3 they were to write the name of the poem we had read that week which they liked best.

By number 4 they were to write the name of the poem they liked least.

By number 5 they were to write any suggestion they had for improving the course.

For the ninth graders the activities that tied for first place in their favor were interestingly enough B and G, listening to each other read and reading aloud alone. Tying for second place were A and C, listening to the teacher read and discussing poems together. (C overwhelmingly won the favor of the teachers.)

Interestingly enough, A, listening to the teacher read, also topped the list of least-favorite activities with reading aloud alone, G, a close second. The vote for favorite activities was heavier than the vote for least-favored. Every student listed a favorite activity. Many wrote "None" for least-favorite.

For the tenth grade, the activities that walked off with favorite honors for students and teachers were the discussion and careful examination of poetry together. Like the ninth graders, the tenth graders registered very few negative votes, but the largest negative vote was directed against choral reading.

The list of best-liked and least-liked poems is appended. The repeated suggestion was for more time for this activity.

The Biggest Failure

Despite other teachers' suggestions that records can be used to introduce units as well as sum them up, I had always found that I used records most successfully at the end of a unit when the students had made the material of the record their own. Flying in the face of this experience because I so much wanted the students to hear Burns dialect poetry done as I could not do it, I presented a part of Untermeyer's "A Treasury of Great English Poetry." The record is so extensive, I found it difficult just to locate Burns, so I decided to play about 20 minutes of it from Blake to Wordsworth. I was dubious about such a long session of unfamiliar poetry, and I tried to prepare for it by having the students examine in detail the day before Blake's "Lamb" and "Tyger" and Burns' "To a Mouse" and "A Man's a Man" and I gave each child a complete script of the poems he was to hear. On the evaluation, the record session just about broke even. Only two students mentioned it; one as the activity he enjoyed most, one as the activity he enjoyed least. Another, however, listed as his least-favorite poem sonnets by Wordsworth. It was obvious during the class period that the session was a failure. The pupils dutifully followed their scripts, but they were bored and bewildered.

Blake (poems on the record):
"How Sweet I Roamed"
"My Silks and Fine Array"
"Introduction to 'Songs of Innocence' "
"The Lamb"
"The Tyger"
"Love's Secret"

Burns:
"My Love"
"The Banks of Doon"
"Sweet Afton"
"To a Mouse"
"A man's a Man"

Wordsworth:
"The Daffodils"
"To a Skylark"
"My Heart Leaps Up"
Lucy Poems
"Strange Fits of Passion"
"A Slumber Did My Spirit Seal"

Sonnets
"The World Is too Much with Us"
"Composed upon Westminister Bridge"
"To Milton"

The Students Speak

Item "Acquainted with the Night" sparked two of the most sensitive responses. Professor H. D. Holland, whose visits always enlivened the poetry classes, had asked how the man of the "Night" would respond to the poet of "Say Not the Struggle Naught Availeth." The class was unanimous in its opinion that he would not respond at all. "Who could speak to him?" Dr. Holland pressed. And a girl replied quietly, "Someone who walked with him."

Item. At another time three or four boys got into an argument about the age of the man of the "Night." One young fellow insisted he was young because "you'd get yourself together as you grew older," and a thin lad returned, "Down on Willow Street, there're lots of old men walking like this every night. They ain't never made it."

Item. One boy loped out of class one day with a verbal expression of his delight in the class, and one of the teachers observed, "He's a nice kid. Not very bright, but nice." The boy selected as his poem "A Father's Heart Is Touched." After he had read it and explained that the father found comfort in his son's being an idiot because life would be easier for him, one of the teachers suggested that the word "idiot" in the poem was not to be taken literally. "No," the youngster maintained (and I wondered how many times he had over-heard himself called "not very bright"), "I think the poet meant a real idiot."

Item. A boy had chosen "Song to the Men of England." He had read it well and with feeling discussed Shelley's call of revolution. When he had finished, a girl asked, "If the country had treated the people so badly, why didn't they go to another country?" The boy returned almost angrily, "You don't want to leave your country. You just want to make it better."

Item. After one introductory session which we had wound up with a vigorous reading of "O What Is That Sound?" one girl closed her book with the exclamation, "That was fun!"

Item. After a student had read his choice, "When I Was One and Twenty," I asked him what had happened to the poet between the first and second stanzas, and the boy answered promptly, "His girl cut out on him."

Item. A boy who had been classified as merely "educable," chose "Song" from *Pippa Passes* as his presentation. When asked why, he answered, "I liked the lines The hillsides dew pearl'd because that makes everything sound pretty and bright and "God's in His heaven" because I guess that makes everything all right."

Poems Used

The following is the list of poems used the first two days of each unit. A dagger before a title (†) means that the poem was used for two groups. An asterisk (*) indicates that a pupil had chosen the poem in a previous group.

"A Kind of Goodby," Theodore Spencer

"A Man's a Man," Robert Burns

*"Abraham Lincoln Walks at Midnight," Vachel Lindsay

†"Acquainted with the Night," Robert Frost

*"Barter," Sara Teasdale

"Bonnie George Cambell," Anonymous

*"Break, Break, Break," Alfred Lord Tennyson

†"Candles," Constantie Cavafy

"Cargoes," John Masefield

†"Chanson Innocente," E. E. Cummings

"Composed upon Westminster Bridge," William Wordsworth

"Dark Girl," Arna Bontemps

"Death Be Not Proud," John Donne

"Do Not Go Gentle into That Good Night," Dylan Thomas

"Do You Fear the Wind?" Hamlin Garland

"East River Nudes," Mildred Weston

†"fate is unfair," Don Marquis

"Fog," Carl Sandburg

"Four Little Foxes," Lew Sarett

†"High Flight," John Gillespie Magee, Jr.

*"Hills," Arthur Guiterman

"I Meant To Do My Work Today," Richard Le Gallienne

"I Never Saw a Moor," Emily Dickinson

"If everything happens," E. E. Cummings

†"I'm Nobody," Emily Dickinson

†"In Waste Places," James Stephens

"Jabberwocky," Lewis Carroll

"Lone Dog," Irene Rutherford McLeod

"Mother to Son," Langston Hughes

"Narrow Fellow," Emily Dickinson

"O What Is That Sound?" W. H. Auden

"On the Vanity of Earthly Greatness, Arthur Guiterman

"Ozymandias," Percy Bysshe Shelley

"My Papa's Waltz," Theodore Roethke

†"Prayers of Steel," Carl Sandburg
"Psalm 23"
†"Richard Cory," Edwin Arlington Robinson
"Say Not Thy Struggle Naught Availeth," Arthur Hugh Clough
"Sea Gypsy," Richard Hovey
"Song of the Open Road," Walt Whitman
"Sonnet 29," William Shakespeare
†"Sonnet to My Mother," George Barker
"Snake," Haiku
"Stanzas Written on the Road between Florence and Pisa," Lord Byron
"Stopping by the Woods on a Snowy Evening," Robert Frost
"The Ballad of the Oysterman," Oliver Wendell Holmes
°"The Coach of Life," Alexander Pushkin
"The Constant Lover," John Suckling

"The Convergence of thy Twain," Thomas Hardy
"The Express," Stephen Spender
"The Lamb," William Blake
"The Listeners," Walter de la Mare
"The Man He Killed," Thomas Hardy
†"The Road Not Taken," Robert Frost
"There Will Come Soft Rains," Sara Teasdale
"To a Mouse," Robert Burns
"To an Athlete Dying Young," A. E. Housman
"To Satch," Samuel Allen
"Travel," Edna St. Vincent Millay
"Tyger," William Blake
"Upon Julia's Clothes," Robert Herrick
"We Never Know How High," Emily Dickinson

The following poems were used to introduce the unit on poetry the last week, but they were chosen by the pupils:

"I Like To See It Lap the Miles," Emily Dickinson
"Casey at the Bat," Ernest Lawrence Thayer
"Interlude III," Karl Shapiro
"Jesses James: An American Myth," William Rose Benet
"Sea Fever," John Masefield

"The Crazy Woman," Gwendolyn Brooks
"The Hammers," Ralph Hodgson
"The Highwayman," Alfred Noyes
"The Raven," Edgar Allan Poe
"All of Us Turning Away for Solace," Delmore Schwartz
"The Ninth of April," Otto Gelsted

Poems Pupils Presented

Ninth Grade

A dagger (†) means that the poem was selected by more than one pupil.

†"A Father's Heart Is Touched,"
Samuel Hoffenstein
†"A Man Saw a Ball of Gold"
from *The Black Riders*, Stephen
Crane
"A Vagabond Song," William
Bliss Carman
"Abraham Lincoln Walks at
Midnight," Vachel Lindsay
†"Annabel Lee," Edgar Allan Poe
"Break, Break, Break," Alfred
Lord Tennyson
"Caliban in the Coal Mines,"
Louis Untermeyer
†"Crystal Moment," Robert P.
Tristram Coffin
"Do You Fear the Wind?" Ham-
lin Garland
"Eldorado," Edgar Allan Poe
†"Fire and Ice," Robert Frost
†"Former Barn Lot," Carl Van
Doren
"Hills," Arthur Guiterman
†"How Do I Love Thee?" Eliza-
beth Barrett Browning
"I Never Saw a Moor," Emily
Dickinson
"Julius Caesar"—Antony's
speech, William Shakespeare
"Sea Fever," John Masefield
"Sea Lullaby," Elinor Wylie
"Solitude," Alexander Pope
"Song" from *Pippa Passes*,
Robert Browning
"Song to the Men of England,"
Percy Bysshe Shelley

"Stopping by the Wood on a
Snowy Evening," Robert Frost
"The Benefactors," Rudyard Kip-
ling
"The Charge of the Light Bri-
gade," Alfred Lord Tennyson
"The Desired Swan Song," Sam-
uel Taylor Coleridge
"The Dismantled Ship," Walt
Whitman
"The Eagle That Is Forgotten,"
Vachel Lindsay
"The Fox and the Grapes,"
Joseph Lauren
†"The Glove and the Lions,"
Leigh Hunt
"The Mountain Whippoorwill,"
Stephen Vincent Benet
†"The Mountains Are a Lonely
Folk," Hamlin Garland
"The Ninth of April," Otto
Gelsted
"The Purist," Ogden Nash
"The Runaway," Robert Frost
"The Spider," Robert P. Tristram
Coffin
"The Wife of Usher's Well,"
Anonymous
"The Wreck of the Hesperus,"
Henry Wadsworth Longfellow
"There Is No Frigate Like a
Book," Emily Dickinson
†"When I Was One and Twenty,"
A. E. Housman

Tenth Grade

†"A Noiseless Patient Spider,"
Walt Whitman
"Abraham Lincoln Walks At
Midnight," Vachel Lindsay

"aesop revised by archy," Don
Marquis
"All of Us Turning Away for
Solace," Delmore Schwartz

†"Annabel Lee," Edgar Allan Poe
†"Auto Wreck," Karl Shapiro
"Barter," Sara Teasdale
"Caliban in the Coal Mines," Louis Untermeyer
"Casey at the Bat," Ernest Lawrence Thayer
"Crossing the Bar," Alfred Lord Tennyson
†"Crystal Moment," Robert P. Tristram Coffin
"Death Be Not Proud," John Donne
"Endymion," selection, John Keats
†"Fable," Ralph Waldo Emerson
"Fire and Ice," Robert Frost
"Former Barn Lot," Carl Van Doren
†"How Do I Love Thee?" Elizabeth Barrett Browning
"I Never Saw a Moor," Emily Dickinson
"Julius Caesar," selections. William Shakespeare
"Loveliest of Trees," A. E. Housman
"Sea Lullaby," Elinor Wylie
"Spanish Johnny," Willa Cather
"The Fox and the Grapes," Joseph Lauren
"The Mountains Are a Lonely Folk," Hamlin Garland
"The Purist," Odgen Nash
"The Spider," Robert P. Tristram Coffin
"The Wreck of the Hesperus," Henry Wadsworth Longfellow
"Without a Cloak," Phyllis McGinley

Pupils' Favorite Poems

Ninth Grade

These are the poems named by the students on the evaluations as their best-liked of all encountered in the course. "Mother to Son" and "The Road Not Taken" were chosen most often, but every poem starred was named more than once.

"A Father's Heart Is Touched"
"Abraham Lincoln Walks At Midnight"
"Annabel Lee"
"Casey at the Bat"
*"Chanson Innocente"
*"High Flight"
*"I'm Nobody"
"Jabberwocky"
"Jesse James: An American Myth"
"Julius Caesar," Antony's speech
*"Mother to Son"
"Ozymandias"
*"Richard Cory"
*"The Ballad of the Oysterman"
*"The Charge of the Light Brigade"
"The Constant Lover"
"The Desired Swan Song"
*"The Glove and the Lions"
"The Highwayman"

"The Lamb"
*"The Man He Killed"
"The Raven"
*"The Road Not Taken"
"The Tyger"

*"The Wife of Usher's Well"
"The Wreck of the Hesperus"
"To Satch"
"When I Was One and Twenty"

Tenth Grade

"Sonnet to My Mother" was mentioned as a favorite poem more often than any other poem. "My Papa's Waltz" and "How Do I Love Thee?" were also mentioned frequently.

"A Kind of Goodbye"
*"A Man's a Man"
"Abraham Lincoln Walks at Midnight"
*"Acquainted with the Night"
*"Auto Wreck"
"Break, Break, Break"
*"Candles"
*"Death Be Not Proud"
"fate is unfair"
*"How Do I Love Thee?"
"Without a Cloak"

"I'm Nobody"
*"My Papa's Waltz"
"Sea Fever"
"Sea Lullaby"
*"Sonnet to My Mother"
"The Constant Lover"
"The Daffodils"
"The Highwayman"
*"The Listeners"
"The Purist"
"The Raven"

Least-Liked Poems

Ninth Grade

These poems were named on the evaluations in response to the query—which poems of all we had did you like least? The poem most often mentioned was "East River Nudes." It is interesting to note that the runner-up was the popular "Annabel Lee." "Fog" was mentioned three times and "Cargoes" twice. Significant also perhaps is that of this list of 17 poems, seven were named in the week the record was used, and five of the seven were on the record.

"A Man's a Man"
"Abraham Lincoln walks at Midnight"
"Annabel Lee"
"Cargoes"
"East River Nudes"
"Fire and Ice"

"Fog"
"How Do I Love Thee"
"Richard Cory"
"The Constant Lover"
"The Glove and the Lions"
"The Lamb"
"The Man He Killed"

"The Mountains Are a Lonely Folk"

"To a Mouse"
"To Satch"

Lucy poems
"Strange Fits of Passion Have I Known"
"A Slumber Did My Spirit Seal"

Tenth Grade

In the tenth grade "Candles" received three negative votes, "Auto Wreck" and "Snake" received two each. All others were mentioned only once.

"A Kind of Goodbye"
"Acquainted with the Night"
"Auto Wreck"
"Candles"
"How Do I Love Thee?"
"How Sweet I Roamed"
"I'm Nobody"
"Lone Dog"

"On the Vanity of Earthly Greatness"
"Snake"
"Sonnet 29"
"The Tyger"
Sonnets by Wordsworth
"Upon Julia's Clothes"

9. Helping Students to Be Pathfinders

PETER P. CARLIN

When teachers think of the improvement of instruction they may think of nonpersonal instruments: libraries, books, charts, globes, films, pictures, gadgets, and the like. This can throw us off the track. The tendency to think of nonpersonal instruments may be a by-product of the extreme materialism which characterizes the age in which we live. I believe that all of these material things have little or no intrinsic power to improve instruction. Collectively or individually they have only such power as teachers and learners impart to them.

The improvement of instruction is a very personal transformation. The teacher's inherent qualities constitute the moving force. The teacher's capacity is central. The physical instruments of instruction are peripheral or subsidiary.

It was my challenge to get the participating teachers to see, to believe, and to act upon the thesis that the power to move instruction up the road of improvement must come from within the teacher.

How do we get teachers to behave in this way? How do we get teachers into a frame of mind which will cause them to think hard and a great deal about the problems of improving instruction? How do we get them to talk seriously among themselves about improvement? How do we help them to arrive at a point where they deeply and sincerely believe that significant improvement is greatly needed, even demanded by our day and time? Can certain types of reading by teachers help us? What are these types of reading? What are some specific examples of the various types? How do we get teachers interested in doing this reading seriously and thoughtfully?

The demonstration classes, seminar planning sessions, and discus-

Peter P. Carlin used Pathfinder Club discussion methods in the 1966 Institute to help students learn from each other about living, and to develop their own methods of meeting daily problems. Mr. Carlin is a Research Associate in the Bureau of Educational Research, Cleveland, Ohio.

sion groups were used to get teachers interested in the improvement of instruction and to challenge them to seek answers to the foregoing questions. To this end the teaching time was used by having critical thinking lessons on character education which allowed the students to gain new insights into their rights and responsibilities.

Background

In 1914, James F. Wright of Detroit introduced a unique and effective approach to character education and at the same time founded the organization known since then as the Pathfinders of America. The techniques developed by Mr. Wright have been used in American schools since 1921. The Pathfinder Clubs have been organized in Cleveland public schools since 1931, based upon the techniques and materials developed by Mr. Wright and his associates.

The purpose of the Pathfinder Club is to help the pupil to explore, to discover motivation for his acts, and to gain insight into his personal life so that he may improve his way of living.

There has been continuous effort to improve both the techniques and materials. Current emphasis is being placed on discovering the needs of young adults and using those needs as a basis for discussion and for providing opportunity for pupils to gain experience in making decisions and experience in living, desirable both to themselves and to our society.

Objectives

The teacher centered his teaching in these aims:

- Developing in each pupil a consciousness of his own personal responsibility.
- Developing an understanding in each pupil of his social responsibility.
- Helping each pupil to enrich his own life, and to maintain and improve the ends of democracy.

In each class, the teacher attempted to create or discuss real, dynamic life situations that call forth common and individual experiences so that children will develop habits of weighing the consequences of their acts by recollection and foresight, leading to purposeful living through development of a *group spirit* and the integration of individual personality.

Technique

The teacher started the discussion with a question that was the key to that session. The question was stated in such a way that members reacted in several ways.

For example, the teacher asked, "Is anger a good thing?." One-third of the class said "Yes," one-third said "No" and the last third held that "It depends on the situation." An ideal climate for discussion was started. A simple question, the group divided, and each group apparently holding convictions. In this situation, skill on the part of the teacher was necessary. He offered no arguments at first—merely asked for discussion—which suggested that the answer to even a simple question is not an easy one, that it can be arrived at only by a process of examining the evidence. All evidence, trivial or not in the eyes of an adult, was given grave consideration and the pupils were led, through questioning by their fellows and the teacher, to arrive at a thoughtful conclusion.

Finally a decision was agreed upon by the students. It was a decision that had been thought out by the pupils themselves. The teacher did not place his approval or disapproval at once upon the decision. However, he did commend the thinking of the entire class, making sure that all expressed thoughts had been evaluated positively while all were seeking a conclusion.

More questions were brought up for future discussion. When might anger be useful? What are some of the harmful effects of anger?

Participation

The classes provided experiences in critical thinking and cooperative effort. Life situations, made graphic by blackboard sketches, gave rise to a lively exchange of opinions. Committee responsibility resulted in leading the members of the class to arrive at conclusions based upon careful exploration of areas related to the problem.

The teacher never imposed decisions or moral precepts upon the class. Rather, he led a discussion of class members, permitting *them* to reach decisions and to suggest action.

Following discussions, it was customary for pupils to write down their own views, criticisms, reactions to the discussion, or evaluation of the lesson.

Classroom Procedures

Although the teacher was in charge of meetings, the following important conditions prevailed:

There was no marking or grading of any pupil.

Each pupil could do anything he desired as long as he did not interfere with the rights of other pupils.

The teacher was "on his own" in the classroom and the pupil could say what he chose in defense of his viewpoint. The teacher exercised no authority and did not punish or did not send any pupil to the office for punishment.

No member made fun of anyone or laughed at any pupil when that pupil was discussing or expressing his views in the meeting. This was a great inducement for free and unhampered expression.

This freedom affords an *immediate opportunity* for any pupil to express any hostility he may feel. This acts as a catharsis, a release, and a help in the pupil's identifying himself in the positive aspects of the day's discussion. These conditions have been accepted by the pupils as being fair to everyone.

It is anticipated that among the students a noticeable development in democratic practices should result, evidenced in the management of their own affairs, increased respect for each individual's viewpoint, and the mastery of individual conflicts.

Through group therapy at least some improved. The quality of the views and conduct of the majority of the class, expressed in free discussion, was almost always an influence for discerning values, and frequently revealed to the teacher an insight into the attitude of any antisocial member.

Materials

Since few textbooks on character education were available and none was completely satisfactory for use in the public school, it was necessary to use materials that had been prepared for classroom use in the Cleveland public schools.

Discussion material consisted of four-page printed pamphlets. Each of the different pamphlets used was easily revised and new material added. Discussion material was carefully prepared to avoid offending any pupil regardless of race, religion, or creed.

When questions came up regarding a controversial subject, the teacher encouraged the pupil to talk the problem over with his father or mother, his minister, priest, rabbi, teacher, or to find help whenever available.

VERBATIM COMMENTS OF STUDENTS

"Teaching Methods—Liked way they worked on lesson. On things around and about you. Stories to prove point discussions."

"It's O.K. The teacher explains it to us and if we want we can go home and read ourselves."

"They were very meaningful and useful. When I go back to school I'm going to show my teachers the pamphlets."

"I wrote about every lesson in my notebook and it was very nice for the institute to furnish them, with other books also."

"The teaching method I liked because the way it was taught made it interesting."

"Class Notebooks—I got a lot out of the notebook and the pamphlets. I got a lot out of them because you wrote the thing on the blackboard."

"It was *meaningful*. It's building us all up to be rightful, respectful, and considerate, law-abiding *citizens*."

"Price Tags—I learned that before you buy things you ask yourself three questions:"

1. Do I need this thing?
2. What is the price?
3. Is it worth the price to me?

"Our Value in Society—I learned to be a plus-value citizen instead of a minus-value citizen.

Rights and Duties—To have your own rights and duties in home, school, community.

Service—To have a great service to your country, town, school, home."

"In this class I like everything we talk about, most of all I enjoy talking about getting an education."

"I like the social studies class very much because it is interesting. I would say that it is anything but boring. In regular school we use books; in this class we are the books, and you learn the other side."

"In this class we did some interesting things such as study 'service,' 'the rights of others' and it is something to know. In my words this class has been very interesting."

"Most of the time in class it was interesting and I learned things too. The movie was fine. I acted the part of Mike—that was really fun."

"I prefer social studies more now because of the things we learn and the way it is taught. I think it will help me more in social studies next year, or history."

"Well explaining our relationship to other people and our attitude toward people and teachers."

"Well my attitude in the classes and the understanding in the classroom's and the teacher's ask me next year and I don't understand it then we can explained it together."

"I think that the pamphlets were a great help to me because my father likes them and he discusses them with me."

"I enjoyed being here with the teachers and discussing the different ideas."

"The pamplets were very educational and the reading lists were very useful. The teaching methods were very good. I didn't keep a class notebook. The institute was very nice."

"What I enjoy most about the pamphlets is the simple fact that they give you examples about everyday people and not like the facts of the books."

"Reading List—It tells you about many books that you may read relating to the pamphlets. Many of the stories are very interesting and you like to find out more about them."

"Teaching Method—That was the most marvelous part of the whole class. It is much more interesting for the students when they are the textbook rather than having textbooks. Another thing is not having to work for a grade, instead to work to gain knowledge for yourself because *you want* it. I do not feel as though there should be tests and exams for students to cram by and lose after the text."

"I had a wonderful time, learned a lot, and it gave me something to do during the summer. I really liked it a lot, and I hope to come again next year. I only wish this course was available for kids all over the world. I also wish school was like the course."

"Well, the other students were helpful in the class decisions as well as the teachers."

"Helped me think things out more."

"I read so far one story on the reading list. I intend to read more of the books on the reading list. It should be interesting."

"I liked the teachers and I thought they made the lesson very interesting for me. I think I learned some things and I had fun in the classes."

"I would like it if they had more books like you gave because they are very interesting. I like them very much."

"I also would like very much to come next year, to have more in my storehouse of knowledge."

OBSERVATIONS AND COMMENTS OF PARTICIPATING TEACHERS

Teacher I

Teaching Techniques

"The method, which may be a variation on that used by Socrates, was new to our students who expected to enter the classroom, sit down, listen to lectures, and be tested on the lecture material with the option to pass or fail, depending on the ability to recall. The first class showed how infrequently these students have been given the opportunity to express themselves and be listened to with any seriousness in the school situation."

Anecdotes

"Annie has made spectacular progress in the group. She entered a shy, young thing who, throughout the weeks, has developed some measure of confidence from class participation. She began by taking notes, which seemed customary with her. Later she grew able to answer questions, and success gave her courage to divulge her fears and superstitions to the group without being afraid they would laugh at her. She has enjoyed the institute and 'wishes school could always be this way.'

"Annie's statement can be interpreted to mean she has gained some idea of her personal worth.

"In regular classes her teachers have gone too fast for her understanding. Moreover, few have taken the time to explain material she has not understood. She had adopted the habit of gazing at the speaker intently with her mind turned off or dreaming of something else. She now listens, and since the discussions are within the area of her experience, she participates. Her walk is straighter or taller."

Teacher II

Teaching Techniques

The social studies coordinating teacher had organized his thoughts and lessons, as well as letting his participating teachers know to what ends they were headed. Here begins a wonderful and worthwhile relationship with the social studies people.

"The format chosen by the coordinating teacher seemed to me to be better suited for guidance, but after viewing and listening a few days I could see and understand its relevancy to social studies. Although I believe the size and temperament of the class made the format workable, I do believe I have been given insight into new techniques of material presentation, as well as use of human resources, up to this time sort of used in moderation by me. The participating teachers also showed me how to get the most out of something, namely, using the children and their role-playing abilities to the hilt. I, myself, hope to use the *Pathfinder* series in both seventh-grade guidance and ninth-grade American history. Likewise, the *Springboards* series is adaptable, in my opinion, to both subject areas.

Working with the six social studies people was a rewarding experience. Perhaps that is the key to successful teaching and satisfaction in teaching. Cooperation in planning class activities or lessons was rewarding in the enthusiasm and 'pitch in' attitude of the social studies group. I would enjoy this cooperation during the coming school year and those that will follow."

Anecdotes

"Gerald has been absent a great deal, as well as tardy on the occasions that he has been to summer school. In the classroom when he's there, he seems to be following the teacher's lesson, as well as the students who contribute to the teacher's lesson. At times, he has volunteered an answer or two or even to be a part of a sociodrama group and has handled himself impressively. Likewise, he has volunteered to be a human resource consultant and appeared voluntarily as a member of Dr. Abramowitz's demonstration class. If he attended regularly I think he would have gained a great deal, as well as contributed much to the others.

"Rosemary started late because she thought she had a job lined up, but fortunately she has attended the summer school and made her presence felt. She participated quite freely in the classroom discussion, and did a very good job in a few parts of a class sociodrama. She, too, was a demonstration class volunteer, but was absent that day. She entered the summer school sessions with a chip on her shoulder. However, as she is given the chance of free expression, either in discussions or acting out parts, the hard core of resistance seems to be melting away.

"Janice has been punctual, neat, and passively interested from the very beginning. She never has much to say, but a few times, being directly confronted by a question, has answered it logically. She keeps herself busy in the classroom by taking notes or copying the information that has been put on the board. I think she will benefit from this type of permissive summer school experience, but it will be in years to come.

Teacher III

Teaching Techniques

"The bright spot in the program was the daily morning sessions that took place at THS. It was the bright spot because it was successful. It was successful because

1. Almost a 100% pupil attendance existed during the six-week program, and the students were interested and participated in the daily activities.
2. The program presented by the coordinating teacher was organized.
3. The cooperation of the participating teachers was 100%. These teachers took on the responsibility of teaching classes, planning activities, and organizing field trips which made the program a success."

Anecdotes

"Harry's physical presence in class is nearly perfect. However, his actual participation in class activity has been far from desirable. In the classroom situation, Harry has been confronted with pointed questions concerning the Institute. The purpose of the questioning was to get him to express an opinion. He will respond if he is prodded into a situation. He seems to pay attention to the other students who are participating in class. Harry is a neatly dressed and well-groomed boy.

"Kathy is a shy young lady who is petite and pleasant. Although she is not an extrovert, she will participate in the class discussion if she is sure her answer will be acceptable. She takes great pride in the notebook she is keeping. Her attendance in class is near-perfect. Kathy gives the impression that she likes school although there is no definite sign of accomplishment."

Teacher IV

Teaching Techniques

" 'A fundamental premise in a democratic society is the belief that human life is precious, regardless of the human's race, creed, or ability.' " It was on such a premise that Mr. Carlin selected and developed the character education series which was presented to the students in a most effective and challenging way. The principles of character education included

1. Instilling a desire for excellence in school work, manners, and achievement.
2. Stressing the values of honesty and respect for truth.
3. Practicing respect and thoughtfulness of others.
4. Raising each pupil's sense of values and standards of behavior.
5. Helping students exercise self-discipline, self-direction and self-evaluation in their lives.
6. Helping students appreciate their education and the school.

"The numerous hours of class work bore fruit because the students soon began to think of themselves as 'pathfinders' discovering the unknown. The real value of the presentation lay in the fact that the students were actually discovering for themselves certain principles of character education. The inductive method helped them to see the connection between the personal problems of the individual and the problems of the school and their society."

"The difficulty that every teacher faces is that of evaluating his efforts or the efforts of other teachers. Unlike the bricklayer who can see results at the end of the day, the teacher must detect subtle changes in attitude, concept formation, comprahension, and, most of all, critical thinking. It was not the role of Mr. Carlin to teach opinions or conclusions; rather he strove to develop the critical faculties of the students to meet the problems confronting them. Junior high school students particularly must be prepared to assume the very difficult educational and social roles which lay before them. I like to believe that PTI program, particularly the eighth-grade social studies curriculum, has in some way met this need.

"In addition to the character education achieved, it seems that there were other outcomes of their experience. Particularly the skill in analyzing problems seemed to have been developed so that students could use character education concepts in their regular school experience. It was clear that in such areas as 'Rights and Duties' where misconceptions abound, analysis was both necessary and fruitful. Certainly, other by-products of this were the development and use of listening and class recitation skills. Still another result was the learning of 'community spirit'—cooperation without sacrificing individual initiative."

Anecdotes

"Rita is from a low socio-economic home environment. She was a very interesting and, at the same time, puzzling young lady. During the early part of the Institute, she was quiet and attentive. Her class activities included careful note-taking and some class discussion. I thought the Institute was of significant value to Rita, although her attendance was highly irregular. Rita did a remarkable job during a class sociodrama; her performance was startling and encouraging. Several times Rita commented that she enjoyed the program and thought that it was very worthwhile.

"Hester took very little part in class discussion, although she seemed quite attentive. Very seldom did she lose eye contact with the teacher or other students taking part in class discussion. She would respond under direct questioning from the teacher, but she never volunteered an answer. Hester's attendance was irregular and tardiness common. I doubt whether the Institute was of any great value to Hester."

Teacher V

Teaching Techniques

"Although this approach was entirely new to the students, they quickly became involved and responded to the questions and problems presented to them by Mr. Carlin with enthusiasm and zest. All of the students for whom I was responsible stated when asked that they enjoyed this approach immensely and wondered why a social studies approach like this could not be used in the regular school. Obviously the answer to this question is that it could be used. It is my hope that I can encourage some of our social studies teachers to adopt this approach.

"Although the complete success of the program cannot be measured in such a short time, some positive attitude changes have already been noticed. Some of these have been quite pronounced. For example, one student thought that to give assistance to a friend during a test, that is, putting it bluntly, to cheat, was a social obligation. However, after the class discussion he had changed his position and was ready to admit that cheating was wrong.

"I thought the first period was the most enlightening and helpful aspect of the Institute. The novel approach was well received by the students and some positive attitude changes were effected. The insights gained by the children should prove helpful to them when they begin their school year in September.

"Besides the regular lessons, one movie was shown, "Mike Makes His Mark." This was very well received by the students and led to a lively discussion. It also showed the students how people react to one another and let us set up certain situations which the student could dramatize in their sociodramas."

Anecdotes

"I think that this program was a real help to Virgil. Unfortunately it ended before a definite change could be noted. It is too bad that there is not a continuation of the approach in regular school.

"Virgil was not too punctual and was absent four times. When first questioned he would not explain these absences but later admitted he had been in a fight and had cut his lip. He was too embarrassed to be seen. Virgil responded to most of his classes but in many instances he seemed to lack insight into the problems being discussed. Virgil said that he liked Mr. Carlin 'because he didn't make me stop chewing gum, he was neat and clean, and he explained things.' His teachers 'didn't act right and don't give no second chance.' Virgil further said that he learned how to control himself better and how to live.

"Harold lives in a project for low-income groups. He is well read, active in sports, popular, and seems to get along well with his peers. He is bright but has an odd attitude in that he does not accept full responsibility for his actions, but would tend to blame faults on environment or peer-group pressure. I think Mr. Carlin has helped him and he has helped himself a great deal through a critical analysis of his own character. Toward the end I felt a definite change in this boy. He seems to have gained an insight into his shortcomings and to be more willing to stand on his own two feet. When questioned about the Institute, Harold said that he enjoyed it very much and asked if he could return next year. He was especially complimentary to Mr. Carlin and his method and, like Don, enjoyed the different teachers and their methods, especially the sociodrama.

"The students all enjoyed the program and profited from it. They expressed a desire for a program of this nature in their own schools."

PART THREE

The Math Science Program

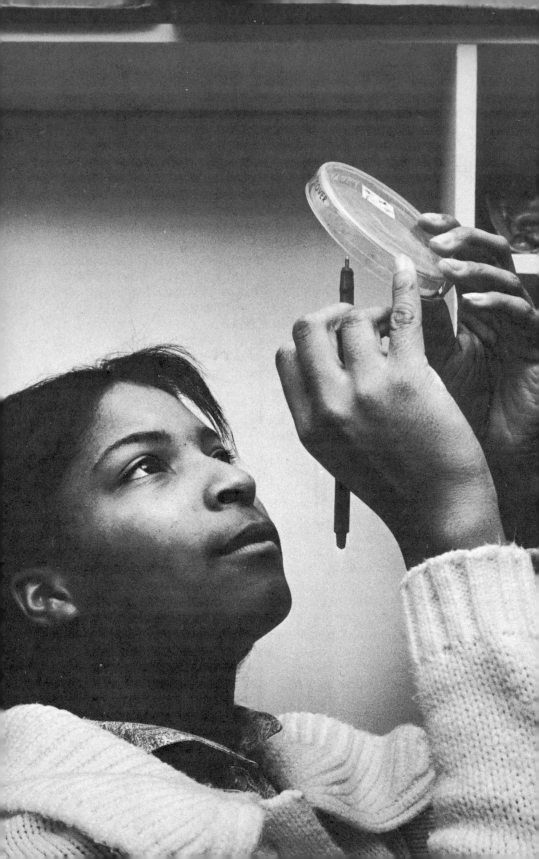

10. The Science-Math Program: An Introduction

CHARLES W. KEITH

The purpose of the 1965–1966 science-math programs was to help teachers do a more effective job of teaching urban youth. The assumptions are made that good teaching will be effective with any group of youngsters and that each teacher possesses skills and uses techniques which others might find useful. The morning program was designed to provide an opportunity for the participating teachers to: become acquainted with some new programs, methods and techniques; demonstrate skills and techniques and practice those that had been observed, using new programs as a vehicle, where available; and interact as a group to offer constructive criticism to one another and plan for future presentations.

The course of study for the science-math program was selected and developed to provide for instruction and experience in the use of new materials as well as proven techniques through the observation of and interaction with master teachers, visiting lecturers, and community resource advisors, and the use of a research center; and to provide an opportunity for the participating teachers to test, in actual classroom situations, these new materials and techniques for urban youth. These goals set the tone for the selection of course content and master teachers.

The probability that learning will take place in the classroom, within the framework of teacher goals, is greatest when students are actively involved in the learning process. It is as fallacious to assume that all students like science and math as it is to assume that all students enjoy reading and writing. If these assumptions are correct, a program

---

Charles Keith introduces this section on some of the science-math experiences at Princeton. Mr. Keith was a science-mathematics coordinating teacher in the 1965 Princeton-Trenton Institute and supervisor of the science-math program in the 1966 Institute. He is chairman of the science department of Lincoln High School in Portland, Oregon.

◀ *Photo credit:* **Ken Heyman**

of studies that provides for many different kinds of activities has the best chance of capturing the interest of the majority of students.

Most students become actively involved in their own education when they are encouraged to express opinions and are permitted to react to those of their peers. Students should be encouraged to explore why they respond as they do. The direction provided by the teacher must assure that the goals which have been established can be attained.

The general goals of the science-math program both in 1965 and 1966 were to help the student differentiate between observation and interpretation, help students learn how to discover answers through observation and interpretation, involve students in scientific inquiry in the classroom, and provide an opportunity for the release of the potential intellectual creativity of students.

The 1965 science-math program of the Princeton-Trenton Institute was composed entirely of a program developed by the Princeton University Secondary School Science Project named "Time, Space, and Matter" initially supported by the National Science Foundation. This program is described in detail in Chapter 11 by Ernest Poll, the 1965 science-math supervisor and the associate director of the 1966 Princeton-Trenton Institute, and by three master teachers who have had experience teaching this curriculum.

The 1966 science-math program built and expanded upon the 1965 experiences and also compiled with the foregoing initial assumptions and goals. The science program was expanded to include a ninth-grade course called "Introductory Physical Science," a tenth-grade course entitled "Special Materials Biology" (BSCS), as well as "Time, Space, and Matter" for the eighth grade.

The math program was also expanded. In the eighth grade it was designed to correlate with science at the same grade level. An attempt was made to reinforce those concepts of mathematics with which students have difficulty in the science course. The course for grades nine and ten stressed developing a "feeling for mathematics," exploring problem-solving from the basis of induction and plausible reasoning, and exploring the structure and deductive aspects in conjunction with understanding terminology, largely via the inductive method of teaching.

11. Time, Space, and Matter: An Overview

ERNEST N. POLL

The course of instruction for the Princeton University-Trenton Schools science-math program during the summer of 1966 was derived from part I of "Time, Space, and Matter," a curriculum developed at Princeton University by the Secondary School Science Project under a grant from the National Science Foundation. Its primary objectives are for the student to acquire an understanding of the processes of scientific inquiry so that he can find out for himself about the physical world, acquire an understanding of the physical world through his own experiences, and, finally, to acquire intellectual tools which will enable him to carry on investigations in any area of study, and attitudes which will move him to become a producer of knowledge. The course, although apparently related largely to geology because of its story line, is in reality an intricately woven fabric of concepts and skills drawn from the fields of geology, physics, chemistry, and mathematics. The story line also describes the course and integrates the various concepts. The Princeton University Secondary School Science Project has developed the story line which follows.

The moon represents a single, isolated system that everyone can see in much the same way. This is the essential rationale for using it as a starting point for an investigation of the physical world. Questions about the moon seem to fall into two broad categories: its size, distance, shape, and motion; and the nature of its surface, composi-

Ernest Poll is in a unique position to describe the "Time, Space, and Matter" program. He was involved in the development of these materials and also supervised their use as Chicago Area Coordinator for the Princeton Secondary School Science Project supported by the National Science Foundation. He is presently on the science staff of the University of Chicago Laboratory Schools. Mr. Poll served as the Science-Math Supervisor in the 1965 Princeton-Trenton Institute and as Associate Director during the summer of 1966.

tion, and age. Unable to investigate these questions directly, students are reduced to speculation.

The earth seems a more suitable place for investigation since specimens can be examined at first hand. Pictures of the Grand Canyon—a large "slice of earth" exposed to view—and rock samples representative of those in the area are observed. But when questions concerned with the canyon's age, size, and origin occur, students find themselves speculating again. The Grand Canyon proves too vast and complicated to be handled at this time. A small, more manageable system is needed for study.

Such a small system is provided in the form of a container of water and ice which is examined after students learn the necessity of distinguishing between an observation and an interpretation. The activity demonstrates the need for employing all the senses in observation and shows that more definition can be arrived at by using devices to refine or extend the senses. Students learn to relate the microcosm situation of the laboratory to the world at large.

Approximation and Precision

The notion of qualitative approximation and precision in observation is developed by providing a situation, a simulated Apollo mission, in which samples of materials representative of a restricted area must be selected within certain limitations of time and space. Precision is found to involve finer and finer approximation, and the degree of precision sought is dependent upon the purpose at hand.

Quantitative precision is then added to observation. Comparing the "heft" of two specific samples of matter from the previous investigation, it becomes apparent that in adding precision to observations of mass, the specimens have to be compared with something else—a standard. A device which enables such a comparison is an equal-arm balance. Eventually students find they can compute mass using the law of moments as they suspend their standard and unknown at various distances from the fulcrum of the balance arm.

After measuring mass, students follow a similar pattern in measuring the amount of space occupied by their specimens. This procedure involves calibrating a plastic vial which is used as a graduated cylinder. When graphed, the mass and volume determinations of class samples reveal a mass-volume relationship—density.

The concept of time is investigated as students make their own timing devices, such as water clocks and pendulums, based on some regularly recurring event. The relationship between the three fundamental physical concepts which students have now investigated—time, space, and matter—leads to an examination of derived concepts such as velocity.

Effects of Running Water

Implicit in the concept of time is change. Running water, though gradual in rate, is found to be the most widespread agent of change on earth. Transportation and deposition are studied by reproducing stream action in the laboratory. Students next examine the effects of running water on common earth materials and plot the different rates of change that these materials undergo. The experiments lead to a recognition of the processes by which the earth materials undergo change—hydraulic action, melting, dissolving, and abrasion. Once again students relate the events and processes of the microcosm to what takes place on the surface of the earth.

Having studied the effects of running water and now able to make relevant observations and measurements, students reconsider questions about the Grand Canyon. They are able to attribute the canyon's formation to the action of running water and to the Colorado River in particular. Using a rate of abrasion established earlier, they make an order of magnitude estimate of the minimum time necessary to cut the canyon. The idea of cycles in nature is suggested by considering the processes at work in the canyon today.

Success in answering questions about the earth encourages students to take up their even earlier queries about the moon and other celestial bodies. Pictures of star trails, the rising moon and sun, and the phase cycles of the moon and Venus enable students to distinguish the daily (rotation or spin) and annual (revolution or orbit) motions of heavenly bodies.

Size-Distance Relationship

After having investigated the relationship between the apparent size and distance of objects, students try to find the size of and distance to the moon. The diameter of shadows produced on the surface of the earth by solar eclipses can be measured directly. Laboratory work leads to a consideration of umbral and penumbral shadows and the geometric relationship of the sizes of and distances to the sun, moon, and earth. The diameter of the moon is seen to approach the value of the radius of the penumbra as the earth-sun distance is increased in relation to the earth-moon distance. Therefore, a measurement of the penumbral radius provides a value for the diameter of the moon. After determining the moon's velocity, the earth-moon distance is found.

Since this distance is too small to help find the earth-sun distance, Venus is used to that end, having been found to be one-third the way from the earth to the sun. Its transit of the sun is treated as a special eclipse, and data from the 1882 transit is used in calculating the solar diameter and the earth-sun distance.

The investigation of the motion and size of celestial bodies proceeded on certain assumptions regarding their relative positions in space. Students are now introduced to the Copernican and Ptolemaic models of the universe. The Copernican model is refined when students discover that the moon's apparent size does change slightly, indicating that its distance from earth varies. That the moon's orbit is not really circular introduces Kepler's ideas of the universe.

Having determined the size and distance values of several celestial bodies, students return to questions about the moon, whose surface may reveal a record of its past. An earth feature, Arizona's Meteor Crater, is observed to be similar to lunar craters. Two different theories of its formation are considered. Laboratory work provides an analogue for an impact theory of origin.

A study of the characteristics and locations of several lunar craters suggests superposition and relative time. Students consider arguments that the earth also must have had immense craters, long ago erased by agents of change. Since the moon does not appear to have running water, it retains its surface features much longer than does the earth. In all likelihood, students conclude, the moon contains a record of events which may help man understand the early history of the earth and solar system.*

The strategy of the course is to maneuver the student into an active role in the learning process. He carries on a sequence of investigations which are initiated through his own questions. As an illustration of how this is actually carried out, on the very first day of the Institute the students were told that the objective of the course was to find out all that they could about the physical world. The students, in discussion, then began to examine the nature of the problem which

---

* *Secondary School Science Project, Progress Report IV, Spring 1966*, Secondary School Science Project, Princeton University, Princeton, New Jersey, 1966, pp. 9–12.

had been set for them by their teachers. They raised questions such as "What is the physical world?" Their responses to their own questions ranged from the vastness of the universe to the nature of the surface of the earth.

As the discussion continued, the surface of the earth was accepted as representative of the physical world, and the Grand Canyon of the Colorado River was seen to be one of the deepest cuts exposing a cross section of the crust. At this point, when student attention was riveted on the Grand Canyon itself, the students were shown colored slides and were given a student booklet containing many different views of the Grand Canyon. They were asked by their teacher to raise questions whose answers would help them to understand the physical world. They were also encouraged to speculate on the answers. Many questions were raised, but their focus generally was "How large is the Canyon? How was it formed? How old is it? What are the rocks or materials of which it is made?"

The teacher led the discussions and variously played the roles of moderator, sounding board for ideas, sympathetic listener, gadfly, and challenger of ideas, but never the authority with glib and ready answers. The students played the role of scientific investigators determining each next step which had to be taken to overcome an impasse or a problem of immediate concern. Each investigation contained a series of activities in which the student observed, manipulated, counted, or measured the very stuff of which the world is made. He then interpreted the objects and events which he had observed. For the student, this was not the blind pursuit of unattainable or unknown goals. He had set them himself. Each investigation pivoted on discussions which in turn fed on the activities of the students.

Each student was issued a kit of scientific equipment so that he could carry on his own investigations. The kit was his to use, either at home or at school. Among the items in the kitbox were an equal-arm balance, a magnifying glass, an ungraded thermometer, and sundry other materials such as the minerals calcite and galena. Student booklets accompanied the investigations. These served several purposes. First, previous investigations were briefly reviewed in the introductory section. Second, the stage was set for the current investigation. Finally, an opportunity was afforded to the student to apply his newly acquired understanding to the world at large. Corollary readings reflecting an expansion of the ideas, some in a historical perspective, are incorporated in a specially prepared paperback reading series. These were available in each classroom for loan to the students.

Finally, each student was expected to maintain a daily log or record of all of his activities: his discussion notes, his observations, his data, and his interpretations. In the absence of a text, the student record book became each student's chronicle of activities and reference book. As the summer term wore on the students took greater pride in their record books and made better entries, even though they knew they would not be evaluated.

The materials and methods of "Time, Space, and Matter" have been tried and tested in a variety of secondary schools from coast to coast. It has been found to be suited for both the advantaged and disadvantaged student, although there is a difference in the outcomes, both in degree and type. By its very nature, the active participation of the students provides many natural outlets for their youthful energy. Discipline problems are reduced or nonexistent. The student may speak to his friends during the class period. He is encouraged to share data and exchange ideas. The classroom atmosphere is relaxed but purposive. With the teacher no longer seen as the authority figure and with the degree of freedom of action and movement which prevails in the classroom, there is little object in adolescent rebellion in the classroom. Another incentive to use this curriculum in the Institute, aside from the fact that it had been developed at Princeton University itself, was its successful inclusion in programs for disadvantaged youth for several summers both at Princeton University and at the University of Chicago.

The effects of the curriculum and methods on the students was noted by many teachers. The amount of class discussion, participation, and the quality of discussions were revealing to the teachers. The gist of their comments toward the end of the program was that this program "seems to bring out the best in the students." Sample comments from critique notes follow.

"The attention of all students at all times was sustained to a very high degree."

"Increased student response in both classes."

"Group work brings the group out."

"Some kids who take copious notes are not participating orally, and vice versa."

"Better reactions from some of the quieter pupils."

"Peer group interaction coming into play."

"Class seemed to be more sure and confident, but bothered because they weren't able to get 'right answers'."

"Students seem to be very careful in their selection of words.

They are using scientific vocabulary. Students seem to be thinking carefully before they speak."

These are not the total commentary, nor are they representative. There were days when participating and coordinating teachers felt the day to have gone badly. The overriding tenor of the teachers' comments is, however, reflected in those quoted.

To call "Time, Space, and Matter" a course of instruction is actually a misnomer. It certainly is a course in which learning takes place. The classroom environment, the teacher, other students, materials of instruction, and lab kits are necessary ingredients. The teaching method is the catalyst uniting student and experiences in often new and varied ways to produce learning. The students come away from the experience seeing science as a means of achieving their goals rather than as an end in itself. It was more a place where teacher respect for students' ideas encouraged reflective thinking and bred self-respect, and where teacher confidence in student ability to do "science" bred self-confidence.

By the very act of the students of assuming some responsibility for their own learning they developed a sense of value and worth in themselves. They found out that "finding out about things" in science is not magic. Student work habits and writing skills developed as they gathered and tabulated data and made other entries in their daily log books.

Students came because they wanted to learn. They kept coming because the teachers treated them as if they cared for them.

In the following three chapters, three educators express their reactions to the subject of "Time, Space, and Matter."

12. The Student as a Scientific Investigator

JAMES PENNINGTON

The general objectives for the students in "Time, Space, and Matter" were: to acquire an understanding of the processes of scientific inquiry so that he can find out for himself about the physical world; to acquire an understanding of the physical world through his own experiences; and to acquire intellectual tools, which will enable him to carry on investigations in any area of study, and attitudes which will move him to become a producer of knowledge.

The strategies of instruction have seven main ingredients.

The student plays the role of scientific investigator. He observes and interprets objects and events. He manipulates materials. He makes things happen.

The student follows a sequence of investigations which have been structured to facilitate student discovery. The student is led to believe that the decision to take a particular course of action has been his decision.

Once a skill has been developed or understanding acquired, the student finds that he must use what he has learned over and over again. Learning becomes purposive.

The completion of each investigation brings to the forefront many new problems. His task never seems to be finished. There is always more to know.

The student is expected to maintain a daily log or record of all

---

James Pennington taught "Time, Space, and Matter" during both the 1965 and 1966 Institutes. Two of his essays, one from each year, are included, beginning with the 1966 experiences. Both are valuable because they show the development of a fine teacher's thinking about his subject matter. The 1966 essay identifies some effective ideas for teachers, whereas the 1965 essay is primarily concerned with the responses to these materials by the children in Mr. Pennington's classes. Mr. Pennington teaches science at James Hart Junior High School in Homewood, Illinois.

of his activities: observations, data, interpretations, and notes. In the absence of a text the student record book becomes his text.

The teacher does not play the role of authority. He too is an investigator and observer. He raises leading questions and skillfully steers the investigations along their predetermined course. He challenges students to prove their assumptions through experimentation or observation. He emphasizes the sciences as ways of investigating the world rather than as ends in themselves.

Investigations are initiated or summed up by student discussion. Discussions also permit the sharing of data and the exchange of ideas.

The role of the student in "Time, Space, and Matter" is to be an active participant in the pursuit of knowledge. He makes things happen, he manipulates materials. He is encouraged to form his own opinions and then to test them by observation and by discussion with the rest of the class.

As the teacher of the class I played many roles, but my main purpose was to draw out from the students their own ideas and encourage the other students to react to these ideas. I was not to be the authority but rather to moderate discussions, listen to ideas, and challenge the students to use their own powers of observation and reasoning.

Each student received a kit of scientific equipment so that he could perform his own investigations. The kit contained an equal-arm balance, several sizes of plastic pill bottles, a calibrated syringe, mineral samples such as galena and calcite, and assorted objects to use as mass standards with their balance.

Student booklets accompanied each investigation. The booklets provided material for review and preview. They consist largely of pictures which provide opportunity for observations related to the current investigation. Corollary readings which were related to the material under investigation were also available for the students to check out.

Each student was provided with a notebook and pencil so that he could maintain a daily record of his class work. Since no textbook was used, his notebook became his own personal textbook to record his observations, questions, and conclusions.

Part I of "Time, Space, and Matter" is designed to provide a series of interrelated sequential investigations which require a full school year to complete. Since 21 teaching days were available this summer, many of the investigations had to be eliminated. The investigations which were included were curtailed in duration and depth so that the participating teachers might see as many investigations as possible. The general plan, developed last year for use in the Princeton University-Trenton Schools Institute, was followed in periods 1 and 3.

Since class periods were roughly half as long as last year this plan had to be modified to be used this year. The schedule that follows seemed to fit the foregoing criteria and also provided some continuity for the students in the course.*

If there is one thing that sets "Time, Space, and Matter" apart from the science course traditionally taught, it is that the emphasis is shifted from content and concepts to skills and an understanding of the process of science.

On the assumption that this change does not necessarily require a new set of activities and problems to work with, I tried to adopt the areas which are traditionally taught as general science to this change in emphasis. Instead of doing an experiment to get a given answer or illustrate a "concept," an experiment's main purpose was to lead the student to work and to think like a scientist. The classroom activity may not have been noticeably different from a content-oriented classroom.

In a unit on light energy, the students worked with discovering that the angle of incidence equals the angle of reflection. My goals for this activity were that students should learn to use a protractor, measure carefully, recognize the need for repeating experiments and recording and organizing data. Students also gained experience in formulation of a theory and recognized the need to test any theory thus formulated. The groundwork that can lead to an understanding of errors in an experiment was also laid.

With all of this in mind the activity was structured so that the skills and attitudes to be developed were needed and used. The student was given what help was needed in order to get started. Some students needed some guidance of a very direct nature before they could get into this. Because of this initial emphasis their attitude remained content-oriented. There was always an answer hanging out there somewhere if the student could just put the pieces together. For him to develop the skills which were listed he needed to use the skills. The teacher posed problems and provided either bridges or obstacles in the path, as the need arose, to assure that the students did need to use the skills the teacher had chosen.

Different skills were developed by other problems. A general rule which seemed to apply is that one must not reach for too large a set of skills and attitudes with any one experiment. Obviously the

---

* A more detailed description of each of the activities listed may be obtained by contacting the Princeton University Secondary School Science Project or the McGraw-Hill Publishing Company.

same skills and attitudes will not all be involved in every experiment. But many will be used over and over again, so an incomplete mastery the first time through need not be considered a failure. It does point up a need for an activity which will reinforce this skill or will build on what had been acquired.

The students need to realize that they are learning as they go through this program. Since they will be learning to work on their own, they may not recognize this as learning. A class discussion was needed to point out to the students that they had grown in their ability to work on problems on their own.

Students will not value the skills highly unless the teacher shows by his attitude and question examinations that skills are important. Tests given on activities should emphasize what students actually did and may be administered before the results of the experiment are discussed in class.

The degree of difficulty of gaining the skills and of the activity which is to develop the skills can be varied. The approach can be applied over a large range of student ability levels and goals can be set which are realistic for the students themselves. Two classes may do the same experiment, but the level of abstraction and the aspirations of the teacher for each group may differ widely. The same situation may be true to some extent of two students in the same "homogeneous" class.

The method does not minimize content because the information acquired is content. The concepts are developed; for example, the angle of incidence is found to be equal to the angle of reflection. He usually develops other ways of identifying these angles and usually concentrates on the complements of the angles of incidence and reflection. While finding this relationship the student has also picked up some of the intellectual tools of the scientist and has begun to see their value. Each experiment, as mentioned before, should have application over a wide range of student abilities. This particular one can lead to the concept of internal reflection and a great deal of abstract thought by considering the multiple images of an object seen in a plane mirror.

The student attempts to account for what he observes and to reconcile this with what he has already learned about reflection. Models are developed to account for the observation, and ways to test these models are suggested. As these models are modified or discarded the process of science becomes very real to the student because he is using it himself. New observations related to the problem are introduced from the students' own experiences and when it all fits together the feeling of accomplishment whets the appetite for the next challenge.

Some students do not get much beyond reading a protractor. Many are content to find the rule for predicting what the angles will be, but for the few who can and will, very many intellectual tools are available.

One of the stated objectives of the Princeton University-Trenton Schools Institute was to provide the participating teachers instruction and experience in the use of new materials and proven techniques. Since the foregoing type of approach can be applied over a wide range of subject matter and does not require much new equipment I chose this approach to use for the second-period class. The participating teachers have taught this class after the first two days.

The first experiment the participating teachers worked with was the one referred to previously. The general set-up may be found in almost any junior high school science textbook series and many high school physics texts. Each of the participating teachers took one class period with the purpose of developing the previously agreed-upon skills.

The first experience of the teachers varied widely. One teacher presented a full 45-minute lecture discussion which was strictly content-oriented. Another gave a five-minute lecture without relating to the experiment at hand at all. One bright note was the lesson developed and presented by one teacher which related the goals of the experiment and the observed student deficiencies to other situations. The need to record data and be precise was developed by a story about a nurse who told the doctor she thought the patient's temperature that morning was around 100 degrees. After doing an excellent job with this, he then tried to show students the need to organize data, which they had not yet collected. But he allowed practically no time to measure and record the data so they might have something to organize. During the third teaching week the participating teachers were asked to plan activities which could develop skills more fully or extend these skills and develop additional ones.

The first activity planned involved linear measurement. A page of rectangles was duplicated and an empty data table was structured. Observed student weaknesses were thus recognized and a new activity initiated to overcome them. Students were provided rulers graduated in sixteenth of an inch and tenths of a centimeter and told to measure the rectangles using each system. After measuring and recording this information they were told how to find the area of a rectangle and asked to compute the area of each one in square inches and square centimeters. The ease of working with centimeters was immediately apparent and thus the value of the metric system was realized in a very practical way.

The idea of measurement was then extended to include indirect measurements. Students were asked to estimate the distance to an inaccessible object by parallax, or sighting from two different positions. The length of the base line and the angles formed were copied onto a piece of paper and an estimate of the distance was obtained. This estimate was then compared with the actual distance. The presence of an error and reasons for the error were considered. Students were finally taught how to determine the percent of error for the method.

Another type of measurement, also indirect, was developed to determine volume. The volume of water displaced when an object was placed in a container of water was determined to be the same as the volume of the object. The volume of the displaced water was measured with a syringe. The need for repetition of a measurement was developed by asking the students how they could tell if they were right. No absolute answer was available to students at this time. Time did not permit us to work with apparent mass loss of an object suspended in a fluid. New ideas of accuracy could be introduced which involved averaging and reliance on the work of more than one investigator.

Volume measurement was then applied by another teacher. The lung capacity of the students was determined by another application of water displacement. A gallon jug was filled with water and inverted in a large container. The student exhaled into the jug through a plastic tube and the amount of air they exhaled could be determined by measuring the volume of the water needed to refill the gallon jug. Data were collected and students were encouraged to speculate about reasons for the differences in lung capacities they measured.

The last area developed by a participating teacher dealt with precision and error in measurement. Data from several of the previous experiments were examined in the light of the measurement errors. The causes of error and its universality were discussed. The relative importance of error as expressed by a percent of error or range of values was related to the work the students had previously accomplished.

The success of the program for the students roughly parallels last year's program. The mastery of skills and techniques was gratifying. The class periods this year were roughly one-half the length of those last year. The student attitudes as reflected by active participation in class did not seem to develop as well as last year. I feel this was due to the decrease in mastery of skills and techniques which in turn was caused by too rapid and superficial a development of each investigation. My zeal to let my participating teachers observe as large a variety of teaching strategies as possible and the reduced time available produced a result with the students which does not fully satisfy me.

It was my original intent to start with the Grand Canyon and return to it to consider questions raised by students relative to its size and possible age. Much time was required for the students to learn to use their balances. The final work with the Grand Canyon had to be omitted and a less logical closure exercise was substituted.

Lest the reader think only the worst let me quickly list a few encouraging bits of information. Regarding student attitude, they enjoyed the work with observation and interpretations. In a teacher demonstration called "hocus pocus," the student is led to distinguish between observation and interpretation by setting up a situation where he is tempted to jump to conclusions and be fooled. The students were encouraged to record in their notebooks what they had learned. The following remarks were taken from the student notebooks. "Interpretations means things that you think you saw. Observations means just which something you did see." "I learned in the experiment about the ice cube and the glass of water that seeing is not believing." "Interpretation is something that you figger out what happen."

The initial work with the balance which led to the need for standard masses was recorded by students in their notebooks. The students initially used whatever they could find to balance their samples of galena and calcite. One student explained the need for uniform standard masses like this, "Pennies or paper clips are better to use for standards than glena or clasite (rocks) because the pennies or paper clips are to weight about the same. The glena and calsite come in different size and shape so they are not." Another student simply stated, "I learned that pennies and paper clips are better than quarters, tokens, keys, gum and etc, etc., etc."

Student quotes have been taken directly from their notebooks and papers. Wording and spelling have not been changed. I regret that the handwriting could not also be included so that the reader could obtain a more complete picture of the students.

The law of moments was arrived at as a result of a quest for a rule to predict where a known number of paper clips would balance another given number of paper clips. After this rule was determined the students were asked to modify their rule so that they could determine how many clips at a known distance from the fulcrum would be needed to exactly balance a given number of clips at a known distance on the opposite arm. A little later after the students had prepared their own copy of a standard ten gram mass, they used their rule to find the mass of their samples of galena and calcite. Some premeasured masses were also made available to the students so that they could check their answers against the "right" answer. They experienced a real feeling of accomplishment and self-confidence when their answer was in agreement with the "right" answer.

Some students' comments on this activity are again taken from the student notebooks. "I learn a lot because I never had experance in weighting thing befor," "I learn two different kind of stone's Caicite and galena and that galena is higher (heavier) than caicite and how to balance thing."

While I am on the subject of student notebooks, one comment was priceless. Students were asked to speculate about some questions they raised regarding the Grand Canyon. For the question, "Has anyone ever lived there?" one girl answered, "Maybe Indians lived there or people who didn't have a home or people who want to hide from the Romans."

Student reaction to the program may be judged by attendance, since it was voluntary, by personal contact, and by class participation. I have already referred to class participation. The same students remained in the room for periods 1 and 2. A second set of students arrived for period 3. Thirty students were enrolled for each period.

The first day 27 students arrived for the first class. Two students transferred into the class and five have transferred out. One new student enrolled the second week. Fifteen students attended on a regular basis. Six students dropped out after only one or two days of attendance. Four students had poor attendance records, having attended on average of only ten class sessions out of a possible 22.

Twenty-six students arrived for the third-period class the first day. Nine students had good attendance records. The rest had fair or poor attendance records. Six of the third-period students had the science course "Time, Space, and Matter" last year. I had intended to involve them in the same type of investigations which were being used second period so I did not transfer them out. As the course developed they revealed several areas in which they were weak so I did not prepare a separate program for them. None of them could use their balance and ten-gram mass to find the mass of an object unless they hung the object at the ten-centimeter mark. They did not know or could not explain why the distance to the ten-gram mass was the same numerically as the mass of their object in grams.

The personal contact with the students has been largely limited to before school. From two to six students arrived regularly before school to talk and help get the room ready for class. This number increased during the institute. The field trip afforded an opportunity for informal contact with the students. They were responsive and relaxed. They still considered me authority, but they were not hesitant to express their own ideas.

The field trip was a very good experience for all. The trip differed from last year's in that only one busload of students went and only two stops were made. The students enjoyed themselves and collected many fossils and rocks. One student painted his fossils with shellac, mounted them on a board, and brought them to school the day after the trip. The bus trip and the stops provided ample opportunity for teacher interaction with the students.

The five participating teachers assigned to me had a variety of backgrounds. Three teach science at the junior high school level. One teaches physical education and health and one teaches social studies.

There was no resistance to the approach I asked them to use. The basic philosophy to be followed was to select one or more scientific skills and then plan a problem or activity that required the student to use these prechosen skills. The shift away from a teacher-telling and content-oriented approach was looked upon with interest. Many questions were raised as the planning progressed and classes began.

An article entitled "Help Stamp Out Non-Behavioral Objectives" by Dr. Edwin B. Kurtz Jr., which appeared in the January 1965 issue of *The Science Teacher* was distributed to each of my participating teachers. It served to supplement some of the ideas which we had discussed and to develop new ideas to consider. Dr. Kurtz's article expressed in a very concise manner much of the rationale for the approach we were using. His key question is, "What do I want my students to be able to do after taking my course that they could not do before enrolling in it?"

The participating teachers have worked this summer within the framework of this approach to science teaching. The success they have had with the material they chose to work with was over-shadowed by the approach they used and the changes which occurred between the first and second time they tried this method of presentation. Where they had difficulty in their last presentation they were able to recognize these difficulties and analyze their own problems.

One teacher missed his goals one day because he failed to plan for the students to need the attitude he was trying to develop. He came back the next day with a modification of the original activity and when the students were done they had decided it was much easier to work with the decimal units of the metric system than with the fractional units of the English system, which was exactly what the teacher had in mind.

Another teacher failed to develop the skill and understanding he was attempting with his lesson. He had failed to concentrate upon his main goal. He was very content-oriented in his first presentation and had made real progress in his last activity. The encouraging thing for me was that he recognized what he had done, and later pointed out a variation of the same problem in another participating teacher's presentation.

To say that the participating teachers have acquired the inductive approach to teaching would be most presumptuous on my part. They have had exposure to the method and some practice with it. They have also recognized that they used some of the methods in their previous teaching experience. Since this approach to teaching grows and develops with usage, I feel that owing to their experience this summer they will be trying more of this approach in their classes.

No science tests were administered during the summer, and the subject of tests was raised. I indicated that I would administer the test after the student had worked several days with a problem or experiment and before the results of the experiment were discussed in class. The test would consist of questions which would determine the student's and the teacher's success with the goals the activity was designed to develop. An article entitled "Preparing Better Classroom Tests" by John W. Lombard which appeared in the October 1965 issue of *The Science Teacher* was distributed to the participating teachers.

It is my opinion that the participating teachers gained in skill and confidence and also have a new understanding of what science is about.

Initially our plan called for helping the students to get acquainted with the course as well as to set the stage for what was to follow. This included a general course description, a short questionnaire,

---

Editor's Note: Mr. Pennington also taught "Time, Space, and Matter" during the 1965 Institute. His observations on this experience throw more light on the effectiveness of these materials. It is interesting to compare the responses of pupils and teachers to some of the similar approaches from one year to the next.

an explanation of the purpose of the student notebook, and work with observations and interpretations.

The questionnaire consisted of three open-ended questions and revealed something of the attitudes, interest, and prior knowledge of the students. Question number one: I think an experiment is. . . . Some typical answers were: "to prove a theory or to help you know how and why this theory is so"; "a hard thing to follow"; "fine"; and finally, "a scientific expression and interpretation that has been performed," whatever that may mean. I would conclude from these kinds of answers that the students' attitude toward science was positive.

The second question was: What would you like to learn about the physical world this summer? The students answered: "How was it made"; "I am very interested in animals"; "chemistry"; "geometry"; "the ocean"; "nothing"; "many things"; "exciting experiments"; "everything there is to know." Their answers revealed a positive attitude again, as well as some confusion about the purpose of the summer program.

The third question was: Ice floats on water because. . . . Representative answers were: "it is lighter"; "it is in a contracting state and it is lighter than water"; "the water is equal to more than the ice's weight and therefore it stays afloat"; "it is water"; "it is a solid"; "it contains air and is lighter"; "the total mass of the ice is more than the water it displaces"; "of its decrease in weight when frozen". The answers to this question revealed confusion and contradictions in the explanation of a commonly observed phenomenon.

In general the answers revealed the same thing as the voluntary attendance of the students. They had some interest in science and a rather positive attitude toward learning.

The classroom atmosphere the first day was not unusual. The students were shy. They spoke very softly when answering questions. They were interested in the pictures of the Grand Canyon but asked very few questions about this region where so much of the physical world can be seen.

After students had examined the pictures I called their attention to a paperback book available in the room entitled *Down the Colorado* by Powell. About a third of the students checked the book out to read. Later when reading the student notebooks I found quite a list of observations from Powell's trip in one girl's notebook. As the students returned the book most of them said that they had really enjoyed it. The method of distribution and student reaction was about the same for each of the Science Reading Series books.

The students were given a notebook the first day and were told that it was theirs to use as they saw fit. They were also given some guidelines to consider if they wanted their notebooks to be really useful to them. There has been only one case of a student losing his notebook and the students have generally taken pride in them. On July 27th, one student cornered me at break time and insisted that I look at his notebook again. He had done a lot of work and wrote that he was now proud of his notebook and asked if I agreed with him. How could I not agree?

I purposely did not define the terms observation and interpretation for them. The way the students expressed the ideas differed but most seemed to be aware of the differences and were able to distinguish between them on a subsequent quiz.

The students were challenged to exercise their own powers of observation upon a system consisting of a container of water with an ice cube in it. I was not satisfied by the quantity or the quality of the observations. Two notebook comments reveal something which I think is significant in regard to this activity. "I learned about how I could get many facts from just looking at something." "I've learned that there are a lot of things you can see if you only take the time to look. For an example I'll use the glass of water with the ice in it. Before this course all I saw was a glass of water with the ice in it. I never really looked at it." Is this something that can be taught with a lecture?

The participating teachers first worked with their students in observing the glass of ice and water. In this role they were generally overly directive. They told the students what they should see and did almost all of the talking. A disagreement developed between one teacher and his students. He was critical and authoritative and succeeded in beating his kids down. A few days later we came at the problem again using different materials and everyone saw that absolutely right answers were hard to find and defend. Productive disagreements were encouraged and things began to move better.

One day while we were working with the previously described material I felt that I did a very poor job with the second class. The next day five of those students cut my class. Fortunately all of the students did not stay out. Four came back and three became regular attenders. There must be a lesson here somewhere.

The work with the student balances involved the selection and testing of standards for mass; the determination of the existence and size of the sensitivity limit for their balances; some introductory work with graphs; and the discovery of the law of moments even though we did not name it.

Student notebooks again reveal some of the pupils' problems

and rewards. In evaluating his first system of standards one student had listed: "Problems in comparison. 1. Had to correct for balance, 2. Units are not related to each other in the same way, 3. Dividing is a problem, 4. Also multiplication is difficult, 5. Sometimes weight is between a number like 9 and 10, 6. Not useful outside the classroom (not a world standard)." With more time one can see many class discussion ideas stemming from his material.

The work we did with graphing revealed several areas in mathematics that were weak. Students used data they had collected with their balances. They listed some of the positions where two paper clips on one arm of the balance were observed to balance three on the other arm. Many could not divide up the spaces between the numbers on the graph. Planning the scale for each axis and plotting points was also a problem, but the improvement in more recent work indicates that students really learn by doing after all.

The students had no idea that a graph could tell them anything. Then we worked with interpolating and extrapolating. This was an activity which led to a discussion that seemed to loosen up the kids. Some who usually had very little to say began to volunteer information as they gained confidence. One boy had attended most of the sessions and often stayed after to ask questions such as: "Why should I study science anyhow?" and "What's the use of all this?" He forgot himself and smiled. That may not sound like much, but it was the first time I saw him smile.

The law of moments was arrived at as the result of a quest for a rule to predict where a known number of paper clips would balance another given number of paper clips. After this rule was determined the students were asked to modify their rule so that they could determine how many clips at a known distance from the fulcrum would be needed to exactly balance a given number of clips at a known distance on the opposite arm.

One student expresses her rule this way.

$$\text{Rule for finding cm } \frac{(\# \text{ of Paperclips}) \times (\# \text{ its on})}{(\# \text{ of Paperclips on other side})}$$

$$\text{Rule for finding paperclips } \frac{(\# \text{ of paperclips}) \times (\# \text{ its on})}{(\# \text{ of cm. on other side})}$$

A little later, after the students had prepared a prototype standard—10-gram mass, the same student included an example showing how to use it and her rule to find the mass of her sample of the mineral calcite.

The students were asked to grade themselves and list what they thought they had learned. These comments about the balance are interesting and informative. "I have learned how to guess how much a rock weighs in grams. I have learned how to use the scale to find the weight of an unknown." "I learned how to scale weights about weight nursing and bring presice in your work." "I learned how to weigh different items without a standard wight." I am not sure what the second quote may mean, but that boy can use his balance. The last quote refers to a problem a boy encountered when he needed a smaller counterweight. He actually made a 1.7-gram mass out of paper clips and then used it to solve his problem.

The students also found out that if they put the object to be weighed on the ten-centimeter mark, the position of their ten-gram mass was the same number as the mass of their object in grams. They had a lot of fun with that and most could see why it worked. One boy got so excited when he figured it out that he just had to tell someone. He found a group and a teacher who did not understand it yet and explained it all to them. Knowledge seems to be worth while when you can share it.

When they wrote up this activity one boy expressed it like this: "Because the little tube with buckshot weighs 10 grams, so you put the object you are weighing on the number as to weight of grams. For example if I had a tube weighing 15 grams I place the object being weight on 15 cm. and balance out." Another boy extended the short cut to objects weighing more than 15 grams like this: "If the weight to be measured is too heavy at 10 move it in to 5 and just double the number on the other side." The wording may not be the best in all cases but they certainly were able to use their rules.

In my opinion student interest was high throughout most of the activities with the balance. They were not too enthusiastic about the work with standards, but when it came to discovering rules for the balance it was just like a game.

During this time the participating teachers became more involved in the course and with the students. The math teachers seemed to come to life and I guess that is natural since there is a lot of math in this material. I did not detect a change in the participating teachers' inclination to direct the students, but four of them were trying to keep from always jumping in with the answer. I have been encouraging them to ask the student the kind of questions that will make him think about his problem in a new way. This is the trick I want the teachers to learn and they have made a real effort along these lines.

Not all of them were able to apply this technique readily. One still talked to his students all of the time and two others bossed their students much of the time. One teacher became rather detached from the whole thing. Apparently she just does not like science. She worked with a group of students who were trying to find rules for their balances. She did not seem to understand the science in it, but the students got along fine. The next day she worked with a student who had been absent. She seemed to enter into the task very well and told me after class that she really enjoyed that day. I think she may have discovered something of herself.

One of the teachers who tends to be "bossy" becomes quite patient and understanding when he does not get in too much of a hurry and will just sit down with the students and let them work. He is beginning to take pleasure in watching how the students work on the problems.

The last focus of our interest was on the universality of change. This involved a consideration of some of the agents of change at work on the crust of the earth. The students investigated changes occurring over short and long intervals of time.

From the students' own experience, including a field trip along the Delaware River, they decided that most of the change in the earth's surface is caused by running water. To study these changes more carefully, ice, halite, and quartz were subjected to running water. Ice changed so quickly it was hard to study at all. Quartz did not change noticeably in the time period we used. Halite lost mass quickly at first and at a declining rate as it became smaller. The students took to this activity readily and did good work. They were careful with the measurements and most of them recorded their data in an organized way. In one group the participating teacher acted as the organizer so I asked him to observe what would happen if he did not direct the group. As soon as the students realized that he was not there telling them what to do they took over and got along quite well. Two students in the group who had not done much work got busy.

The students graphed the results of this experiment and were asked to suggest reasons for the halite curve. After a little help to get them started they developed some good interpretations. They were told that they did not have to believe their interpretations and this is the kind of thing they wrote: "The halite was harder on the inside and softer on the outside." "The water could have come too filled with small particles of halite thus slowing down its dissolving." "Particles are more loose on the outer crust." "The one doing the swishing got tired and slowed down." "The smaller the piece the slower it goes."

When these interpretations were discussed by the whole class, I asked the students what was meant by smaller. As we all talked about this word the ideas of volume and surface area came out. The class decided that the change in surface area was probably the best explanation for the change in the rate of mass loss.

We next considered the quartz and they felt that it probably did change a little bit but they just could not measure the change. Each student selected a quartz pebble and determined its mass and any identifying features. The pebbles were then placed in a plastic tumbler with some water in it and then tumbled for six days. Each day the students determined the mass of their pebbles and put them back in the tumbler. During this time we used part of the class period to develop some intellectual tools: an understanding of first approximations, orders of magnitude, scientific notation, density, and map reading. Regarding first approximations, orders of magnitude, and scientific notation one student wrote: "I learned about how to cut a problem down to size so I could figure it out myself."

A concept of density was developed during this time. Volumetric measurement of irregularly shaped objects as described by one boy was: "How to measure by volume. Take a flask full of water mark it off and put rock in and take water out till you hit the mark where the water is inside of the syringe and you have how much water by volume the rock has taken up." Mass and volume data for samples of galena and calcite were shared by the whole class. They had already realized that galena was somewhat "heavier" than calcite and now they were able to determine the relationship more precisely.

Since surface area was so important in understanding the rate of mass loss, the students needed a method for measuring the surface area of an irregularly shaped object such as a quartz pebble. The same student described his method like this: "How to measure the surface area of a irregular object. Take cloth or tape and cover the object cut of excesse pieces measure the cloth that is on the rock in cm or place it on a piece of paper that is marked out in cm." He said he got the idea of using the graph paper from the teacher working with him and probably picked up the spelling of measure the same way.

After the data for the rate of water of the quartz was collected we returned to questions raised by the students about the Grand Canyon. Questions about the size and age were chosen for attack at this time. Topographical maps of the Grand Canyon were made available to the students after they had worked briefly with a simpler map and a model.

They determined the length and width of the river and the depth of the canyon. Their measurements had to be converted to the units we would need later. One student described the activity like this: "I learned to measure a map by using a scale and to change different measurements like miles to centimeters."

The age of the Canyon was determined by a comparison of the total amount of material cut from the Canyon by the river with the rate at which this cutting action occurs. The rate was extrapolated from the students' data relative to the rate of wear for quartz determined earlier by tumbling rocks in the abrasion mill.

Student reaction to the last area of study and to the entire course was largely favorable. I think this was the result of the high degree of student involvement and the success the students had with the material of the course. There is a question I have been asked by several students which I think reveals something about the success of the program with the students. The question is: "Will there be a course like this at high school next year?" I consider something else unusual. Five days before the end of classes this summer, one of my students told me that his mother wanted him to go to the shore with her and he would not go because he wanted to come to school. His attendance record was rather spotty and he had been in the habit of cutting class earlier in the summer.

The most gratifying comment was written by a boy who has done consistently good work. He wrote: "I have learned how to break large problems into simpler ones, and not to make everything complicated. For example: I learned that instead of writing large numbers I can just put down an exponent. I know when to take approximate answers and when to strive for accurate ones. I also learned to trust my answers, not always thinking someone's is better because it is different, yet to work with others also."

The patterns of behavior described previously for the participating teachers persisted for the most part to the end of the institute. Five teachers have become able to lead their students without having to dominate them. Seven teachers have established a good relationship with the students they sponsor. One teacher commented to me that his relationship with his students had broken down, but from what I have observed things are not as bad as he thought they were. He was more understanding and he had learned that criticism, to be effective, must be accompanied by large doses of deserved praise.

13. Reactions to the Discovery Method in "Time, Space, and Matter"

ALAN D. SEXTON

The initial response of the students to "Time, Space, and Matter" (TSM) was the same as that of other students whom the writer has taught. This reaction can best be described as one of confusion, indecision, and bewilderment. Students are so accustomed to being told what to think that they are quite perplexed when they must really think themselves. This first reaction was somewhat surprising to the writer because for some reason he had expected these students to be "different." Some of the early responses of the students seemed to be given only for the purpose of determining whether or not their opinions were actually important. The students were quite surprised to find that their individual thoughts were important.

Near the beginning of the Institute some students became almost hostile because they wanted the teacher to give them *the* answers. When their questions were answered by other questions, they did not grasp the fact that they could offer answers which were (in most instances) as acceptable as those of the teacher. One girl stated that she had seen crystals falling from the ice cube which she observed and demanded to be told what they were. When the teacher only asked her questions about them she became very upset. This girl was so concerned over "the answer" to this situation that she approached the teacher after class. The teacher explained that he had

---

Alan Sexton was initially more concerned with the idea that a classroom experience should be structured so that a student's opinion would be considered worthy of consideration, rather than whether students thought the teacher knew any science. Mr. Sexton was a science coordinating teacher in the 1965 Princeton Institute. He teaches science at Council Rock Intermediate School in Richboro, Pennsylvania.

reacted as he did because of the fact that he was not going to give direct answers and that the other students were not concerned with her observation. This student had an "ah ha!" reaction. She said, "Maybe the ice cube which I was observing was different from those that the others were observing."

This girl reported the next day that she had observed four additional ice cubes and that she had *not* observed crystals which had previously been a subject of concern for her. Whether or not she had observed the crystals before was not important. What was important was that she had grasped the idea that definite conclusions should not be based upon the observation of one sample or specimen.

Some of the participating teachers stated that the girl had probably been frustrated to the point where she would withdraw from active participation. Actually this student did additional work on her own.

Near the end of the first week of the Institute one of the students reported to one of the participating teachers that the teacher (coordinating teacher) was not answering questions because he did not know the answers. The participating teacher reported this incident with apparent concern to the coordinating teacher. The lack of concern on the part of the coordinating teacher seemed to be quite a surprise to the participating teacher. The following statement was offered by the coordinating teacher for consideration: "What the student thinks of the teacher's competence is not so important at this time as is the concept that the student's opinions are worthy of consideration." The participating teacher considered this comment and remarked at a later time that the students would, in time, realize that the teacher did know something. This teacher also remarked that leading students to making their own conclusions was better than the teacher's telling them the conclusions.

Some students were definitely uninterested in TSM at times. However, when the teacher could question these students individually, he found that their interest was soon revived. These students seemed to want recognition as individuals. The point to be made here is that a small amount of time spent with individual students is usually well worth the effort in terms of the improvement of student attitudes toward learning.

At the beginning the students accepted the comments of their classmates, and they would state their own reactions to particular questions. After a few days they began to challenge each other rather strongly. "How can you say that, when . . . , or when thus and so happens?" Some of the participating teachers regarded this reaction as argument for the sake of argument. The writer believed that this was an acceptable mode of behavior because, in effect, the students were challenging each other to think before they made conclusions.

One new opinion of the writer is that interest in TSM is not always expressed with enthusiasm—a situation (interest) which could be taking place unobserved. A student was cited by the participating teachers as one who was not participating to a great extent in class and who was not interested. The coordinating teacher made a special effort to observe this student and at first agreed. However, this student was observed to be one who finished the routine matters very quickly (massing the pebble each day) and then turned his attention to investigations on his own. He was observed to be calculating the mass of his pencil and the mass of one of the balance pans which he had filled with water. This activity was apparently not noticed by the participating teachers.

The students were extremely interested in the abrasion mills. Most wanted to know why the water turned milky. When asked if they had an explanation for this phenomenon, most replied that the milkiness must have been caused by the particles which had been knocked off the pebbles. Some of the students remarked with enthusiasm, "We are making sand!"

Near the end of the Institute two of the students brought friends (adolescents who were not members of the Institute) into class. The reaction of these student members and of other student members was most interesting. The visitors were treated as ping pong balls. The members who had brought them were intent on showing them what they had learned. Other members of the class were equally intent on showing the visitors that they had learned something. One girl (who had not brought a visitor) "cornered" one of the visitors and was intent on showing the visitor her balance. The visitor asked, "How do you weigh something with this balance?" The reply was, "You can't weigh anything on this balance; you determine its mass." This reply was a good one in light of the fact that this girl was not participating much in discussions. She evidently did understand what was going on.

The students were introduced (through discussion) to the concept that graphing is a means of organizing data. Several graphing patterns (as done by the students) were discussed. One of particular interest was done when graphing the relationship of the distance of two paper clips on one arm of the balance to the distance of one paper clip on the other arm of the balance. One of the patterns was for students to connect every dot in a sawtoothed fashion. One student questioned this practice. He said that if the relationship between the number of paper clips and the distance from the center was constant, the graph could not be sawtoothed. "If the graph (trend line) were sawtoothed, one distance could be increased and the other (distance of the number of paper clips) could be decreased." This point of the student was not seen by the participating teachers as an understanding of the graphing of the relationship of the distance of two paper clips as compared to the distance of one paper clip. Yet this statement by *one of the students* probably had more effect on the class than would have the same statement by the teacher.

The students like the idea of having certain equipment in their investigation kits and enjoyed the experience of using this equipment. They also enjoyed the abrasion mill investigation. After the abrasion mills were started, two girls suddenly started reporting to class early so they could stop the mills, remove the bottle, and shake out the pebbles. The students were also fascinated with the syringes. Two of the boys used them for squirt guns, but most students were using them properly and seemed to enjoy a piece of apparatus of this type.

The Field Trips

The field trips were a valuable part of this Institute. The participating teachers seem to feel that class time should have been spent in preparing the students for the field trips and that one or two succeeding class periods should have been spent discussing these trips. If the purpose of a field trip is to prepare for a test, then the participating teachers are correct. However, if the purpose of a field trip is merely to extend the students' knowledge, the trips were of great benefit to the students. The possible "association" benefits of field trips are innumerable.

There was a general feeling among the participating teachers that the students should be held accountable for every possible gain of knowledge which *might* occur in (or from) their observations of the field trip situation. The fact is that some students did gain meaningful information from these trips. The success of field trips should be determined by those concepts which the students might gain as a result of looking at the situations through their own eyes and interpreting those concepts in the light of their own experiences. What is wrong with the idea of taking the students on a field trip with the only thought in mind being the broadening of the students' views of the world around them? Must *we* hold the students responsible to the nth degree for those things related to the field trip which *we* consider to be important? Aren't the students supposed to enjoy field trips? Will the enjoyment of the students be reduced if they know that they are going to be tested on the minute details of the field trip experience?

The participating teachers stated that the first three field trips (Princeton, Philadelphia, geology) were not organized well enough. They felt that the students were not given the proper number of specific directions and were allowed too much freedom. They stated that the fact that "nothing serious" happened to any of the students involved was very unusual.

The discussion of the process of abrasion as it had taken place in Nassau Hall was one of the best of the summer in terms of student interest and participation. The students were delighted to study pictures of a building which they had actually visited, and to relate these pictures to their laboratory investigations.

Teachers' Observations of Students' Reactions

The teachers were favorably impressed with the initial student participation. One teacher remarked that one student (whom he had taught) participated more in the initial class discussion than he had during the entire previous school year.

Some of the participating teachers seemed to have difficulty distinguishing between antisocial behavior and normal adolescent behavior. The following example is offered as support for this statement. One of the boys was arguing with one of the girls about her "observations" of the Grand Canyon. Although the boy was not actually rude, he was sure that the girl's statements were not correct. One of the participating teachers approached the writer and told him that this was typical of the boy's poor attitude toward school. "He will argue for the sake of argument. He will dominate the class. He may come up with a few ideas, but he will not work to test them." The fact remains that this boy *did* make some valuable contributions to subsequent discussions, *did not* dominate the class, and *did* work to test some of his ideas. The writer does not wish to imply that this boy has been made into a model student, but rather that a good relationship has been established which could lead to a great improvement in the attitude of this boy toward learning.

One of the participating teachers remarked to the writer that he was not a science teacher. This teacher felt that he could concentrate on approach and student reactions to a greater extent than someone who was concerned with the content that was presented. The quality of his observations supported his statements. This teacher was far more perceptive of student reactions than are teachers who are overly concerned with content.

Some of the participating teachers were inclined to label a class unsuccessful if one or two students were uninterested for part or most of the period. However, this is one of the problems of education. It is difficult if not impossible to interest all students at all times. By using the methodological approach the teacher can interest most students most of the time.

There were times that worthwhile student reactions were not noticed by the participating teachers. There were probably two reasons for this lack of observation—first, some of these reactions were misinterpreted, and second, some of the teachers wrote their weekly reports during the class. At times participating teachers working with students would make such comments as, "I wouldn't do it that way," or "Don't do that, do this." The reaction of the student to these statements was usually one of embarrassment. Even though the participating teachers did not realize it, they had failed to allow the students to work out laboratory techniques of their own.

The Critique Sessions

The Human Resources Seminar (June 29, 1965) was valuable in setting the pace for the subsequent critique sessions. This session was probably too long, but it did "break the ice" by getting teachers involved in discussions. There seemed to be an initial reluctance to accept TSM's approach to science. This was probably associated with its lack of emphasis on testing, facts, and direction. This was interesting in light of the fact that these teachers had not yet observed this approach in action.

Early in the Institute the teachers were observing the coordinating teacher more than they were observing student reaction. Many of the early questions from the participating teachers were of the following type: "Why did you do that when you could have done . . . ?"

Some participating teachers became increasingly concerned over TSM's lack of emphasis on "the facts." When these teachers were asked what "facts" should be included in a science course, however, their replies were quite vague.

At about the midpoint of the Institute the teachers could have been classified into three groups. Some teachers were not receptive to the different techniques which they had seen. Others stated that the techniques could be useful, but that they could not be used for an entire school year. Another group of teachers was fairly well convinced of the usefulness of the techniques and was concentrating on devising ways to implement these techniques.

As the Institute progressed there was a tendency for teachers from the first group (unreceptive) to shift to the second group. Some of the thoughts of the teachers in the second group are worthy of comment. Some felt that these techniques were too demanding on the teacher and that keeping up such a pace would be physically impossible on the part of a teacher. That a pace such as this had been used with classes for entire school years in the past did not seem to convince these teachers that these techniques had merit. Another thought was that the coordinating teachers were teaching under very unreal conditions and that they (the participating teachers) questioned the effectiveness of these techniques when used under "normal" conditions. The writer's comment is that these techniques have been tried under "normal" conditions, and they have been shown to be effective.

The discussion of topics which were to be presented the next day was sometimes quite revealing. Some teachers were quite willing to dismiss as too difficult topics which they had not even seen presented. These teachers seemed to believe that if the method which they had used to present these (or similar) topics had failed, the topics were too difficult for the students.

As the participating teachers discovered that the coordinating teachers did not intend to change their techniques to make them more traditional, they (the participating teachers) began to give more consideration to the application of these different techniques.

The Institute was, in general, successful. The teaching methods used by the coordinating teachers were successful with the students. The writer offers the following information from one of his classes in support of this statement. Fourteen of the first 18 students to turn in rate of abrasion data had determined acceptable values. To obtain the data the students had to be able to use their balances properly, be able to record these data in their record books, make careful observations, and be able to estimate with a reasonable amount of accuracy. After they had the data, the students then had to be able to perform the necessary multiplication and long division.

The success of the Institute with reference to the participating teachers could not be easily determined. The writer is firmly convinced, however, that the observation of different techniques forced the participating teachers to take a careful look at their own teaching methods. The writer is confident that most of the participating teachers will try some of the different techniques which they observed in actual situations during the Institute.

The success of this Institute's influence on the participating teachers could best be studied by determining how much the methods of these teachers were influenced in actual classroom situations.

14. More Reactions to Discovery

LUCY V. SMITH

The problem that the students were to solve was to find out some things about the physical world. The problem was reduced to trying to find out something about the crust of the earth. Attention was directed to the Grand Canyon because it represents an exposed area in the earth's crust.

Synopsis of Lessons Taught. Included are comments regarding pupil response and teacher reaction.

Lesson on Speculation. This was the first lesson. The students were not sure of what was expected of them. They did not know how they were to go about discovering for themselves anything about the Grand Canyon. They showed this by their reluctance to state what they saw in the slides of the Grand Canyon. They were reluctant to speculate on how some of the different features of the Canyon were formed. They wanted me to tell them about it. All of the students participated. However, there were only a few volunteers.

The Trenton teachers did not understand why I did not tell the students when their speculations were incorrect. It was explained that the idea was to get the students to think about what they saw.

Lesson "Hocus Pocus." The students were excited. There was a lot of student participation. The students exclaimed that I had "fooled" them. One student in the second class had been told by a student in the first class that the liquids would be vinegar and water. In the second class I used alcohol and water. The student who was positive that she knew what was in the containers came up front with another student to prove that she was correct. She was disgusted when she found that she was incorrect. The class was surprised and excited.

Lucy Smith recorded pupil and teacher reactions to the discovery method in "Time, Space, and Matter" and presents them here. Mrs. Smith was a science coordinating teacher in the 1965 Princeton Institute and teachers at Springfield Gardens Junior High School in Springfield Gardens, New York.

The students in both classes became very careful in making observations.

The science teachers liked this lesson. However, they did not feel that it was anything new.

Lesson on Observing a Simple "Ice Water System." Students were challenged to make 20 observations in one class and 30 observations in the other class. In both instances, the students made several more than the number given. They were enthusiastic. Several called out that they had gotten more than the number set. They made good observations. Where interpretations had been made, clarification was obtained through class discussion.

The teachers felt that it was a bad procedure to challenge the students to reach a certain goal. They thought that it would frustrate the students. It was pointed out to the teachers that the challenge was meant to motivate the students.

Lesson on Qualitative First Approximation. The students followed the reasoning of first approximation of color and shape of objects. They applied the idea to numbers and got the idea of first approximation in numbers, the order of magnitude.

There was active student participation. The teachers felt that the students already knew the order of magnitude of numbers.

Lesson on India Ink Demonstrations. The students discussed India ink in water in terms of first approximation in regard to composition and appearance. They showed that they understood the concept of qualitative first approximation by explaining their answers.

As a follow-up the students looked at the cover of the book "From the Moon to a Pebble." They discussed it in terms of first approximation. It resulted in a very lively discussion in which the teachers became involved.

The teachers did not react orally to this lesson.

Lesson on Measurement and Precision. The meaning of precision was developed. It was related to instruments. The students were given a balance. The students worked carefully to see that their balances were properly adjusted.

The teachers did not react to this lesson.

Lesson on Student Development of Standards. Sudents worked diligently to set up their standards. The students were interested in this task.

The teachers felt that it would have been better to just tell the students about standards.

Lesson on "A New Way to Use the Balance." The students liked doing this. Many of them did make up a "rule" on how to use the balance in a new way.

The teachers felt that it would have been better to just tell the students about the law of moments.

Lesson on Change. The pictures in the book resulted in an excellent discussion. The teachers became involved.

The teachers now recognized that the students are interested. However, they do not feel that the course is really teaching science.

Lesson on Effects of Running Water on Halite and Ice. The students liked this activity. Several of them told me so. They worked diligently and carefully.

The teachers felt that it was a waste of time.

Test on Observation and Interpretation. The students' answers were challenged by some of the teachers. The students proved the teachers wrong. The discussion was extremely lively and thought-provoking. The students as a whole did very well on the test.

The Abrasion Mill. The students enjoyed working with their pebbles. They would come in with their pebble and record their data without being told. They kept their records up to date.

Lesson on the Grand Canyon Analogue. The teachers worked with the pupils. This activity was enjoyed by the pupils and the teachers.

One teacher stated that he has used a small model to show erosion.

Lesson on Usage of a Topographic Map. The teachers worked with the pupils. The teachers and the pupils enjoyed this activity.

Lesson on Gathering Data to Find the Age of the Grand Canyon. The information needed to find the age of the Grand Canyon was obtained from the students in class discussions. The discussion was thought-provoking. The students were attentive. Many students entered into the discussion.

Lesson on Calculating the Age of the Grand Canyon. This lesson was developed with the class because of limited time. The class was interested. Participation was excellent. The students were pleased at having been able to find the age of the Grand Canyon. I felt from the reaction of the class that it was a worthwhile, meaningful, and satisfying terminating activity for them. It gave them a feeling of success and accomplishment.

In the beginning, several teachers in my group were very critical of the philosophy behind the curriculum of "Time, Space, and Matter." They believed that it was a waste of time to permit students to discover things for themselves. One said that there were too many facts to learn to permit students to discover things for themselves.

Later on the teachers decided that the philosophy was good. However, they felt the teaching of facts is much more important. Therefore, there is simply not enough time for this kind of curriculum.

At a later date the science teachers all assured me that they often used the discovery method in isolated instances.

At the conclusion of the course all of the teachers now seem to feel that the discovery method is excellent. However, it really isn't teaching enough facts. One teacher called it "games." The science teachers still feel that it is more important to teach facts. One teacher has asked to teach the course this fall. He wants to learn more about it by doing it.

I believe that all of the teachers' attitudes have changed except one. My other science teacher, who previously has had no time for slow students, told me that he has asked his principal for a slow class in September. His principal has agreed to change his schedule and give him a slow class. In conversation they mention their responsibility to slow learners. In the beginning they negated this responsibility.

The program as scheduled went smoothly. A story line was there. The students start by trying to find out something about the physical world by studying the Grand Canyon. I related all of the student activities and discussion to their problem of studying the earth's crust as exposed in the Grand Canyon. (I had the students make this relationship.) The teachers felt that hearing this relationship (story line) was repetitious. They stated that there was too much repetition. I found that the program, as set up for science, presented a compact, meaningful unit. I believe that it was necessary to cover sufficient related material so that the pupils could have a long-range goal. It was then desirable to have the students achieve this goal to provide them with a feeling of accomplishment, and when a student has a sense of accomplishment and a sense of discovery then that course is a success.

15. *Mathematics as Plausible Reasoning and Guessing*

RUSSELL ABRAHAM

The main theme of the program we pursued was the role of plausible reasoning and guessing in mathematics. With proper choice of topics it was hoped that all students would be able to participate in this central theme, each according to his own experiences. In so doing, it was further hoped that he would begin to learn methods and appreciate the role which guessing at mathematical truths and solutions of problems plays in the creation of all mathematics. The approach lent itself especially well to the inductive method of teaching, the whole idea of plausible reasoning and guessing being based upon examining one's experiences, determining what additional information is needed, determining how to go about getting this additional information, and then proceeding to accumulate this information in order to make better and better guesses to the solution, or approach to the solution of a problem.

Being free from any pressure to cover a prescribed amount of material, we were able to pursue our course of study at a pace wherein the students were constantly encouraged to contribute their reactions and feeling about any point. If one takes time to let a student express why he feels about a particular point as he does, no matter how absurd or illogical his reaction or opinion may seem to you as a teacher with vastly richer experiences in your field, it may still in many instances represent a beautiful and logical interpretation in light of his own experiences. Basically, this is precisely the thing we were looking for in carrying out the theme of our program, plausible reasoning and guessing. You must bring what you presently possess into focus, determine what is lacking in what you possess in

---

Russell Abraham demonstrated to his students during the 1966 Princeton-Trenton Institute that there was room for guessing even in an exact course like mathematics. Mr. Abraham teaches mathematics at Portland Community College in Portland, Oregon.

order to arrive at the solution of a problem, and then proceed to acquire that which is missing but necessary in the solution.

I feel that two major reasons for lack of success on the part of students are lack of time to work at their rate of learning, and lack of opportunity to contribute their efforts to the development of the work. We attempted, and I think were quite successful in the attempt, to provide an atmosphere and pace in which students were able to think at their own rate, be better prepared to contribute to class discussions, and do creative thinking at their level. Although most students were low in basic mathematical background, they proved to possess active imaginations. Questions which were developed around student responses proved to be a productive technique in furthering learning.

Through providing a program wherein the student was constantly encouraged to be active, to be important in the development of what we were doing, and to be aggressive in an acceptable manner we achieved a degree of success in eliminating emotional blocks which some students have against contributing to classroom discussions. This program helped them to gain in prestige, and to know the feeling of being respected for their opinions and judgments. They in turn could then learn what respect means to others.

A very simple example might help to illustrate. We had reached a point where we were ready to write a formula to be used in calculating the number of unique ways in which any number of objects can be arranged.

Teacher. How would you write "one less than m"?

Student. "l."

Teacher. Why would you write "l" for "one less than m"?

Student. Because "l" comes before "m" in the alphabet.

Teacher. Have you ever studied algebra?

Student. No.

Teacher. Then in light of your past experience, I think your response was a very logical one. But do you see any way in which this might relate to what we are doing here?

Student. No, I guess not. I really don't understand what you are trying to do.

Teacher. How would you write "one less than 5"?

Student. "4."

Teacher. How would you write "one less than 5" without actually subtracting 1 from 5?

Student. "5 minus 1."

Teacher. If "*m*" was the name of a number just as "5" and "4" are names of numbers, how would you write "one less than *m*"?

Student. "*m* minus one."

The discussion was carried on, involving the rest of the class directly, developing the idea of variable and use of variable in mathematics.

One of the first topics we chose to discuss was permutations and probability. Our basic source of material for this topic was *Introduction to Secondary Mathematics* by Haag and Dudley. Since this book uses set language and notation in its presentation, it was necessary to first lay a foundation in this. I led the class in the discussion of set notation, measure of a set, equal sets, and equivalent sets. Emphasis was placed upon the importance of the role of language in mathematical communication. This was followed by one of the participating teachers leading the class in an introduction to probability. His presentation was built primarily upon gathering experimental data through tossing coins and dice. After this experimental phase, I took the class back into a discussion of sets. The idea of one-to-one correspondence between equivalent sets was introduced. Talking about the number of one-to-one correspondences which can be set up between two finite equivalent sets, a discussion of permutations, led into the examination of such questions as

How many ways can a certain number of books be arranged on a shelf?

How many distinct license plates can be made using various arrangements of letters followed by digits?

How many telephone numbers can be made using various arrangements of letters and digits?

Up until this point all problems proposed were of such a nature, or else were led into in such a way, that the students either possessed background experiences or were provided with experiences in the classroom. Each student had some feeling about how he might begin a solution to the problem before the problem was proposed, and in many instances proposed a reasonable solution. In the discussion of finite and infinite sets which followed, the question "Is the number of grains of sand in the earth at any given instant finite?" was proposed. After a discussion of what was meant by a set being finite and agreeing that the number of grains would be finite, the next question proposed was "How many grains of sand do you think there are in the earth at this instant?"

The purpose of this question was to present the class with a problem of such a nature that a reasonable guess would be virtually impossible in light of any experiences they may have had. This was a question, the answer to which could never be determined precisely, but a question which, with careful consideration, would provide us with a variety of mathematical experiences in arriving at what might be considered a plausible estimate, and conducive to classroom participation. Various plans of attack were offered by students. One settled upon involved answering two major questions: "How many grains of sand would it take to fill a sphere the size of the earth, and "what part of the earth is composed of sand." Answering the question "How many grains of sand would it take to fill a sphere the size of the earth?" led into a discussion of the discovery and use of some mensuration formulae, denominate numbers, conversion from one unit of measure to another, and methods which might be employed in approximating the number of grains of sand in a cubic inch.

We began by drawing circles of various diameters, measuring the circumferences by using a string, and tabulating the results. The students observed that the circumference of any circle always turned out to be a little more than three times the diameter. We then had a basis for conjecturing a technique for determining the circumference of any circle. We knew the diameter, and could then multiply the diameter by some number a little more than three. This led to a discussion of the name of number, distinguishing between numeral and number, and to giving a name to the number which was the ratio of the circumference of a circle to its diameter. Historically this number was given the name "Pi" in honor of the mathematician Pythagoras. Assuming that the ratio between the circumference of any circle and its diameter is constant, and by giving the name "Pi" to this ratio, we could conclude that a formula for determining the circumference of any circle would be "C = Pi d."

A discussion of linear measure, square measure, and cubic measure followed. The students were left with the problem of discovering a technique for finding out if any relationship exists between the area and radius of any circle. We experimentally approximated the areas of various circles by dividing them into square inches; we tabulated data and arrived at the conclusion that the area of a circle always appeared to be a little more than three times the square of the radius. We conjecture this to be true, and concluded that a formula for determining the area of any circle would be A = Pi r².

The next problem proposed was to devise a technique for arriving at a formula for determining the volume of a sphere. It was suggested that we could approximate the volume of a sphere by filling it as completely as possible with cubes measuring one inch on an edge, and then by counting the cubes we arrived at an approximation of the number of cubic inches in the sphere. Since we did not have equipment to perform the experiment, the formula for determining the volume of a sphere, V = $\frac{4}{3}$Pi r³, was given. In questioning the students, they decided that if they had performed the experiment of filling various-sized spheres with cubes, they would have found that the volume would have been a little more than four times the cube of the radius.

It was decided to calculate the volume of the earth in cubic inches, since it would be more practical to approximate experimentally the number of grains of sand in a cubic inch than in a cubic foot or cubic mile. A technique settled upon for approximating the number of grains of sand in a cubic inch was to count the number of grains of sand it would take to extend through a linear inch and then cube this number. Students carried out this experiment as a weekend assignment. We settled on an approximation of one million grains per cubic inch for very fine sand. In coming to some decision as to what part of the earth is sand we worked from the premise that sand would only be found in the earth's crust which is about ten miles deep on an average, and that about 60 percent of the earth's crust is silica dioxide. We then calculated the volume of the earth's crust and determined that on the basis of the information we had accumulated there could be at most (.60)(1,000,000)(volume of the earth's crust in cubic inches) grains of sand in the earth. We actually carried out the calculation, had a discussion on the reading of large numbers, and the use of scientific notation. Discussion followed as to how we could go about arriving at a more accurate figure by getting an approximation as to the part of the silica dioxide in the earth's crust which is actually in the form of sand.

A follow-up question "How many stars do you think there are in our galaxy, the Milky Way?" was proposed. One student responded with a number he remembered reading. Speculation was made as to how one might arrive at an approximation for the number of stars in our galaxy. Such questions as the following were discussed:

Was the approximation to the number of stars in our galaxy a better approximation than that to the number of grains in the earth?

How might a technique for determining the number of stars in our galaxy be similar to the technique we employed for determining an approximation to the number of grains in the earth?

Which do you think could be more accurately approximated?

I emphasize again that the main objective of our program was not to accumulate the knowledge of a collection of theorems contained within the structure of some mathematical system, but to develop an appreciation and understanding of the role which the process of plausible reasoning and guessing plays in the building of such a structure.

That this approach was successful was borne out by one of the participating teachers who expressed a concern of those observing the class. "We can give testimony of student progress and interest in mathematics. Many students will now risk an answer and a majority of students will participate in discovery of solutions without fear of being wrong. The student has found out we are interested in his thinking and in him."

The demonstration teaching finally pointed out quite strongly that a good teacher must try to offer his class experience that will establish confidence and a sense of adventure in mathematics.

16. A Handful of Area

LILLIAN KOLTNOW

The mathematics most people use is related to very real objects in
their lives such as handling money, measuring various objects, and
estimating space relationships. But in school, beyond the first or second grade in most cases, an understanding of the meaning of number
is assumed, and the ideas of the basic arithmetic operations are often
determined abstractly. Yet we continue to wonder why so many students have trouble *even in simple arithmetic* even though we know
that a great many students have difficulty generalizing. Therefore
I wanted a course which would give a maximum relationship between
numbers and real things, I wanted to make available a variety of
experiences in which students would measure distances, count squares
and cubes, record and summarize their measurements, and talk about
what they were doing and the conclusions they had reached. In our
classroom, although there was much activity, the number of topics
covered may have seemed small. But it was important that the class
progressed at the rate the students were able to advance, rather than
at the rate at which the teacher could present new material.

There were certain advantages inherent in this technique which
helps the child learn. He became actively involved in *doing*—measuring, counting, pouring, stacking. His results were therefore more
meaningful to him. In addition, he determined the sequence of his
activities through class discussion, under the teacher's guidance. It
is sometimes highly informative for the student to explore an idea
which will lead into a blind alley. It is informative not only because,
having reached an impasse he will not repeat the mistake again, but
also because he learns to evaluate his mistakes, to learn why and
how his idea was incorrect. Even more important the student learns

---

Lillian Koltnow was concerned with teaching abstract mathematical concepts
through concrete examples. Mrs. Koltnow teaches science and math at Springside
School in Philadelphia and was a coordinating teacher in both the 1965 and
1966 Institutes.

that a mistake is not the end of the learning process. He can back off, take a second look at a problem, and try again from another approach.

In discussing methods of this type the question perennially arises, "But how can we cover all the necessary material?" The only useful answer is, "What is the value of complete coverage if the student has learned little or none of the material covered?" Isn't it better to proceed more slowly with results that produce real understanding rather than temporary memorization? Unfortunately the 20 periods per class we had in Trenton this summer were really too brief for a clear picture of the effectiveness of this method, but it is essentially one I have used successfully for several years teaching "Time, Space, and Matter." This summer it took a certain amount of time for the students to realize that the ideas had to come from them—that the teacher just asked questions and gave out very little information. They quickly became involved in the various activities, learning somewhat slowly how to make informative records of their measurements. Opportunity to try several variations of one activity, to enable them to compare results, improved their understanding even more.

The mathematics program for the eighth grade in this summer institute was designed to accompany the eighth grade science course "Time, Space, and Matter" in order to make available to the students some of the mathematical concepts and skills which they would need for that course. The two basic ideas I therefore planned to concentrate on were graphing and determining areas and volumes. My own experience teaching "Time, Space, and Matter" during the 1965 Institute had convinced me that the students at this grade level would have very limited experience with graphing and would have a great deal of difficulty understanding formulas for finding areas and volumes. Being firmly convinced that "laboratory" work that leads to discovery is a more fruitful source of knowledge for the student than the same information falling as pearls of wisdom from the teacher's lips, I had planned a set of activities which would send the students in a direction where discovery would be possible.

In the very beginning it was very difficult to get much in the way of responses from the class. When the discussion was opened with the question, "Suppose by some magic all the numbers disappeared, how would you like that?" there was very little reaction. I had not taught them anything, so they did not see how they could answer any questions. I also suspect that because numbers were so much a part of their lives they could not imagine life without them and did not bother to try. I baited them with "Just think, no math!"

but still no response. Finally somebody suggested that telling time, counting money, and remembering a birthday would be hard without numbers.

A somewhat more successful question in eliciting discussion was: "Which would you rather have, a barrel of silver dollars, or a barrel of dimes?" The idea that the silver dollars as coins represented more money was most appealing at first, until someone said that dimes were smaller, so the barrel would hold more dimes than dollars. Then someone else asked, "but would this be more money?" At this point the discussion of this question was temporarily halted, and I said we would find out the answer by the end of the summer. By this time the students realized that questions would be asked that required some thought, and that they had ideas that would be listened to.

Bringing the discussion around to my first big topic, I asked, "What is a graph?" Most of the students were at a loss in trying to answer the question, but none of them had ever thought of a graph as a picture. What would we do if we wanted a picture showing the heights of the children in the room? They suggested that the children could line up and we could take a picture, but they did not see how a graph could do the same thing. What would they need to make such a picture? They agreed that they needed to measure their heights. They were therefore provided with metersticks, divided into four groups, and sent to measure their heights with no further instructions than to make a record of their heights for the groups.

I find it very useful to give the students limited instructions about what to do, and let them acquire some experience handling the equipment they have to use before they get down to the real task at hand. It gives them time to learn something about the equipment and their own ability to use it—a time when they can make some mistakes and either learn to correct them or ask intelligent questions. They might also answer my questions, which might direct their thinking. For instance, because a meterstick is too short to measure the height of anyone in the class they had to mark a length and lay off an additional distance. The problem for most was the fact that a meterstick is not a yardstick, which many had not noticed, and so they treated one length as 36 in. We tend to think of our own heights to the nearest inch, and many of the students could not read fractions of an inch correctly, so we did not worry about the precision of the measurements.

The next lesson began with a discussion of what they had done, what difficulties they had encountered (such as the length of the meterstick), how they could overcome the difficulties to get correct measurements, and what other suggestions did they have about collecting the information before they tried it again. They suggested that they would like to separate boys' heights and girls' heights, and that it would be a good idea for each person to have a chance to do some measuring. As a group lined up, each student measured the height of the person next in line. This time the measuring was done with considerably greater efficiency, although some students had a little trouble with the arithmetic ($36 + 27 = ???$).

A very important characteristic of a lesson was how much the students were involved in its progress. To this end suggestions for what to do next were frequently sought from the class, and sometimes acted upon even if they did not necessarily lead in the direction the teacher thought most desirable. For instance, when I asked how we could arrange the information of the heights of the students, each of which had been recorded on a small card, their first suggestion was "Alphabetical order." There were no names on the cards but this was an order with which they are very familiar. We had placed a large sheet of paper covering a bulletin board across the back of the room on which to thumbtack the height cards. The class decided the paper needed some lines and numbers with heights to help them place their card accurately, so a base line was drawn 48 in. from the floor. A vertical line was drawn along one side with heights marked off every 2 in. The students lined up alphabetically in two rows, separated in groups of boys and girls. In that order each placed his own height card on the chart. A line was then drawn across the top of each card and the cards removed. They agreed that the zigzag pattern of the lines was very uninformative and possibly very inaccurate.

The suggested improvements included additional horizontal lines on the chart to help in locating heights, and a rearrangement of the height cards according to height rather than to the alphabet. This produced two good charts or graphs from which they were able to deduce a considerable amount of information about frequency and range of heights in the class. They were also able to make comparisons between heights of boys and girls in the class and to read similar graphs made by another class. At this point they saw the need for an informative title identifying the horizontal and vertical scales.

We moved from this kind of graph to one which might give similar height information for the entire school. Plotting a frequency distribution was discussed, following suggestions from the class, after which they made their own graphs, both broken-line and bar graphs, with questions from the teacher which served as guidelines. The relative merits of these two kinds of graphs were examined. Various kinds of errors which showed up on individual graphs were discussed because they were all posted on the bulletin board. The importance of careful plotting of points was made clear. Students were encouraged to color their bar graphs. The value of various kinds of coloring techniques was discussed in terms of whether or not they helped to make the information of the graph clearer.

All of the preceding work was a preliminary to a graph which showed a relationship between two different properties, such as weight and volume of different amounts of some material. I wanted the students to learn that it was possible to graph two different kinds of measurements against each other and find a relationship. In introducing this idea we talked about the meaning of the phrase "How big is . . . ?" and discovered that this is a very general kind of question and might refer to area, volume, height, or length. Two different ways of answering this question could mean something quite different for the same object.

For this activity I had obtained a variety of different kinds of containers having different shapes. The students could pour unit measure after unit measure of water or fine sand into them. They were to record the height of the material in the container after each additional measure was added. The graphs they obtained of height against volume in terms of numbers of measures poured were, of course, different, depending upon the shape of the container. The graphs did not, as some students thought, actually have the shape of the container.

Some students measured the length of a row of small cubes after each cube was added to the row. Because the cubes were 1 in. on an edge, measurement in inches would have obscured my purpose, so I had them make the measurements in centimeters, which also gave them practice for their science class activities. This turned out to be a straight-line graph like that of the heights of water or sand poured into a cylindrical container.

The next topic we explored was the measurement and calculation of areas and volumes. When asked to find the size of a table top the students said they needed the length and width of the table. They suggested a variety of different things we should do with the measurements. Even though they had once learned area formulas most could not remember them. I finally put $A = lw$ on the board and pointed out that we measure length and width in inches. Someone then remembered that areas are in square inches—but no one knew why.

I gave each student a small square cut out of light cardboard, and asked what it was. The answer was " A square, because it has four equal sides." How big was the square? They measured the edges and decided it was a square inch. Could they use it to measure a table top, or some other similarly shaped object? Yes, they could, either by laying it off over and over again, or by using many of them. They each then received about 50 sq.-in. pieces and a page with several rectangles drawn on it. They found the size of each rectangle using the square-inch pieces, and then tried to find a connection between their answer and the area formula. They saw that a square inch is quite different from an inch measured on a ruler, and finally discovered that the area formula is really just a short cut for counting all the squares needed to cover the space inside a rectangle.

The next experience was to mark off a line $\frac{1}{2}$ in. away from the long edge of the paper and find the area of this strip using smaller squares they received. They had to find out how big these small squares were, and how many it took to cover one of the square-inch pieces. They learned that each small square was one-quarter of a square inch. They then tested the area formula on the little square and discovered that $A = lw$ gave them $\frac{1}{2}$ in. $\times$ $\frac{1}{2}$ in. $= \frac{1}{4}$ sq. in., the same answer.

The next operation was more difficult and required that they extend the sides of a 2 in. $\times$ 5 in. rectangle by $\frac{1}{4}$ in. in length and in width and find the area using their inch squares, making still smaller ones as they needed them. They had to find how many of the smallest squares it took to cover 1 sq. in. They also had to find the area of the enlarged rectangle by calculation, doing the multiplication both in mixed numbers and improper fractions. This gave the class an opportunity to compare the relative difficulty of calculation with different kinds of numbers.

Class activity ranged between laying out and counting squares and calculating areas by multiplying measured dimensions, to making concrete the meaning of the area formula as a short cut for a very tedious counting job. They also had an experience with one such tedious task—finding the area of a square a foot on each side by laying out the necessary number of 1 in. squares. This followed the question, "How many square inches do you need to make a square one foot on a side?". The immediate response was 12. Told to "Try it!", they soon discovered it actually took 144. Because I had found that a number of students did not know how many pieces one would have if something was broken in half, we explored some relationships between a part and the whole. We worked on the idea that if it took

144 sq. in. to make 1 sq. ft., each square inch was therefore $\frac{1}{144}$ of 1 sq. ft. If it took four small squares $\frac{1}{2}$ in. on an edge to make 1 sq. in., then each of these small squares must be one-quarter of a square inch, and if something was one-quarter of a square inch it would take four of them to cover a whole square inch. We explored the same kind of relationships for the pieces formed when a small square was cut in quarters, checking a matching of pieces against answers found from the formula, until the students felt that they really knew and could trust the formula for any size of measurements.

We then did the same sort of thing with 1 in. cubes—stacking them, counting them, measuring the edges of the stacked pile, and discovering the formula $V = lwh$ as a short cut for counting cubic units in a rectangular solid. They also learned the characteristics of a cube and the important differences between a cubic inch and a square inch.

In the course of getting acquainted with the students I gave a short diagnostic arithmetic test and discovered that their achievement in the simple arithmetic operations ranged from excellent to poor. Division produced poorest results with multiplication a close second. This test did not include fractions or percents. As a consequence I sometimes tried to fit in some practice in arithmetic skills in the limited time available. I feel that a future program for this grade level should emphasize arithmetic competence, presented in terms of handling things, and activities should be performed to give point to the arithmetic. Many children drift through school, learning things only to forget them very quickly. In many cases in mathematics the manipulation of numbers is so far in the realm of the abstract, so far removed from physical activity, that the numbers have little meaning for students.

Formulas are even more removed, an abstraction of an abstraction, and therefore never really understood. I think I pretty largely succeeded in making concrete for the students some notions about areas, volumes, and measuring, and about the usefulness and meaning of graphs, that had not been clear to them before.

All the units presented to this class by the participating teachers fit together very well except for the unit on the introduction to algebra. This topic was selected because the teacher wanted to try teaching algebra using some new techniques. By the time it was her turn to teach she and the students knew each other well enough so that a topic that was quite different from the rest of the curriculum was acceptable. The students took change in stride and participated very well.

The first topic presented converted the classroom into a city. The teacher took a typical urban situation in which the members of the class might find themselves. Students became storekeepers, bankers, or consumers, with cash in hand and in the bank, to withdraw, deposit, and spend. The activities produced some understanding of the use of banking materials, the responsibilities of operating a business, and their role as consumers. The unit culminated with a circle graph which was an effective tie-in with their other lessons on graphing.

The teacher reported, "I became more and more involved with the lesson as it progressed and became aware of the fact that I was enjoying teaching this lesson. The class was also reacting favorably. I was pleased that at no time did I refer to a textbook, nor did the students. It was different." His lesson was drawn from life, from the students own actual or potential experience. He continued, "I was pleased to see the interaction between the students, and I remained in the background. . . . My experience was very beneficial to me. I taught a lesson very differently from my regular teaching. The students reacted well and I enjoyed teaching."

The second unit was devoted to teaching measurement of fractions of an inch. There was a variety of activities in which the students divided a paper disk into fractions, built up larger fractions from smaller subunits, used a large model of an inch, and finally made a small box from a diagram and measurements. Again they were all involved, but in this case it was a more individual involvement rather than as part of a group. This teacher, in an evaluation of his own experience in the institute, said, "During my teaching sessions I attempted to perform a new aspect of teaching fractions and measurement to my students. . . . I feel I received much more professional value and advancement from the institute than I was able to add to it."

The third topic was fractions, decimals, and percent. After the first lesson the teacher had to modify his program to fit the more limited abilities and experience revealed by the class. At the end of his unit he reported that he felt a sense of accomplishment, that most of the students seemed to understand more of the material than they had earlier. He said, "I can safely say that in being part of the math class I have also grown in areas of teaching. More time will be devoted to getting pupils to arrive at concepts via their own action rather than arriving (hopefully) at that point via teaching 'instruction.'" This teacher also made a strong effort to know the students assigned to him better. He reported changes in attitudes toward school on the part of two of his four pupils, and noted a slight opening up of a very reticent student in a third case.

The biggest change in the students has been in their attitude in class. Whereas they had sat silently during early efforts to arouse discussion, they now volunteer when questions are asked. If an answer is wrong they do not feel rejected or dejected, but try again. Even though frequent answers sometimes mean that the tongue is involved and not the mind, there is greater hope for improvement than when a child remains in, but not a part of, a class. There is also a warm, friendly relationship that exists between the pupils and teachers which is evident almost all the time. It may be a result of what one participating teacher observed when he said, "I didn't expect to see miracles. What I do see is a group of teachers who are *really* working at their jobs." This was a comment which another participating teacher amended by saying, "A group of teachers who treat their students as human beings and are really working at their jobs."

17. Introductory Physical Science: Foundation for the Sciences

COROLYNNE G. BRANSON

In recent years, tremendous effort has been spent on improving science teaching in the secondary school. As a result the curriculum-improving projects have had revolutionary effects on science curricula at all grade levels, especially in the areas of biology, chemistry, and physics. As if by chain reaction, one curriculum change has triggered another. It was thought that the newly developed secondary school curricula would be even more effective if they were preceded by a curriculum designed to teach the student the basic laboratory skills, give them experience in collecting and analyzing data, and in drawing conclusions.

The Introductory Physical Science course that I have taught in the Princeton-Trenton Institute was developed in response to just such a demand. Developed at Educational Services Incorporated under the direction of Dr. Uri Haber-Schaim, the course was constructed to serve two purposes: ". . . on the one hand, to be a sound foundation for future physics, chemistry, and perhaps biology courses; and on the other hand, to furnish sufficient nourishment in the essence, the spirit, and the substance of physical science to be a good terminal course for those who will not study physical science later on."*

The theme of Introductory Physical Science is the development of evidence for an atomic model of matter. This is done by means of sequential experiments which make use of specially constructed equipment.

During the five-week period of the Princeton-Trenton Institute, the

---

* Uri Haber-Schaim, "Objectives and Content of the Course." Adapted from a lecture given at Florida State University, Tallahassee.

Corolynne Branson demonstrated that an introductory laboratory course in physics could serve as a sound foundation for future physics, chemistry, and possibly biology courses. Mrs. Branson is Chairman of the science department at Backus Junior High School in Washington, D.C.

portion of the course taught had to do with the characteristic properties of matter such as density, solubility, thermal expansion, and boiling and freezing points as means by which substances may be either identified or distinguished from one another.

As a laboratory-centered course for which there were no prerequisites it was ideally suited for the disadvantaged or inner-city students. It provided them with daily physical experiences in the laboratory, made use of inductive methods of problem-solving, gave the students opportunities to collect and analyze data, and draw valid conclusions which they expressed both in oral and written form. It also proved challenging to students with a broader range of experience in that it raised questions and opened avenues for research which led away from the central theme of the course itself.

In the Princeton-Trenton Institute, Introductory Physical Science was taught to students who had just completed the ninth grade. The four participating teachers assigned to work with the program visited the homes of these students on Thursday and Friday of the week preceding the opening of school at Trenton High School. Of the 30 students contacted by them on those days 26 appeared in class on the opening day. Of this number approximately one-third said that they had not had science the year before, whereas the other two-thirds had had general science. None of the students were working for credit or to make up a failing mark received in the regular school session.

On the opening day of school, after a brief get-acquainted session where students and participating teachers introduced themselves and gave the names and locations of their schools, the students chose lab partners and immediately set to work assembling their peg boards, alcohol burners, and clips. Working together to assemble equipment provided teachers and students an excellent opportunity to become better acquainted. As on many opening days, all the necessary tools were not on hand. To compensate for this lack even the girls devised makeshift screwdrivers and pitched right in to do their jobs.

The second day of school found us assembling equal-arm balances, cutting the strings of beads which were used as weights with the balances, and hoping that the rest of the equipment would arrive in time so that we need not delay our first experiment.

The first experiment, "Distillation of Wood," was performed as scheduled on Thursday and Friday. For the student who had had no experience in the laboratory, this was quite an exciting experiment. He discovered that to find out about matter you must do something to it. In this case heating the wood produced a gas, a mixture of liquids which required further separation, and charcoal. Student reactions to this experiment were mixed: the shy girl who felt very insecure and seemed almost afraid of all that was happening; the two rather squeamish girls who thought the odors quite nauseating, especially the smell of the alcohol burners which, they laughingly confided, smelled nothing like the alcohol they had tasted somewhere; the boy who had a laboratory set-up at home, thought it was great, and talked in a superior manner about what he thought each fraction contained.

Out of the activities of this first week there developed excellent rapport between the students and teachers. The spirit of cooperation which was so evident during those first days prevailed throughout the course, helping to make it a pleasant and profitable learning experience for all.

The role of the teacher in the Introductory Physical Science program has been changed by the nature of the material used and the laboratory-type classroom situation. In place of the traditional authoritarian type of teacher who dominates the scene on all occasions, the Introductory Physical Science teacher has emerged as a guide of student activity who encourages the student to work out the answers for himself, and who avoids bringing in new concepts which are not needed to develop the central theme of the course. In short, he tries to tell as little as possible rather than as much as possible.

An awareness of the change in the role of the teacher in the Introductory Physical Science program, together with a knowledge of the course content and the teaching method used, are listed by the authors of Introductory Physical Science as prerequisites for teachers planning to use the program.

Since the participating teachers in the group at Trenton High School had not worked in the Introductory Physical Science program before, they each received a copy of the text and the teacher's manual which they scanned during the first week of school and from which they selected blocks of material to teach. Using the suggested time allotments for the material which had been selected we made a teaching calendar. The fourth period in our daily teaching schedule which had been left free by the institute for conferences or planning was used to set up and try out experiments before attempting them in class. The teachers also found it convenient to carry equipment home for further experimenting since a rigid bus schedule demanded a prompt departure at noon for Princeton and the afternoon program. Some items and materials such as Geiger counters, sand, and additional chemicals which were needed to make the student laboratory sessions more meaningful were either borrowed by the teachers from their own school bases or bought for use in class. As a result of this planning, the Introductory Physical Science class periods were interesting and challenging to both students and teachers.

The enthusiasm of the participating teachers for the program was further evidenced by their desire to try as much of the new equipment as possible and to teach more than the required number of lessons. They seemed most impressed by the simplicity and sensitivity of the equipment designed for the course. Since the four participants were experienced teachers, they appreciated the student response to the laboratory situation, the ease with which such a program lends itself to good lesson planning, the lack of discipline problems because of the keen student interest in the work, and the student growth in both communicative and manipulatory skills.

Through the efforts of one participating teacher a trip was made to the Thiokol Chemical Corporation where pupils were conducted in small groups through the plant. Highlights of the trip were the specially constructed high-pressure laboratories, the huge vats in which plastics were being made, the guide's explanation of how a glue produced by the plant had been discovered to be the prime ingredient needed to make rocket fuel, the refreshments served in the plant's cafeteria, and finally the gift of a plastic portfolio to each student. On the morning following the trip a representative from the plant came to Trenton High School to talk to the class about employment after graduation and about Thiokol's tuition-free program designed to encourage employees to acquire additional training while working on the job.

Evidence of student growth in the Introductory Physical Science course has been observed in several areas. The students acquired some basic laboratory skills which included handling glassware, reading thermometers, collecting gas by means of water displacement, and separating substances by distillation and filtration. They have learned to use the equal-arm balance and to calibrate a rider. They have plotted a graph to show equivalent gram and bead weights. They have kept laboratory notebooks in which they carefully recorded data and conclusions. They developed a polaroid film on which they had placed radioactive samples of matter. Most important of all they have shown improved ability to do critical thinking in pre- and post-lab sessions.

In summary, the Introductory Physical Science program taught at Trenton High School provided students with an opportunity to work in the laboratory and to observe and enjoy some of the scientific phenomena which are too often simply described to them. It provided participating teachers a new curriculum which can be used either in junior high school or senior high school with academic or terminal students, along with a new philosophy and objectives for their classroom teaching.

18. Laboratory Biology

JAMES McCRACKEN

Our approach was determined by recognizing that our students had limited reading skills, a short attention span, and an undeveloped ability to abstract and generalize. By concentrating on these learning difficulties rather than on cultural differences we hoped to overcome the child's educational deficiencies.

The level and abilities of each of the students varied. The job of the teacher in each case was the same—to be enthusiastic and concerned with the worth of each individual child and to make biology interesting, meaningful, and worthwhile. In order to accomplish these goals the teacher must draw upon and master basic teaching skills such as motivation and an ability to pace a lesson. He must be well grounded in the principles of the laboratory method and also be firmly convinced that these pupils will benefit by laboratory experiences.

The teacher must let his students learn to handle equipment, collect data, interpret data, and draw conclusions. He must help them structure their work, give praise, and help to tie abstractions to concrete everyday examples.

The teacher must have a good background in modern principles of biology and not water down concepts, but be more selective and more thorough with fewer concepts with reading material geared to the students' reading level.

The key to this biology course was to tell the students nothing and do nothing for them that they could not do for themselves. The teacher was a guide to the child's discovery of biology, always encouraging participation and building into the course some success for each student each week.

James McCracken has been involved in experimental biology programs for the past three years while being biology instructor at Dixie Hollings High School in St. Petersburg, Florida. As a 1966 coordinating teacher, Mr. McCracken demonstrated a laboratory approach to biology.

In order to help the class atmosphere, the participating teachers introduced themselves, and gave the students some of their own personal backgrounds. In turn, the students stood and introduced themselves. The students were then asked to fill out a simple questionnaire. The questionnaire included name, address, telephone; number of older and younger brothers and sisters; interests and jobs after school and on Saturdays; reasons for studying biology; hobby and other interests; and lastly, ambitions after graduation.

Each participating teacher used the questionnaire to get better acquainted with his students. All teachers were asked to make an evaluation sheet for each child so that they could make notes of changes in attitudes, skills, and abilities. They were to date each observation in order to compare notes. Three or four students were selected by each teacher as ones to whom they could give help when needed. These evaluation sheets were used as a guide so the teachers could see which students were and which were not having the desired success in the classroom.

Each participating teacher compiled a list of the qualities they thought a good teacher should have. All of the teachers had the opportunity to observe the work of their colleagues. In group meetings strong and weak qualities were noted, and suggestions were made to help the particular teacher improve his methods.

The two most frequent mistakes teachers made were that they failed to ask leading questions which would encourage student discussion and they would ask questions without giving students a chance to respond.

The text used in the course was the BSCS (Special Materials) *Biological Science Patterns and Processes,* published by Holt, Rinehart, and Winston, Inc. Each student was given a binder and compiled a notebook of materials distributed, student laboratory reports, discussion notes, and quizzes.

Our original plan was to spend one week on the topic of ecology, one week on evolution, two weeks on cells and cell processes, one week discussing growth and development, and the final week on heredity. The participating teachers, however, wanted to know if one unit of work could be fully developed so they could see the over-all approach used; therefore the ecology unit was covered in 11 days or 22 class hours. We developed many ideas. We looked at the fact that men find it useful to arrange things in meaningful groups. We saw that grouping systems help in communication when based on the same or nearly the same observations. Biological classifications were seen as flexible and under constant revision. Curiosity was indicated as the force which has led to new ways of studying groups. Population and population change were studied emphasizing individual interaction within their environments. Our studies of populations and communities led to a concept of succession. Finally, interactions of populations and communities led to the idea of an ecosystem.

Fifteen laboratory exercises were selected for the remainder of the Institute. Each participating teacher chose to conduct three exercises in order to put into practice some of the methods, ideas, and techniques they had acquired. They were asked to choose exercises with which they were not familiar. Two exercises were done each day. The laboratory exercises were selected to illustrate or introduce the following topics: evolution, natural selectivity, cell structures, comparing plant and animal cells, cell processes, energy, cellular energy, diffusion, and burning versus respiration.

Almost all the course was based on laboratory work by the students. In the 42 hours the students were with us, they did a total of 19 exercises in the laboratory. They were presented with a problem and set to work doing the various exercises to see if they could come up with a possible answer or solution. Each student received a great deal of personal attention during which time he was shown how to write a laboratory report. They were taught how to collect data by making notes, sketches, and jotting down anything that had happened during the exercise, no matter how insignificant it might have seemed. Students were shown how to present their data in narrative form, to use charts and graphs, and to make predictions as to lab results. We pointed out that some conclusion must be drawn from all that was done in an exercise. Must of the students did a creditable job. We kept stressing the idea of control in an experiment, why it was important, and that without controls one had nothing with which to compare results.

One of the strongest factors in this program was the interplay between the teacher and students. Small group discussions were used very effectively. Many times, after the small group discussions or individual attention, a large group discussion was used by the teachers to get small groups or the various individuals to speak out and help develop a whole idea. The teacher's role during discussion was to lead, guide, direct, and most of all to *Listen*. Our main aim at this time was not to obtain the "right" answer immediately, but rather to help a student use his raw data and through reasoning arrive at an answer. We demonstrated respect for student opinion. It was a slow process, and often we had to rephrase the question in order to get responses, but it was the heart of our teaching.

Each student and participating teacher was asked to evaluate the course. Some representative comments from the students follow:

"I learned some tips on studying biology."
"The way this course was taught was almost perfect."
"We had a chance to learn and not just skim the topic."
"I wish we could have studied more of what we wanted to."
"All is A-ok."
"I wanted to dissect small animals."
"If we could have studied the brain and human body, it would be nice."
"This was fun."
"You made us talk too much."
"I think what I learned is not what I anticipated."
"I would like to study marine life."
"The study of ecology is less needed than the knowledge of other stages of biology."

The evaluations made by the teachers are as follows:

"As a teacher I talk too much; I ask the question and then don't give the students a chance to answer."
"Be fully prepared before you go into the laboratory, because you never know what they will ask if given a chance."
"This lets the student do more demonstrations."
"I like the philosophy and approach."
"I learned to seek criticism and not take it as a personal offense."
"The personality of the teacher will determine success or failure."
"The rapport between the teacher and the student was good."
"The students seemed to gain self-respect and confidence."
"This course made me take another look at myself as a teacher."
"The success had by the students made them belong."
"I liked the climate; it was open, free, relaxed, and the students felt like expressing themselves."
"This type of teaching sure keeps you on your toes."

PART FOUR

Essays in Urban Education

19. Human Relations: An Overview

DONALD K. CAREW

To capture on paper the flavor of a dynamic, exciting, frustrating, depressing program such as PTI would tax the talents of an accomplished artist. The program was people interacting, questioning, competing, cooperating, searching, rejecting. The program was a process that wound its way through a maze of teacher-student, teacher-teacher, and teacher-administrator relationships that were constantly complicated by philosophic ideals and practical day to day problems.

The function of the writer as a member of the Institute staff involved a focus on the human relations aspects of the program. Specific responsibility included the Human Relations Laboratory during the first week of the Institute, work with individual teachers and with minor groups, guidance, and teacher-pupil relationships in the high school, working with other staff members, and evaluation of the Institute. Chapter 24 contains an evaluation of the program by Dr. Margaret Fleming and the writer. The present chapter will focus on the process and outcomes of the first week of the institute which set an important tone for the institute program.

The First Week—Human Relations Workshop

This $2\frac{1}{2}$-day Human Relations Workshop which started at noon on the first day of the Institute was designed to help each individual

---

Dr. Donald Carew was responsible for the human relations and research of the 1965 and 1966 Institutes at Princeton University. One of his major responsibilities was the organization and administration of a Human Relations Workshop which initiated the Princeton-Trenton Institute. Much of the flavor of a workshop, which is both an inspirational and intellectual training experience, is retained in his article. Dr. Carew is Associate Professor of Education at Ohio University.

realize his own potential for growth more fully and to increase his ability to work with others in a variety of situations. The core of the workshop was the T-group which is a relatively unstructured group composed of from eight to 15 people who meet for long periods of time and who have no external topic on which to focus the discussion. The data for learning are the transactions among the members, their own behavior in the group as they struggle to create a productive organization and work to stimulate and support each other in their learning. The T-group is concerned with self-diagnosis and is intended to provide an opportunity for group members to look at themselves as they relate to each other and to the group as a whole.

The success of laboratory or sensitivity or t-group training programs has been widely acclaimed. After an initial stage of ambiguity, people begin to express themselves more openly and honestly, defenses are lowered, and honest reactions to one another are possible.

T-groups have been extremely effective in creating a climate which encourages learning, understanding, insights, and skills in the areas of self, group, and organization.

The laboratory training design seemed to fit especially well into the structure which had been planned for the Institute. Since the Institute was centered around teams composed of ten participating teachers and two coordinating teachers, and since these teams had been scheduled to meet regularly in critique sessions and to work together in the classroom, it seemed appropriate to begin the Institute with a program that was designed to encourage effective team organization, break down interpersonal barriers, and develop insight into the dynamics of small groups. The Laboratory for Applied Behavioral Science, which is affiliated with the Graduate Division of Newark State College, was contacted and agreed to provide trainers and material for the workshop.*

The use of the T-group seemed appropriate for another reason. Although the methods used in the T-group are not necessarily the same as those methods used in inductive or nondirective teaching, there are, however, many similarities in philosophy and technique between the two. Generally, inductive teaching might be described as student-centered, participative, democratic, and group-centered. Education becomes a cooperative endeavor in this atmosphere. The

---

* Trainers who worked with the T-group throughout the workshop included Mark Atwood, Lawrence Barclay, Donald Carew, Robert Chasnoff, Donald Leveridge, Wilton Pruitt, and Alice Sargent.

teacher is not an authoritarian nor a disciplinarian. Inductive teaching groups may have an externally imposed task and in this way they differ from laboratory training groups; however, the interactions and process with the group are often utilized as part of the educational process. In this way inductive teaching is very similar to the T-group. Since the summer school for the children was to concentrate on the inductive approach to teaching, the Human Resources Seminar seemed like a logical introduction and an approach which might stimulate a *cooperative involvement* in the search for *new ways to facilitate* learning in our public schools.*

The schedule for the workshop follows.

HUMAN RELATIONS WORKSHOP SCHEDULE

PTI JUNE 27–29, 1966

Monday, June 27th

1:00– 1:30	Orientation	McCormick Auditorium
1:30– 2:30	T-group	Seminar rooms
2:30– 3:15	Intergroup observation	Seminar rooms
3:15– 3:30	Break (coffee)	Seminar rooms
3:30– 4:15	Intergroup observation	Seminar rooms
4:15– 5:15	T-group	Seminar rooms
5:15– 5:45	General session	McCormick Auditorium

Tuesday, June 28th

9:00–10:30	Human Resource Consultants (Boys from Essexfields)	McCormick Auditorium
10:30–11:00	Break	
11:00–12:15	Group demonstration (Boys from Essexfields)	McCormick Auditorium
12:30– 1:30	Lunch	
1:30– 3:15	T-group	Seminar rooms
3:15– 3:30	Break (coffee)	Seminar rooms
3:30– 5:00	T-group	Seminar rooms

---

* For a more thorough description of the laboratory method the reader is referred to the following publications: Schein, E. H. and W. G. Bennis, *Personal and Organizational Change through Group Methods,* New York: John Wiley and Sons, Inc., 1965. Bradford, L. P., J. R. Gibb, and K. D. Benne, *T-Group Theory and Laboratory Method,* New York: John Wiley and Sons, Inc., 1964.

Wednesday, June 29th

9:00–10:30 T-group   Seminar rooms
10:30–10:45 Break (coffee)
10:45–12:00 T-group   Seminar rooms
            (Preparation for home visits)
12:15– 1:15 Lunch
 1:15– 2:00 Final general session   McCormick Auditorium
 2:00   Preparation for home visits,
            meeting with coordinating
            teachers

A word should be said about the Human Resource Consultants who spoke with the Institute participants on Tuesday morning, June 28th. These consultants were seven teenage boys and their supervisor. They were sponsored by Science Resources Incorporated (SRI) of Union, New Jersey. The boys were graduates from Essexfields and had been hired by SRI to act as consultants to educational groups. The Essexfields program is a new approach to the social treatment of juvenile delinquents and it "designed to rehabilitate 16- and 17-year-old delinquent boys who are referred by the Essex County Juvenile Court."*

The boys spent the first part of the morning talking about themselves, how and why they had gotten into trouble and how Essexfields had helped them. They also discussed how they felt that school had contributed to their delinquency. Finally they suggested how schools and teachers might improve in their efforts to help young people.

During the latter part of the morning the boys demonstrated group process by engaging in a spontaneous group session on stage. Their skill in communicating and in listening was amazing.

This session generated excitement and enthusiasm in some, and hostility and skepticism in others. On one occasion during the morning session one of the boys reminded a group of teachers, who were not listening courteously at the time, that although teachers demand attention from students, teachers did not seem willing to give it to the boys. Some teachers thought the boy insolent. Others felt that the boy's scolding was deserved. At any rate the morning program generated a great deal of discussion and thought during the T-group sessions which followed.

---

* Pilnick, S., A. Elias, and N. Clapp, "The Essexfields Concept: A New Approach to the Social Treatment of Juvenile Delinquents," *The Journal of Applied Behavioral Science,* Vol. 2, No. 1, 1966, p. 112.

The Human Relations Workshop was followed by preparation for and visits to the homes of the students who were to attend the summer school of Trenton High School. There was a great deal of apprehension about these visits and an effort was made in some of the T-groups to work through these fears by role-playing and discussions of what to expect. The visits were made on Thursday of the first week. Friday was devoted to reports and discussion of the visits and planning for the school activities which were to begin the following week.

The Outcome

The goals of the laboratory training included helping the participants become more aware of their attitudes and the attitudes of others, especially toward inner-city youth, and encouraging an openness and honesty among the teachers in each group in order to provide the basis for cooperative efforts and productive relationships throughout the remainder of the program.

How successfully the goals were reached varied from person to person and from group to group. For some teachers the experience was extremely rewarding and affected them deeply. For others it had some, but not an extraordinary, value. A few felt it was a total waste of time.

At the end of the week the teachers were asked to fill out an open-end questionnaire. It asked for their reactions to the activities of the first week. Sixty-one teachers responded to the question which asked for a reaction to the Human Relations Laboratory and *47, or 77 percent, gave responses which were totally positive in nature. Eleven, or 17 percent had positive as well as negative things to say about the laboratory. Only three people or five percent were totally negative* and felt that the workshop was a waste of time.

Positive comments included statements such as

· Helped us to know each other and to examine our feelings about inner-city youth.
· Of course it was helpful. In examining ourselves we discovered our own personal weaknesses as well as weaknesses in our educational ideologies.
· It was very helpful but we needed more time in the T-group in order to be completely honest.
· Very worthwhile experience. It gave me a deeper insight into the feelings and personalities of my group members and myself.

· Would be even better if we repeated it again at the end of the Institute.

· It was helpful to me because I became more aware of some of my attitudes and of the attitudes and feelings of the other teachers.

The comments made by those who had positive and negative things to say usually included some suggestions for change. Some examples of comments in this category follow:

· Some sessions interesting but some unproductive.

· Helpful in establishing relationships within our group but was a bit labored—too long.

· Interesting but I don't like to share my thoughts with a group of strangers.

· Has potential but was disorganized and some groups were dominated by three or four people.

The three totally negative comments indicated that the workshop was a total waste of time.

The reactions to the Essexfields boys were very similar to the reactions to the workshop in general.

41	Totally positive	67.2 percent
11	Positive–Negative	18.0 percent
9	Totally negative	14.8 percent

Those that were totally positive were very impressed. Some thought it was the best experience of the week. Others felt the Essexfields practices should be introduced into the schools. They saw in the boys some hope for the future of the schools' rejects. Those who expressed negative comments almost unanimously felt that it was unreal, a fake, and that the boys were just good showmen.

The home visits too were viewed positively by a large majority.

47	Totally positive	77.0 percent
5	Positive-Negative	8.2 percent
9	Totally negative	14.8 percent

Those who felt negatively felt as though they were prying or intruding or that it was absolutely unnecessary. The positive comments indicated that those teachers felt that the experience was very worthwhile and enlightening and that home visits should be a part of the regular school program. Many of the teachers who felt apprehensive before the visits were surprised and pleased at how well received they were by parents.

Teachers' comments certainly suggest that the goals of the Human Relations Laboratory were realized for most of the participants and that the Institute was off to a good start by the end of the first week.

Conclusion

As was true in last year's PTI a great deal of conflict and resistance as well as excitement was experienced during this summer's program. The conflicts arose over many of the same issues, such as controlling or not controlling the kids, standards of dress, and grades.

As I reflect on the conflict that we experienced during this summer's program, it seems to me that it is closely related to what, in my opinion, is the most serious problem in education today. I think that it is related to the problems that higher education is facing, as evidenced by occurrences in Berkeley and other recent events. I think that we have for so long been convinced that we know what is best for students, that we know what they should do, we have forgotten to recognize that they too have some ideas about what they need and what they want, and, in fact, what they will do. We have talked about individual differences and the importance of meeting the needs of the people with whom we are working, but we have established our institutions as though everyone was the same, and without regard to the way the world looks to the youth.

It seems to me that it has been very clearly illustrated by a variety of forces in our society that if we are to make an impact, if we are to fulfill the American dream of providing the opportunity for all people to realize their potential, we must begin to look at the needs of the various people about whose welfare our educational institutions are supposedly concerned. It seems to me that the major conflict that we experienced in our Institute revolved around the same question—the difference between what teachers think students should be like and what, in fact, students are like; the difference between what we think is important and what, in fact, is important to the young people who are our clients.

I think, therefore, that the conflict in general is a healthy one for it forces us to concern ourselves with the world as it seems to the students, instead of just the world as it seems to us. I think that this approach which we call inductive or discovery, which seems to excite and involve students, does so, not only because it is a good technique or method, but also because it communicates an attitude, an attitude which says that I value you as a person, I value your feelings, your needs, your ability to learn and to grow, and your right to be involved in decisions that affect you. In general, I think that a great deal was accomplished by this summer's experience, and I feel as though I personally have gained much as a result of my involvement with the staff, coordinating teachers, participating teachers, and students in this exciting program.

I think my role differed somewhat from what I expected for a variety of reasons. I had anticipated having more time for individual conferences with the participating and coordinating teachers, or for meetings with these people in small groups. I found that a great deal of my time seemed to be taken up with staff meetings, planning sessions, and problem-solving. However, it is very likely that whatever contribution I might have made in terms of attitudes, relationships, and values was as important in this area of the operation as it might have been in individual conferences with teachers. I had the feeling at times that it was not possible to do the things that I would like to have been able to do during the Institute. I often felt, for example, that I should be at all five critique sessions at the same time in order to really understand what was happening to the people. This, of course, was an impossibility.

I do think that since one of the major purposes of the Institute was to focus on interpersonal relationships, attitudes, and values, there were not nearly enough staff members who could devote themselves solely to these things. In other words, I think that there was an imbalance in the staff in favor of curricular areas. We often found it difficult to get away from the specifics of methods or subject matter and on to the philosophical and psychological issues about which we were especially concerned. I would therefore recommend that future Institutes add more staff who could devote their time to dealing with human interaction which was the richest source of data throughout the summer program.

I think that we have learned a great deal about what to do, as well as what not to do, in future Institutes, and I feel that as a result of this experience, future efforts will be more effective. It has been a real privilege for me to have had the opportunity to work with the staff and the coordinating teachers of this Institute. They have been a source of inspiration and enlightenment, and I am sure my future will be greatly affected by this summer's opportunity. If it affected everyone as I think it has affected me, it should be scored as an outstanding success.

20. The Community as an Extension of the Classroom

MARSHALL STALLEY

Ever since the conception of free and compulsory education, teachers and school systems have recognized the importance of the so-called "whole person," a term which is something of a cliche, but a concept, however, meant to underline the importance, in fact, the necessity of reaching the individual student and being concerned about his health, mental and physical, and his attitude or readiness to participate in the learning process.

The teacher is concerned not only with cognitive learning but also in relating to the person—dealing with intangibles, attitudes, understandings, and the illusive "motivation." As difficult as it is to define and identify conditions for learning, nonetheless this can be regarded as the *sine qua non*. Students do not learn history or English or anything else unless they are there physically and have a mind and a so-called "attitude" conducive to learning.

This theory is not new. It may have, however, some extensions or adaptations in present-day society and in the educator's role in working with "educationally disadvantaged." Based on this theory the school historically has provided the services of truant officers, attendance officers, and home and school visitors; and, in its concern for dealing with the student as a "whole person," the school has developed a variety of supportive services including counsellors, a guidance staff, school social workers and school nurses.

The teacher has two roles (at least) to perform: (1) the substantive teaching role and (2) the personal role or helping role of relating

Marshall Stalley, Assistant Director of the Rutgers University Urban Studies Center and Visiting Lecturer to the Princeton-Trenton Institute, developed the theme that the community should serve as an extension of the classroom. His paper outlined some strategies that teachers may employ in order to make more effective use of the resources in their communities.

to the student and endeavoring to do what is necessary directly or indirectly to facilitate the learning process.

Teachers require supportive services provided internally within the school system and they need to make effective utilization of such services and help to bring the student to the point where learning can take place or be enhanced. If the child is nearsighted and cannot read the blackboard, it is obvious that his condition needs to be corrected before he can do much about learning to read and write and do arithmetic.

The school system, in its concern about the "health and welfare" of its students as an element in the climate for learning, can look to the home, to its own institutional resources, or to the community. The "community" is an easy and glib word to use, but is increasingly hard to identify, especially if we are seeking to locate meaningful health and welfare resources which can be effectively utilized by the school system to meet the human needs of the students.

Our health and welfare system* is unbelievably complicated. It is both public and private, that is, a system provided by government and through a variety of voluntary health and welfare services. Publicly supported health and welfare services involve the participation of governmental units at various levels including local, county, state, and federal, and further through administrative units or districts with a geographical area which may cut across municipal and county boundaries or include groups of counties where services are provided on a regional basis.

In New Jersey, for example, public assistance, sometimes referred to as "general" assistance to distinguish it from the various categories in our public welfare system, is the responsibility of the local unit of government, the municipality. And, in a state where there are 567 municipalities, there are 567 different systems because each local unit interprets its role to provide general assistance in a somewhat different manner.

The county, through the Board of Chosen Freeholders, like the municipality, is the "creature" of the state, and in New Jersey the county has the responsibility of administering the categorical forms of assistance such as aid to the blind, aid to dependent children, etc.

Further, the extent, quality, quantity, availability, and accessibility of health and welfare resources varies from community to community

---

* Classification of Social Welfare Agencies, a chart prepared by Mrs. Kate Silver of the Social Service Council of Greater Trenton.

Classification of Social Welfare Agencies*

Auspices

Governmental (Public) Tax supported	Voluntary (Private) Supported by contributions (United Fund and Others) and Tax supported

Geographical Areas

Municipal	County	State	National

Functional Fields

Family welfare	Child welfare	Health	Physically handicapped	Mental health	Aged	Recreation and informal education	Adult offenders	Planning, coordination, and program development	Other

Consumer services	Nonconsumer services

Institutional	Non-institutional

Case work	Group work	Community organization

---

* Chart prepared by Mrs. Kate Silver of the Social Service Council of Greater Trenton.

and even in those communities relatively well equipped for the provision of such services there are gaps and areas which might be regarded as "no man's land."

Who, for example, deals with children with suicidal tendencies and what are the procedures and practices necessary to bring to play the utilization of such community health and welfare resources as are available?

In brief, the community resources, complicated and as inadequate as they may be in central cities, constitute a significant "extension of the classroom," and the school needs to establish cooperative relationships with community agencies and with the urban community of which it is a part.

The family's affairs are fragmented among various agencies—housing authorities, welfare departments, case work agencies, hospital and health agencies, settlement houses, and juvenile courts. These services are uncoordinated and there are gaps. This situation limits the usefulness of each agency.

It is the school itself which has more experience with children, and more children, than does any other institution. Because of the universality and continuity of the school's interest in children it has more "knowledge" of children. It can put this to work by constructively influencing other agencies.

The school uses its own personnel and it should work toward the coordinated use of the resources of the community. It avoids treating symptoms and closing cases. It participates with other community agencies in getting at the root causes which prevent families from helping their children.

In discharging its responsibilities in this area, the school system in a sense has to look in three directions at the same time: (1) to the students, (2) to the teachers, and (3) to the community.

But what is everyone's responsibility is frequently no one's specific assignment.

We may acknowledge the school's role, the teacher's role, the community's role, but unless we provide in our school system an office, a place, and personnel whereby this function can be performed, the task of relating the social and health needs of the individual child to strengthen the teaching role may be lost in a shuffle of bureaucracy. The skillful utilization of supportive services within the school system and the potentially available resources within the community are not likely to happen without an arrangement for effective integration of effort.

Who has this generic role: the school nurse, the guidance person, the social worker, or the "principal's office?" In some schools it is not clear who, if anyone, has the role. This is not a regulatory function but one of facilitating and implementing and having a working knowledge of what community services are available for what specialized needs and how and when they can be called upon. Certainly the administrator has the obligation to see that effective linkages and communication exist between needs and resources.

A policy issue is the extent to which the school system should "do everything" or turn to the resources of the community. Should the school system try to meet all these personal, family, social, and health problems directly through its own resources and, if they do not exist, enlarge its own resources, or should it look to the community for such supportive services?

In our commercial life, for example, the retailing and the distribution of food and related products, our system has developed a facility known as the "supermarket." Here the shopper has readily and conveniently available and accessible in one central place most of his shopping needs for food and related commodities on a day-to-day basis.

In the area of health and welfare services there is no comparable supermarket facility available. Frequently, but not always, there exists a central information and referral service. But even the location of such a facility, the name of the person who runs it, and the telephone number is not always known to the teacher or the school system.

It may be that such an information and referral service is provided by the community welfare council where it exists in a given community, or by a local voluntary agency such as a YWCA. The local public welfare office may serve as a general referral agency, although more times than not it will stick to its "general assistance" business.

Most of the larger communities have catalogs of community health and welfare resources in the form of directories* of agencies and the services available. Such directories are often issued by the community welfare council.

Some of the emerging nonprofit corporations concerned with developing economic opportunities for people under the provision of the Economic Opportunity Act of 1965 are beginning to offer information and referral services either on a central or neighborhood basis. Within the last decade or so England has developed neighborhood

---

* *Directory of Community Services,* Social Service Council of Greater Trenton; *Community Resources Directory of Essex County and West Hudson,* New Jersey Council of Social Agencies, Newark, New Jersey.

service centers where people can go for information, and guidance, service and referral, regardless of the nature of their problem or interest.

In dealing with the particular problems of educationally disadvantaged students and their families, it is recognized that special problems exist, extremely difficult and complicated special problems.

Our society generally is regarded as a highly organized society with a multiplicity of organizations, agencies, and groups providing a wide range of opportunities for our citizens to participate. Indeed, we are regarded as a nation of "joiners" with an association, group, or club for any and every interest and an agency for every need.

It has been discovered, however, that one of the central characteristics of the educationally disadvantaged and of low-income families is nonparticipation in the life stream of the nation and its community resources and living patterns. This condition has been referred to as the state of "functionlessness." In brief, this means that many persons, especially the educationally disadvantaged and the urban poor, are not participating members of society.

Perhaps in the long run (and this we can achieve only by decisions taken on a day-to-day basis, for the short-run sequences constitute the long-run situation) the most creative role for the school system may be to help people help themselves and help them to make use of existing resources or seek out new resources where none are available. This might be regarded as a creative brokerage service where the school through its faculty and supportive services seeks to provide an "introductory service" for the nonparticipating members of society, frequently "newcomers" from a rural or nonurban background.

It is a role of matching the needs of people with the community resources for health, welfare, education, and employment, and in general helping the nonparticipating members of society to become involved as participating members of society.

Educational systems are now in trouble partially because, as Paul Ylvisaker* has said, they are faced with the necessity of serving a generation "brought up on Dr. Spock," expecting individual attention and special services which educational institutions have neither the organization nor the manpower to provide.

Such "supportive services" are clearly needed. But generally they are not all available in the needed quality and quantity at the right time and at the right place, either within or outside of the school system, that is, "the community."

---

* *Community Progress,* Vol. 3, No. 3, March–April 1966, New Haven, Connecticut.

This is especially true in schools and among school districts serving predominately the educational needs to the urban poor. Where the needs are greatest the resources are least. This has been pointed out by James Bryant Conant in "Slums and Suburbs."

We are still plagued with a myth that grass-root problems require only grass-root solutions and that local community needs can be equated with local community resources. To deal effectively with the social needs of students in central city areas, their special needs which exist because of their living conditions and community environment, will require new ways of relating needs to resources and getting around the current mismatch between these needs and resources.

School systems and teachers, like people in general, in dealing with their problems can always endeavor to make the most of what they have, and to utilize skillfully and fully what resources, for example, community health and welfare resources, are available. It should not be denied, however, that the resources, inside and outside the school system, are simply not available to deal with the nature of the situation which teachers face.

It is not possible for the local unit of government, the school system, and its local public and voluntary health and welfare services in a central city to deal adequately with the nature of the problem which exists without being able to tap more extensively the resources of the larger society.

The central city seems to be becoming subordinate to the so-called suburb and the suburb is becoming central to our new way of life.* Statistically, for most of us, our way of life and, increasingly, the way of life of all of us, may be more like that of the so-called suburban-type communities than what we have traditionally thought of as "central city living."

If the central city is to be viable in this new society, including its school system and its public and private community health and welfare services, a profound change in thinking and new institutional arrangements will be required. Not only is population size stabilized in the old central cities, but it is declining, both in terms of percentages and in terms of absolute numbers of persons. New institutions and changes in existing institutions, including substantially larger resources for school systems and supportive community services, are needed to meet the crucial and serious needs of the urban poor living in such areas.

---

* Popenoe, David, *The Church and the Urban Condition*, New Jersey Council of Churches, Department of Research and Church Development, East Orange, New Jersey, 1965.

Urbanization has produced striking changes in patterns of behavior and in the kinds of experiences with which central city dwellers must deal. Special skills are needed by the central city resident, frequently a newcomer to the urban area, Negroes from the traditionally agricultural south and whites from the hills of Appalachia, to take advantage of the various resources—economic, health, welfare, cultural, and social—of the place in which they live. The central city resident may live across the street from a hospital, but he may not know it is for him and he probably is not informed as to how to go about using it. Indeed, he may need to be "taught" where and when and what is available in a highly complex and irrational gamut of institutional and agency facilities and services, public and private.

This calls for a recognition that urban school systems have not only the traditional educational role but, of increasing importance, the role of helping relate the urban poor to their urban environment. This role has been described in *The School in Contemporary Society* by David A. Goslin as follows:

> "Urban school systems . . . have a special responsibility to train and motivate students to participate actively and intelligently in local governmental affairs and to accept their responsibilities as citizens for the welfare of the community in the absence of external sanctions for antisocial behavior. Perhaps more than in any other social environment, the urban dweller must be his brother's keeper if our cities are not to turn into jungles where order is maintained only by force of arms. In relation to this aspect of the urban school's functions, it should be noted that the diversity of beliefs and cultural traditions characteristic of the city makes it of critical importance for schools to put special emphasis on increasing students' awareness, understanding, and tolerance for the beliefs of groups other than their own."[*]

Over and above all these additional nontraditional school functions, one can ask what institution, if not the urban schools, has the role of attempting to teach children something about maintaining relatively stable and meaningful social relationships in order that as adults living in an increasingly complicated technological and urban environment they will be able to participate and have some measure of control over the community factors which are likely to affect their own lives.

---

[*] Goslin, David A, *The School in Contemporary Society*, Scott, Foresman, Chicago, 1965.

21. Designing Compensatory Programs: Some Current Programs

HARVEY PRESSMAN

The past five years have witnessed a fantastic growth of "compensatory" programs for disadvantaged urban students. Stimulated at first by the "great cities" projects supported by the Ford Foundation, and accelerated by the substantial sums of money made available under Title I of the Elementary and Secondary Education Act of 1965, these programs have now become a major feature of the American urban and educational scene.

To the casual observer, these developments may seem quite promising. Is the student from the low-income inner-city area at last getting the educational break so long denied him? Are the huge inequalities that have persisted for so long between educational opportunities in the slums and educational opportunities in the suburbs finally being corrected? Is the poor city kid at last getting a "chance for a change," as the title of one Office of Education publication suggests?

The only honest answer to all these questions has to be a resounding "No." The truth is that compensatory educational programs sponsored by urban public schools are simply the latest example of their inability to cope with the problems of educating disadvantaged youth. The

---

Dr. Harvey Pressman, who has been in the forefront of developing programs for urban youth, devised a unique scheme that teachers can use to analyze their communities' social and economic conditions. At the Princeton-Trenton Institute it was called "The Princeton Game," but its application definitely is not limited to the Princeton community. His observation in the development of compensatory programs is one which stresses innovation. Dr. Pressman is Program Director of the Lincoln-Filene Center at Tufts University and served as a Visiting Lecturer at the Princeton-Trenton Institute.

billion dollars allocated by congress for the improvement of education in 1965–1966 for low-income students has been largely wasted.

Part of the problem lies with the very notion of compensatory education. Just what are we supposed to be compensating for, inadequacies in the children or inadequacies in the schools? It is not surprising that the usual answer that the schools give to this question boils down to inadequacies in the students. They may no longer hold that certain children are by nature inferior educational raw material. They are more sophisticated than that. They talk about cultural deprivations, the lack of exposure to "verbal stimulation," the problems of "auditory discrimination. "None of these things are the fault of the children who are, in the current jargon, "innocent victims of inferior circumstances." But whether we attribute inadequacies to heredity or to environment, is not the end result the same? For whatever reason, we still believe that low-income students come to school without the necessary learning equipment, and that we have to change the children *before* we can teach them.

In fact, there is considerable evidence that we have to adjust the schools to the children, rather than vice versa. One of the pieces of evidence which Kenneth Clark has pointed up suggests that the learning problems of disadvantaged children may have more to do with the schools' inability to teach than the students' inability to learn. Disadvantaged students do not usually fall behind grade level in achievement until the third or fourth grade, that is, until the schools have had a few years to mess them up. The longer they stay in school, the further behind they fall. Does this not suggest that we would not need compensatory programs at all if the city schools did their basic job well in the first place? And does it not suggest that all the compensatory programs at all if the city schools did their basic job well in the first place? And does it not suggest that all the compensatory programs we can devise may be doomed to failure unless the regular school program is radically altered?

If we accept the foregoing view, we would not need, in the long run, extra compensatory programs. If we could dramatically change the character and quality of the school system so it could succeed with the disadvantaged in its regular program, we would not need all the special programs. We would probably, however, still need them in the short run, in the catch-up period. It then becomes relevant for us to examine not only the need for compensatory programs, but their quality in actual operation. Unfortunately, it is difficult to find much to praise in the operation of current compensatory programs. Some of the most glaring inadequacies follow.

Inadequate Objectives

The very conceptualization of many compensatory programs is evidence of negative attitudes toward the disadvantaged. The fondest goal is often getting children up to some minimum standard, rather than producing an achievement distribution similar to some of the so-called better schools in the country, or even doing better than those schools. Too many programs merely seek to make educational misery bearable rather than to achieve significant educational breakthroughs. The emphasis is too often on remediation rather than on excitement and enrichment.

Emphasis on Quantity Rather than Quality

Too many compensatory programs simply seek to give children more of the same (wrong) program rather than to make significant improvements in the quality of what happens to the student.

Too Little Money Is Spent

Too often federal money is used to replace local expenditure rather than to supplement it. What should be happening is that the proportion of local, city educational funds expended in low-income areas ought to be increasing at the same time that federal funds are being injected into these areas. The cities had, after all, been spending much less in such areas than in more advantaged areas until the 1960's. What seems to be happening is that the cities are using the federal funds to support most of their special programs in low-income areas.

Poor Educational Strategy

Most urban compensatory programs reflect a very poor conceptualization of the strategy of helping disadvantaged students. Some reflect no concern for strategy whatever. One obvious error in many programs is the spreadout problem—as the program expands, the number of students served expands even more quickly, resulting in an actual reduction of expenditures per student. The failure of New York's Higher Horizons Program is an obvious case in point, but the trend is as obvious in such a "showcase" city as Pittsburgh. Another strategic error is the frequent neglect of the high-potential student. For some reason, there is a masochistic urge to deal with the most difficult problems first, rather than to help those students for whom relatively small inputs of assistance might open up real educational opportunities. The lack of Head Start follow-up in the face of growing (and obvious) indications that Head Start gains will be dissipated without some form of follow-up is a national case in point.

One of the reasons for strategic failures is the simple lack of educational strategists. To paraphrase the Pentagon, we need to show more concern with how to get "the most boost for a buck."

Personnel Problems

Personnel may be the key to the inadequacies of compensatory education. Jobs in compensatory programs are already too often the moonlighting substitute of the 1960's for urban teachers. New higher-paying jobs created by the new federal programs are filled with the friends of those in power. The programs call for experts who simply do not exist in sufficient abundance (for example, reading experts), so the expert jobs are filled by nonexperts.

Most important of all, the attitudes of the staff of compensatory programs may be at the core of the problems. More and more people are pointing out that the negative attitudes of teachers and supervisory personnel toward their disadvantaged students are frequently the major cause of their failure to teach adequately. Yet, at the same time, many of these same teachers and supervisors are getting jobs in compensatory programs. There is probably no better way to insure the failure of such programs.

In summary, it is wise to ask now, even though some compensatory programs are just getting off the ground, whether we don't need a thorough re-evaluation and reorganization of the direction in which we are heading. The evidence so far is not encouraging. If we do not ask such questions, the ultimate losers, as always, will be the children of the poor.

Appendix. The Princeton Game

One of the most necessary requirements of a successful pre-service or in-service training program for teachers of inner-city students is to provide a proper exposure to the community which is served by inner-city schools. Too often the inner-city school and its staff constitute an island which is physically within, but spiritually and culturally removed from, the surrounding environs. The need is for direct experiences which give the teacher a better feel for the problems *and* the strengths of the people in the kind of community in which he teaches.

The Princeton Game is an exercise which was devised to get teachers-in-training out of the classroom into a community which had similarities to the areas in which they taught. The questions represent only a first effort which can be refined each time teachers play and evaluate the game. They are designed to develop skills in finding things out as well as to obtain certain basic information. Although the exercise seems useful in and of itself, it is probably even more valuable when it is also utilized as a springboard for discussion sessions in which teachers' attitudes toward the communities in which they teach can be probed more deeply. As is suggested by the last question, there may also be some value in the exercise as an illustration of a game technique which can be used to get students out of the classroom discovering answers for themselves about crucial local issues.

Instructions to Participants

On Thursday, you will go out in teams of three to explore a low-income section of Princeton, New Jersey. This section comprises approximately 15 blocks.

Your first task will be to fill in the attached outline map of the area, according to the following color code:

Red, for any schools in the area
Orange, for any public community service agencies
Yellow, for any private service organizations
Green, for any religious or political organizations
Blue, for any places where children and teenagers play
Purple, for any places where unemployed men gather
Brown, for any places where women shop for necessities
Black, for any condemned buildings in the area

Label the Red, Orange, Yellow, and Green spots on your map.
Besides filling in your map, you must also fill in the attached questionnaire. Part of the game is to figure out the most efficient way to discover the answers to these questions. The members of the team

preparing the best answers will each receive a copy of Jerome Bruner's *The Process of Education*. Teams should work independently of one another.

The Princeton Game Map. Draw in street names and boundaries of the 15-block area of the low-income section of Princeton, New Jersey, in the following outline map.

1. Names of team members:_____

2. What is the average rent for a four-room apartment in this area? $_____

3. In what condition is the typical apartment renting for the above sum?_____

4. What attitudes do teenagers in the area really hold toward the schools and school teachers of Princeton?_____

_____

5. Where do residents of the area buy most of their food?_____

6. How much do typical food staples cost in this area?_____

7. How does the cost of those staples compare with costs in stores you usually shop in?_____

_____

8. How does the quality of the meats, fruits, milk, and vegetables compare?_____

_____

9. What are the outstanding physical problems of the area?_____

_____

10. What, if anything, is being done about these problems, and by whom?
    a._____
    b._____
    c._____
    d._____
    e._____

11. What attitudes do the mothers in the area express toward the schools of Princeton?_____

_____

_____

12. List how a typical welfare recipient of the area spends her monthly allotment, by major category:
Food_____per month
Clothing_____per month
Heat_____per month
Utilities_____per month
Other (specify)_____per month
Other (specify)_____per month
Other (specify)_____per month
13. What are the major social problems of this area?_____

_____

_____

14. What, if anything, is being done about these problems, and by whom?

a. _____

b. _____

c. _____

d. _____

e. _____

f. _____

g. _____

h. _____

15. Who owns most of the property in this section? _____

_____

16. How good are the municipal services in this section? _____

_____

_____

17. What were the principal methods you used to get the answers to the above questions? _____

_____

_____

18. What do you think of The Princeton Game? _____

_____

_____

19. Would it be helpful for you to explore the area around the school in which you teach in the same fashion? _____

Why or Why Not? _____

_____

_____

20. Would you have your students play this game in your area? _____

Why or Why Not? _____

_____

_____

22. The Home Visit

LAWRENCE BARCLAY

The home visit is not an entirely new or unfamiliar concept in education. The reasons for my being an advocate of the home visit, however, may not be traditional ones.

As a former classroom teacher and guidance counselor who has spent 20 years visiting the homes of his students I see the home visit as a valuable defensive and offensive weapon in the war educators are waging against poverty and the plight of the disadvantaged.

Colleges and universities are becoming increasingly aware of the need to better prepare teachers who are going to teach in disadvantaged areas of urban communities. Many educators, sociologists, and psychologists have done a more than adequate job of accurately describing both the disadvantaged and their environment. That is to say the descriptions are adequate in relation to the environment as a whole and the disadvantages as a group.

Frequently our pat feeling of "knowing" the disadvantaged because we are so familiar with information available in the best books, by the best authors, dealing with the disadvantaged causes us to forget we are in the business of educating and planning the education of *individuals* who are disadvantaged but who do not necessarily fit the general descriptions of authorities in urban education.

When a teacher visits the home of one of his students he can focus on the individual student. For example, the Hough Area of Cleveland has been described in the 1960–61 Annual Report of Great Cities Gray Areas Program as "overcrowded, noisy, not too clean. It covers about 2.2 square miles and holds about 80,000 people. . . .

Lawrence Barclay was primarily concerned with developing a guidance program for the pupils in the Princeton-Trenton Institute. He also organized a series of home visits for the participating teachers which was a resounding success. The step-by-step procedures for developing a successful home visit are described in his paper. Mr. Barclay has recently assumed responsibility as Director of the Western Reserve University Upward Bound Program. Formerly he was a Guidance Counselor and teacher in inner-city schools in Cleveland, Ohio.

It leads the city in crime, in delinquency, in murder cases. It rates high in relief recipients and in cases involving family neglect." Despite this description of Hough, with which I concur, the more than 300 home visits I have made during the four years I worked in the area have always revealed to me some way that the student involved and his home differed from that very accurate, but nonetheless general, description.

A properly conceived and executed home visit can be of great value in acquainting the teacher with the individual student and dispelling stereotypes caused by generalizations.

The Hough Community Project which was a part of the Great Cities Gray Areas Program made excellent use of the home visit. This project used home-school visitors who were nothing more than classroom teachers in most instances. It was felt their visits accomplished among other things: bringing the home closer to the school, helping to break down resentments and barriers in attitudes of parents and children toward the school, and establishing home and school channels of communication. The home-school visitor was expected to bridge the gap between the home and the school and called within a few days after a new student enrolled in a Hough Area school. The Annual Report for 1960–61 for the Hough Community Project-Great Cities Gray Areas Program agreed with these conclusions and stated that "The Home Visitation Program was considered one of the most effective and desirable aspects of the entire project."

Individual teachers can effectively use the home visit if he or she prepares properly, but even so it should not be used indiscriminately. Nor is the home visit advisable for every new or experienced teacher.

A check list for a teacher who is about to conduct a home visit might include the following:

· Discuss the visit with the student.
· Either by phone or letter inform the family of your projected visit and its purpose.
· Stress the positive aspects of the projected visit.
· Agree upon a time when the whole family can be present if at all possible.
· Know as much about the student before the visit as possible.
· Know three or four favorable aspects of the youngster to use as conversation starters.
· Your manner of dress should be appropriate for the season.
  a. Don't carry a briefcase.
  b. Don't have clip-on pencils in pocket.

· Be willing to accept the home as it is.
· Be businesslike but informal in your approach and let those visited set the tone.
· Don't be patronizing.

The female teacher who intends to visit a student should do some special planning by trying, if at all possible, to make and complete her visit during daylight hours.

Any teacher who intends to regularly visit the homes of students should have some well-defined reason beyond curiosity. Obviously all parents are not willing to be visited by the teacher unless something is wrong. No teacher can be expected to visit all of his or her students in their homes. If as a teacher I developed any standard policy for home visiting it was to concentrate on my home-room group. I visited the homes of only those class students who gave some indication, by one means or another, that a home visit would be beneficial. The potential class trouble maker's home was usually visited as early as possible before he or she had a chance to really cause any trouble. That way the visit could be totally positive. The homes of young people who seemed to be capable of more than they were achieving were also usually first visited. The visits were always made after consulting with and getting the permission of the student involved and were never used as a threat.

My major objectives in visiting the home of a home-room student were to get to know the student better and more quickly and to allow parents to become acquainted with me in a setting where they would feel most comfortable.

The major objectives in visiting the home of a subject-class student might be, in addition to the foregoing reasons, to attempt to prevent a situation that might jeopardize the student's best development and to establish meaningful rapport with parents and student.

In certain instances where students are in trouble or are causing trouble, a home visit may bring better results than a letter home or a demand that the parents come in to see a school authority.

Students, particularly those from disadvantaged homes, are aware of the appearance of their homes and of their parents. This means a teacher planning a home visit must expect a reaction from the student that will be influenced by age, sex, and economic status.

The general feeling toward the individual teacher is positive. A family is usually flattered that the teacher has taken the time to be concerned enough to visit. No teacher should be afraid to use the home visit if he plans it and establishes a well-defined reason for it. The feeling toward strangers is not nearly as warm. The youngster who lives in a disadvantaged area is accustomed to seeing strangers go to his door, knock, and wait for an answer that never comes. This does not bother the child since he knows this just may mean: "Mama didn't have this week's insurance money," "Daddy ain't home to pay that bill anyway," "We ain't got money for that anyhow, whatever it is he's selling. It doesn't bother the youngster to say simply, "I don't know," to any questions asked by a stranger. It becomes extremely important then for the teacher to make himself known before the visit.

The utilization of a home visit can be invaluable, but a well-organized system of teacher-conducted home visits could be even more important to an inner-city school and could be a most significant step in accomplishing involvement with disadvantaged students rather than developing pseudo-relationships with "the disadvantaged."

PTI Home Visits

Each participating teacher was given four to six names of youngsters who were to be in their classes and were asked to visit the homes of these students on Thursday of the first week of the Institute.

The participating teachers were prepared for the home visit with a formal presentation of the methods and procedures of a home visit, discussions, and structured role-playing situations in seminar groups. Teachers were set up in teams so that no teacher was compelled to go into any neighborhood alone. Each team of teachers was given a street map of Trenton even though there was an attempt to include a Trenton teacher familiar with the area on each team.

No single assignment given participating teachers seemed to draw as much opposition from them as the home visits. The basic reasons they gave were:

· Home visits should be made after they got to know the students and the students got to know them.
· They had made home visits before and home visits did not do any good.
· The teachers who were from out-of-town would get lost because they did not know the city.
· Some of the neighborhoods were unsafe for white women.
· They had made home visits before and there was nothing they could learn from a home visit.

Despite the rather elaborate preparations by the PTI staff for home visits they were made in many instances reluctantly and with a great deal of trepidation.

The home visits however, proved to be most beneficial to the participating teachers and the Institute on several counts:

· Teachers found that they were considered to be people of importance and that students and parents were flattered to have them in their homes.

· Very few of the homes they visited in very obviously depressed neighborhoods were not clean and did not show some effort on the part of the inhabitants to keep them clean and presentable.

· Parents were most appreciative of this extra effort on the part of teachers. The interest parents felt was reflected in their children.

· The obvious privations of some of the homes pointed out students who might have school problems.

· In several instances students could not be found because of an incorrect address, the family had moved, or the house had been torn down.

Information on and impressions of the students were recorded on 4 in. $\times$ 6 in. cards. Reactions to the actual visit were far different to anticipated reactions of the projected visit. Even teachers who felt they had not "learned" anything by the visit felt that it was an excellent method for most teachers of the disadvantaged to gain some awareness of the students' environment.

The home visits were to bring forth a complaint that was to be repeated time and again. Some of the students recruited by the junior highs and high school were not disadvantaged. There was some truth in this. Nonetheless a very informal and nonscientific check of this complaint revealed some interesting situations.

A knowledgeable Trenton High teacher chose the names of 12 students who on the basis of address would appear to be from economically disadvantaged homes. Also chosen by the same teacher were a similar number of students whose addresses would indicate they came from homes that could not be called disadvantaged. The results of this little experiment were as follows. I was able to visit only eight of the 24 homes. I selected three from the group deemed "disadvantaged" and five from the group thought not to be "disadvantaged." Two of the first group would qualify for the term "disadvantaged" in every way. The third case was open to question. The house was located in a changing neighborhood that had seen better days. The inside of the home was well furnished. The family consisted of father, mother, junior high-age son, and a daughter who was away at a college summer session. My acceptance of refreshments led to an accepted invitation for supper. Conversation revealed that both parents worked. The father was a registered pharmacist and had graduated from a Negro college in North Carolina. The mother had attended the same school for a year and a half and was a practical nurse.

Dinner conversation covered PTI, civil rights, Viet Nam and Negro theatre. All, including the son, participated. Middle-class signs such as books and magazines were well distributed in the upper part of the house. The father mentioned that he planned to move to a better neighborhood when the daughter finished college.

A superficial conversation and the general appearance of the parents would probably lead one to believe that here was a nice colored family with a bright son who could benefit as a result of some of the help available to the "disadvantaged." But I did not think that family qualified as "disadvantaged."

None of the other four visits were as long as the aforementioned visit but they were lengthy enough for me to ascertain that three of the families considered middle class by the Trenton teacher would by several criteria be considered "disadvantaged." Two of the group, a white and a Negro girl, lived in neighborhoods that were obviously in the higher economic bracket. If the young ladies involved were "disadvantaged" it was not economic and it was well concealed.

If there is any conclusion to be reached by my personal experiences it is that sometimes teachers tended to characterize students as "disadvantaged" on the basis of color and address. Home visits can help remedy this misconception. This factor alone will justify the expenditure of time and effort the home visit requires.

PART FIVE

An Evaluation of Teaching Practices and Teacher Training

23. *Princeton-Trenton Institute Evaluation, Summer 1966*

DONALD K. CAREW and MARGARET FLEMING

EVALUATION PLAN

Purpose

The evaluation will attempt to describe the degree to which the 1966 institute met its objective of fostering the development of effective teachers of disadvantaged youth through building pertinent understandings and attitudes. Although the program is teacher-oriented, the evaluation will also examine what effects the program may have produced on the pupils who participated in the demonstration classes associated with the Institute. It is considered that pupil changes are also indications of the Institute's effectiveness.

It is acknowledged from the onset that conclusive judgments about this program cannot be made immediately upon the close of its activities. Real judgment lies in the years ahead when the participating teachers work in the classrooms of the inner city. The achievement of their pupils will be the true evaluation. Plans for the evaluation of this Institute do not include such follow-up procedures.

Dr. Donald Carew and Dr. Margaret Fleming attacked one of the most crucial areas in education. They sought to identify changes in teacher attitudes toward working with disadvantaged youth. Two new instruments were developed by Dr. Fleming for this purpose, and are included in Chapter 23. Although Doctors Carew and Fleming do not claim that their attempts at research are the final word, it should be noted by the editors that it is a significant beginning. Dr. Carew served as Director of the Human Relations and Evaluation Sections of PTI in 1965 and 1966. He is Associate Professor of Education at Ohio University. Dr. Fleming was Research Associate during the 1966 PTI and is also Assistant Chief in the Bureau of Educational Research in the Cleveland Public Schools.

◀ *Photo credit:* **Ken Heyman**

Research Design

Within the framework of a program of limited term and scope such as the Institute, the evaluation will compare certain characteristics considered to be indicative of teacher behavior on a before and after basis. Such comparison presupposes that such characteristics can be at least nominally classified. It trusts that these factors do constitute distinguishing characteristics of the effectiveness of teachers—particularly teachers of disadvantaged youth. In addition, the evaluation will examine student and teacher appraisals of their experiences during the Institute.

Although descriptions of teaching models have been presented in the literature, little evidence has been produced to confirm that the procedures advocated actually do produce optimal response among pupils—especially disadvantaged pupils. Educators find it difficult to measure the effects of changed attitudes of teachers on the achievement of their pupils which, in the final analysis, is the goal of training programs for teachers of disadvantaged youth. Observation appears to indicate that certain teacher attitudes and teaching styles, however, are more conducive to pupil achievement than others.

As a working hypothesis for the evaluation of teacher change, it is believed that certain characteristics may distinguish effective teachers of culturally disadvantaged youth from teachers in general. It proposes that aspects of these differences can be found in the following:

· Understanding of psychological and socio-economic factors operating in the inner-city school climate.
· Attitude toward minority groups and their culture.
· Dominant personal values.
· Perception of role as teacher.
· Perception of disadvantaged pupils.

In addition, it is anticipated that participation in the Institute program may develop for enrollees a more sensitive understanding necessary for effective teaching of disadvantaged youth.

It is admittedly an elusive task to determine any person's attitude with the most sensitive instrument or interview scheme. It is also possible that a person might possess "highly rated" understandings, attitudes, value, and perceptions, but still be an ineffective teacher.

One of the major qualifications of this evaluation is the lack of observational information about the classroom teaching performance of the participants previous to and during the Institute program. With-

Table 23.1 Plan for Evaluation

Objectives	Product and Process Outcome	Instrument	Schedule
1. To promote understanding of the psychological and socio-economic environment of disadvantaged youth	Teacher sensitivity and understanding of disadvantaged youth	Teacher Questionnaire	Post administration
	General effectiveness of the institute	Teacher survey	Pre- and post-administration
2. To provide instruction and experience in the use of new materials as well as proven techniques	Teacher knowledge of methods, techniques, and materials	Teacher Questionnaire	Post administration
		Teacher Survey	Pre- and post-administration
		Pupil Questionnaire	Post administration
3. To provide an opportunity for the participating teachers to test in actual classroom situations these new materials and teaching techniques for the disadvantaged	Teacher performance	Pupil Questionnaire	Post administration
		Pupil Survey	Pre- and post-administration
4. To encourage these teachers to assist in the training and counseling of their colleagues and newly recruited teachers in their school systems	Not evaluated		
5. To develop in the attitudes toward working with disadvantaged youth that will help to promote growth and change	Teacher attitude toward self and others	Teacher Questionnaire	Post administration
		Teacher Survey	Pre- and post-administration
		Study of Values	Pre-administration

out such data, it cannot be definitely stated that a teacher's behavior in the classroom has actually changed. As has been indicated previously, no arrangements for follow-up of the future teaching performance of the participants are possible under the funding arrangements of the program. The participants' teaching performance is after all "the heart of the whole matter" in making judgments about the effectiveness of the Institute program. Perhaps the most to be anticipated with the data that are at hand is communicating to other educators the experiences of one group of persons who have given themselves to the study of their problems as teachers in schools serving disadvantaged youth. There is some comfort for teachers in knowing that many problems in inner-city education are mutual. There is always hope too that these experiences can add some dimensions to the approaches to be considered for these youth.

The plan for evaluation of the Institute appears as Table 23.1. It relates to the program objectives, the dependent variables or behavioral outcomes which are considered indicative of the attainment of the program objective. It also lists the instrumentation used to document these outcomes and the schedule for administration of the instruments.

Two types of objectives are seen as being appropriate for the evaluation: product and process. Product objectives are those having to do with changes in the behavior of the participants. Process objectives are those concerned with the operation of the program.

Instruments

Information for this evaluation report was obtained from the following instruments:

· *Teacher Questionnaire* administered at the close of the program.
· *Cleveland Teacher Survey* scheduled at the opening and close of the program.
· *Cleveland Inventory of Student Self Attitudes* used at the opening and close of the demonstration classes.
· *Pupil Questionnaire* administered at the close of the program.
· *Study of Values* by Allport, Vernon, and Lindzey given at the opening of the program.

Copies of the these instruments are included at the end of part five.

The instruments were used to obtain both "self-report" information and what has been arbitrarily designated as "third-person" data. This was done in an attempt to check both sets of information against each other for validity. The participants were asked direct questions about the effectiveness of the program. They were also requested to react to opinions and situations which hopefully would provide a mirror of their feelings. Multiple-choice questions and open-end questions were combined to draw out all the meaning possible in a rather limited situation. Neither teachers nor students were asked to sign any instrument. A number system was used to relate the data between instruments and between points in time (pre- and post-program).

The Teacher Questionnaire attempted to sample teacher opinion about the implementation of the program and record a self-appraisal of changes.

The teacher survey sought to describe the teacher's degree of acceptance of the stereotypes of disadvantaged youth, his appraisal of the problems of teaching these youth, his estimate of success in teaching them, his rating of teaching methods and techniques, and the degree of his agreement with the statements of authorities about teaching in the inner-city schools.

The pupil inventory was intended to secure pupil ratings of their abilities and feelings for and against school, teachers, and friends.

The Pupil Questionnaire solicited information about pupil reactions to the demonstration classes specifically and to school generally. The questionnaire also contained a personal data sheet which the pupils completed.

The *Study of Values* was used to obtain an objective rating on a standardized instrument of "personal values" held by the participating teachers.

Teacher Sample

Sixty-nine teachers participated in the Institute. They came from New Jersey school systems indicated in Table 23.2.

Fifty-five teachers responded to the Teacher Questionnaire. For the teacher survey, a sample of 56 participants was secured. The group had a median teaching experience of 8.5 years and a range of from one to 31 years in teaching. The range of teaching experience is summarized in Table 23.3.

Fifty percent of the sample hold master's degrees; almost all of

Table 23.2 Participants' School
Systems (N = 69)

Number	School Systems
25	Trenton
27	Newark
12	Burlington
1	Princeton
1	Freehold
1	Hoover
2	Flemington

Table 23.3 Participants'
Teaching Experience (N =
55)*

Number	Years of Teaching
10	1–3
9	4–6
8	7–9
8	10–12
5	13–15
3	16–18
6	19–21
1	22–24
2	25–27
2	28–30
1	31–33

8.5 median; 10.2 mean.

Table 23.4 Participants' College Credits
(N = 55)

Number	College Credits
4	Bachelor's degree
22	Bachelor's degree and graduate work
4	Master's degree
24	Master's degree and graduate work
1	Doctor's degree

those of master's degree status have additional graduate credits. The educational levels attained by the sample appear in Table 23.4.

"Professional improvement" was selected by a majority of the participating teachers as the reason for attending the Institute. Eight teachers list "degree credits" and "stipend" as their reasons. Responses to the question on the Teacher Questionnaire: "Why did you come to this Institute?" include:

"To keep pace with the new developments and improve professionally"—47
"To check on myself"—6
"To gain credits"—5
"To get income (stipend)"—3

One of the purposes in obtaining the responses of the participants in this Institute to the *Study of Values* was to describe their dominant interests. The manual for the *Study of Values* reports information about the norms for various occupational groups for the instrument. The Institute group was compared to the teacher group described in the manual as "126 teachers in Wisconsin junior and senior high schools." It appears that the Institute group was significantly different from this group of educators in five of the six areas. The participants did not significantly differ from the Wisconsin group in political value. The t-values obtained in a comparison of the average scores of the Wisconsin and Institute groups appear in Table 23.5.

Table 23.5 Summary of t-Tests

Group	Theoretical	Economic	Aesthetic	Social	Political	Religious
I Institute:						
Means	39.10	37.03	38.92	40.25	42.12	40.90
S.D.	5.91	7.38	7.80	7.74	6.24	8.06
N	55					
Wisconsin:						
Means	40.10	41.71	32.85	37.32	41.32	44.75
S.D.	7.50	7.91	8.02	5.69	5.78	7.43
N	126					
t-ratio	2.94	4.03	4.67	2.51	.81	2.40
Outcome	< .01*	< .001*	< .001*	< .02*	> .40	< .02*

* significant

It would appear, therefore, that the Institute participants hold aesthetic and social interests to a greater degree than their Wisconsin counterparts, whereas the Wisconsin group is more interested in theoretical values.

An inter-group comparison of the Institute group average scores produces the following t-values:

Table 23.6 Inter-Group Comparison of Dominant Interests

Interest Areas	t-values	df	Outcome
Theoretical vs. Economic	1.69	54	> .05
Theoretical vs. Social	.13	54	> .80
Theoretical vs. Aesthetic	.13	54	> .80
Theoretical vs. Political	1.00	54	> .30
Theoretical vs. Religious	1.35	54	> .10
Economic vs. Aesthetic	1.32	54	> .10
Economic vs. Social	2.26	54	< .05*
Economic vs. Political	3.94	54	< .001*
Economic vs. Religious	2.66	54	< .02*
Aesthetic vs. Social	.88	54	> .30
Aesthetic vs. Political	2.38	54	< .05*
Aesthetic vs. Religious	1.32	54	> .10
Social vs. Political	1.41	54	> .10
Social vs. Religious	.48	54	> .60
Political vs. Religious	.88	54	> .30

* significant

On the basis of this comparison, the Institute participants held higher social, political, and religious values than economic values. They also appeared more politically oriented than aesthetically motivated. Following Spranger's formulation of values reported in the manual, the participants held their highest values in:

· Interest in power (political),
· Love of people (social),
· Quest for unity (religious).

As the manual describes these areas:

". . . The highest value for this type is *love of people*. . . . The social man prizes other persons as ends, and is therefore himself kind, sympathetic, and unselfish. . . . The political man is interested primarily in *power*. . . . Leaders in any field generally have high *power* value. . . . The highest value of the religious man may be called *unity*. He is mystical, and seeks to comprehend the cosmos as a whole, to relate himself to its embracing totality. Spranger defines the religious man as one 'whose mental structure is permanently directed to the creation of the highest and absolutely satisfying value experience.' "[*]

The information from the *Study of Values* is intended to provide a general description of so-called "values" of the Institute participants as a group. It is recognized that any further interpretation should be made with due caution.

Student Samples

A sample of 121 students was obtained on the instruments administered. These are the students who were in attendance during the third period of the next to the last day of the demonstration classes at Trenton Central High. It must be noted that this group generally represents those students who continued to attend the classes throughout the Institute. The results of the first administration of the attitude survey indicate that those students who dropped out rated their abilities significantly higher than those students who continued to attend.

The personal data sheets provide the following information about the student sample:

· Median age is 14.5 years.
· 65 percent were born in Trenton.
· 70 percent hope to attend a college or university.
· 39 percent are from broken homes.
· More than 50 percent have four or more brothers or sisters.
· 72 percent live in separate, detached houses or row houses.
· More than 50 percent of their fathers hold unskilled, semi-skilled or skilled labor jobs.

Significantly, not one of the students responding to the data sheet states that he plans to drop out of school at age 16.

Table 23.7 presents the breakdown of the personal information that was collected from each student.

---

[*] Allport, Gordon W., Philip E. Vernon, and Gardner Lindzey, *Study of Values: Manual,* Boston: Houghton Mifflin Company, 1960, p. 5.

Table 23.7 Description of the Sample* (Number of students = 121)

Item	Number of Students	Item	Number of Students
1. Age		5. How long have you	
11	1	lived in Trenton	
12	2	All my life	71
13	22	Ten years or more	18
14	35	Five to nine years	17
15	44	Two to four years	11
16	16	Less than two years	1
17	1	No answer	3
(mean age—15.51)		6. School plans	
		Drop out at age 16	0
2. Year in school—		Finish high school	23
Sept. 1966		Go to a trade school	12
Seventh grade	1	Go to college or a	
Eighth grade	6	university	85
Ninth grade	36	Other	1
Tenth grade	44		
Eleventh grade	32	7. Occupational plans	
Twelfth grade	1	Professional—law,	
No answer	1	medicine, teaching, etc.	47
		White collar—	
3. Last year's school		Clerical	22
Jr. No. 1	19	Skilled labor	20
Jr. No. 2	17	Nursing	15
Jr. No. 3	25	Entertainment, sports,	
Jr. No. 4	11	politics, modeling	3
Jr. No. 5	12	Small business	1
Trenton H.S.	28	Undecided	10
Other	3	Military	1
No answer	6	No answer	2
4. Place of birth		8. Parents occupational	
Trenton	79	plans for students	
Southern state	19	Parents agree with	
New Jersey	8	my choice	45
Eastern city	11	Parents disagree with	
(not Jersey)		my choice	18
Other U.S. city	2	Parents don't care	40
Puerto Rico	2	No answer	2

Table 23.7 (*Continued*)

Item	Number of Students	Item	Number of Students
9. Parental relationship		13. Type of dwelling	
Live with mother only	32	Separate, detached house	40
Live with father only	6	Row house	48
Live with both parents	75	Duplex	10
Other (uncle, aunt, etc.)	12	Apartment	17
10. Number of siblings		Other	2
None	4	No answer	4
One	20	14. Father's place of birth	
Two	21	New Jersey	26
Three	19	Southern state	38
Four	16	Other U.S. area	11
Five	15	Foreign	12
Six	10	No answer	34
Seven	6	15. Father's occupation	
Eight	4	Unskilled	13
Nine or more	7	Semi-skilled	21
No answer	11	Skilled labor	30
11. Number of people in home		Driver	3
Two	2	Owns small business	6
Three	7	White collar	1
Four	26	Military	5
Five	26	Professional	6
Six	16	Retired or unemployed	2
Seven	15	Deceased	4
Eight	7	No answer	30
Nine or more	17	16. Mother's place of birth	
No answer	5	New Jersey	42
12. Number of bedrooms in home		Southern state	32
		Other U.S. area	13
Two	10	Foreign	4
Three	37	No answer	30
Four	36	17. Mother's occupation	
Five	17	Housewife	27
Six or more	10	Domestic	9
No answer	9	Professional	20
		White collar	9

Table 23.7 (*Continued*)

Item	Number of Students	Item	Number of Students
17. Mother's occupation (*Cont.*)		19. Mother	
Skilled labor	20	Works for someone else	61
Unskilled labor	4	Is self-employed	19
Other (student)	1		
Deceased	4	20. Do you have a part-time job	
No answer	27	Yes	17
18. Father		No	65
Works for someone else	61		
Is self-employed	19		

Institute Program

Although a description of the Institute activities appears elsewhere, it is appropriate to the evaluation report to note briefly the offerings of the Institute.

The initial week of the Institute involved a $2\frac{1}{2}$-day Human Relations Workshop, visits to the homes of the demonstration school students, and preparation of class materials for the school program.

After the first week, 11 of the 69 participants were involved in the Princeton Cooperative School Program which is a residential "upward bound" program held on the university campus. The remaining 58 teachers observed and taught classes of inner-city youth at Trenton Central High School every morning. They formed teaching teams consisting of a coordinating teacher and five participating teachers. For the most part, the teams were organized on the basis of a teacher's subject area. These teams worked together in the classrooms in the morning. They spent the last 40 minutes of each morning in a critique session of the day's activities and a planning session for the following day's classes.

In the afternoons, two teaching teams combined to form a seminar group. In addition, lectures were scheduled in the afternoon and teachers pursued individual study and research.

A resource center was available to all participants. Books and materials from leading publishers were loaned and distributed to the teachers. A number of mimeographed papers relating to disadvantaged youth, the facilitation of learning, and teacher-student relationships were distributed to all the teachers.

EVALUATION DATA

In order to discuss the data in some meaningful way, it was decided to organize the results in terms of the goals of the Institute program. This section of the report presents the data in the following format:

- General effectiveness of the Institute.
- Teacher sensitivity and understanding of disadvantaged youth.
- Teacher knowledge of methods, techniques, and materials.
- Teacher attitudes toward self and others.
- Teacher performance.
- Recommendations.
- Conclusions.

General Effectiveness of the Institute

The reaction of the Institute participants to the program appears to be an overwhelmingly positive one. Data from the Teacher Questionnaire indicate that

- Almost two out of three teachers (61.7 percent) attending rate the Institute as being "much" and "great use" to them in terms of their work as an educator.
- More than nine out of ten teachers (93.2 percent) would recommend this training to colleagues in their school systems.
- Almost nine out of ten teachers (87.2 percent) indicate that their teaching will improve because of the Institute.

Most participants tend to view their contribution to the effectiveness of the Institute as having been in one of five ways:

- Exchanging ideas and sharing views.
- Sharing teaching experiences and demonstrating techniques.
- Bringing honest opinions and an open-minded attitude.
- Helping other participants to be positive in their attitudes.
- Showing a willingness to learn.

The following list of responses show the number of teachers making the foregoing and similar comments to item 4 of the Teacher Questionnaire.

Exchange of ideas, sharing views, active participation (14)
Sharing teaching experiences with others (7)
Helping others to be positive in attitude (7)
My honesty and open-mindedness (6)
Worked with and helped students (4)
Willingness to learn—honesty in evaluating program (3)
Myself (3)
Very little (3)
Demonstration of my techniques (2)
Organization and planning (2)
Try new ideas, experiment (2)
Excellent listener, fair observer (1)
Use of socio-drama (1)
Bringing in community resources (1)
Participation in Trenton High (1)
Did best I could (1)
Meeting different type of Negro (1)
Nothing (1)
Catalytic agent (1)
Constructive criticism (1)
Sincere concern and respect for young people (1)

Almost one out of every two educators (47.2 percent) attending the Institute considered the timing of the Institute to be "good, any time." An additional 29 percent rate it as "just right." The teachers' replies to question 5 of the questionnaire show these choices:

	Percent
"Too late"	5.4
"Too early"	3.6
"Good, any time"	47.2
"Just right"	29
"None of these"	7.2

"Demonstration teaching by the coordinating teachers" is rated as the most effective activity of the institute by the teachers. It appears that teachers are looking for concrete teaching practices carried out in reference to a particular student group. In line with this, they place their own "teaching of the demonstration classes" next in order of effectiveness in contributing to their understanding and growth of experience as a teacher working with the disadvantaged. Third most effective activity is the "home visit" according to the teachers and fourth is the t-group sessions.

The teachers assign the least value to the "critique and planning sessions" and "individual study and research."

The average ranks resulting from those ratings assigned by the responding teachers are summarized in Table 23.8.

Table 23.8 Summary of Averages of Ranks Assigned to
Institute Activities by Participants

Average Rank	Activity
3.1	Demonstration teaching by coordinating teacher
4.1	Teaching the demonstration classes
4.5	Home visits
4.9	T-group sessions (first week)
5.2	Lecture series
5.6	Seminar group meetings
6.7	Resource materials
6.9	Meeting and knowing various individual pupils
7.0	Field trips
7.1	Critique and planning sessions
7.7	Individual study and research

The participants' high opinion of the demonstration classes is also apparent in their majority choice (60 percent) that the classes be continued just as they were this summer. Not one teacher responding says these classes should be eliminated. Ten teachers (18 percent) state that the classes should be continued but that the participating teacher should teach more frequently. Nine teachers would have the classes continued but with a minimum of 25 pupils per class. Responses to question 9 of the Teacher Questionnaire were:

	Percent
"Be continued just as they were this summer"	60.0
"Eliminate them"	No replies
"Be continued, but allow participating teacher to teach more"	18.1
"Other"	16.3
"No answer"	5.4

Some estimate of the degree of effectiveness of the Institute can be gleaned from the responses of the teachers to the question: "What is the most significant thing that happened to you during the Institute?" Apparently most feel that they developed a sensitivity toward students which they did not know before. The sharing of problems with other teachers evidently provides a support teachers are seeking. Learning new teaching techniques as well as seeing "great teachers" influenced other teachers. The teachers name the following significant things:

	Percent
"Sensitivity toward students"	21.6
"Discussing problems with other teachers"	16.3
"Learning new techniques"	10.9
"Chance to see myself as a teacher"	5.4
"Warm friendly feeling, enjoyed working with other participants"	5.4
"Criticism of participating teachers helped me"	3.6
"Seeing great teachers—Mrs. Trout, Mr. Sohn, Mr. Carlin"	7.2
"Positive attitude toward improvement"	5.4

Single responses were obtained for these statements:

"Teaching Time, Space, and Matter program"
"Teaching at Trenton Central High School"
"My association with 12 boys"
"Atmosphere of T-groups"
"Realized I was a better teacher than I thought"
"Nothing"
"Learned how not to teach"
"Trying to influence change"
"Terrorized by T-groups"

Pupils are most positive in their opinions about their experiences in the summer demonstration classes, according to the information supplied by the Pupils' Survey. They consider they will be *more interested in learning than they used to be* as a result of the program.

The pupils report that *they will take part in their classes more than they used to* and *are more sure about speaking up in class.* The responses in Table 23.9 show this positive pattern.

The ingredients which the students consider to be the best thing about the summer school include

· The lab work experiments in science class.
· The afternoon classes and programs in performing arts.
· The understanding and interested teachers.
· The field trips.
· The morning classes in English, social studies, and math.

Table 23.9 Students' Perceptions of Personal Growth

Question	More	About the Same	Less
9. After this summer I think I will take part in classes . . .	84	32	0
13. Because of this summer's work I think that my interest in learning will be . . .	78	31	0
14. Because of this summer's work I feel I will be speaking up in class . . .	70	45	1

Table 23.10 summarizes the student responses in terms of curriculum, teachers, methods, field trips, and general comments.

A close look at the comments seems to indicate that the students appreciate a school climate which communicates an understanding, friendly, respectful, and relaxed atmosphere. This atmosphere, they feel, encourages their open and free participation in the school activities. Perhaps their emphasis on these qualities represents a criticism of the way they feel they are received in their regular school programs. The students appear to be asking that the "threats" be removed from the school situation. They seem to be saying:

· "I need to be respected."
· "I need to be involved and it's easier in a friendly atmosphere."
· "I need to express myself without fear of being ridiculed."
· "I need teachers to be interested and to care about me."

Student perceptions of the pressures in their regular school program are also evident in their responses to the item asking for a description of the differences between regular school and their summer experiences. In addition to some of the obvious differences such as a shorter day and more teachers to help them, they seem to value a freer organization and structure to their school experience. In their comments there is an emphasis also on a *curriculum which is interesting and challenging, a classroom climate which is warm and involving,* and *teachers who are understanding.* There seems to be an appreciation of the fact that schools and teachers can be fun. In the survey, the pupils are less concerned about methods than any of the other categories. They voice a relief at not being burdened with thoughts such as "What will I get next marking period?" Table 23.11 includes the responses to question B-2, organized in terms of five categories.

Table 23.10 Question B-1: The *Best* Thing about this Summer School
Was: (Total responses—282)

Category or Factor	Student Responses	Number of Responses
A. Curriculum		95
	1. The lab work experiments in science class	24
	2. The afternoon classes and programs	20
	3. I learned a lot more than in regular school	9
	4. The interesting topics we studied	9
	5. The English classes	8
	6. The morning classes	6
	7. The math classes	6
	8. The social studies classes	5
	9. The films we saw	4
	10. Learning English in a different way	2
	11. The biology	1
	12. I learned some algebra	1
B. The Teachers		29
	1. The understanding teachers	110
	2. The teachers because they were interested in you	8
	3. The many interesting teachers	8
	4. My teacher	2
	5. Everyone seemed to want to help you	1
C. Teaching Methods		22
	1. The debates and discussions	4
	2. The classes were informal	4
	3. It was easier to participate in a friendly atmosphere	4
	4. Teachers tried to make school pleasant	2
	5. The individual help and attention we got	2
	6. The teachers didn't holler at you	1
	7. We spoke more openly than in other schools	1
	8. The method used in teaching	1
	9. That you could speak up in class	1
	10. We could say what we thought	1
	11. Gave me a chance to express myself	1
D. General		25
	1. The fun we had	5
	2. Not being too strictly supervised	4
	3. The entire idea	3
	4. The small classes	2

Table 23.10 (*Continued*)

Category or Factor	Student Responses	Number of Responses
	5. It was never boring	2
	6. The teachers and the students	1
	7. My classmates	1
	8. You could dress as you pleased	1
	9. The books we got	1
	10. "The whole course was relaxed, fun, and interesting"	1
	11. The free lunch	1
	12. The student council	1
	13. I could get extra credit	1
	14. That it was well organized	1
E. The Field Trips		11
	1. The field trips	11

As a result of the summer program, the majority of students report that they feel better about themselves in a variety of ways—*they can express themselves better in a group; they act better toward others; they do not feel as lazy.* Their attitudes toward school indicate more interest in school and more determination to succeed in college and in life. They find that school can be fun and not just a "drag." They say that they understand and get along better with teachers. They see themselves as having gained in knowledge and responsibility. Table 23.12 summarizes the student appraisals of the ways they have changed this summer.

There is an attrition rate that needs to be considered when any interpretations are made of the student data in relation to this program. Initially, there were 245 students enrolled in the program. On the second day of classes, 228 pupils participated in the initial administration of the Cleveland Inventory of Student Self-Attitudes. For the final administration, 121 students were in attendance during the third period of the next to the last day of the institute. Daily attendance averaged approximately 180 students. Often throughout the course of the Institute, many pupils left at the end of the second period. The students (121) completing the final administration of the inventory do not necessarily represent all of those who regularly attended.

It might be anticipated that those who stayed in the program would be those who felt more positively about themselves. This does not

Table 23.11 Question B-2: This Summer Was Different from Regular School Because: (Total responses = 151)

Category or Factor / Student Responses	Number of Responses
A. Organization and Structure	54
1. It was a shorter day	15
2. There were more teachers to help us	10
3. We had more freedom	7
4. The classes were smaller	5
5. We could dress like we wanted	4
6. There were no grades	4
7. We had a chance to do what we wanted to do	2
8. It was less formal	2
9. I didn't have to come if I didn't want to	2
10. We didn't have to do what we didn't want to	1
11. Free lunch	1
12. There was no recreation	1
B. Curriculum	35
1. The work was more interesting	9
2. There was less homework	8
3. It was easier	6
4. We did more things	4
5. We had a chance to do experiments	4
6. We didn't learn as much	2
7. We learned more	1
8. We went on field trips	1
C. School and Classroom Climate	25
1. It was more fun	15
2. There was an understanding between teachers and students	3
3. Kids are respected more	1
4. We were more relaxed	1
5. Students really worked to learn	1
6. It was more helpful	1
7. It wasn't as strict	1
8. "Everyone seemed lighthearted, not burdened with thoughts such as "What will I get next marking period?"	1
9. "You could let yourself go"	1
D. Teachers	22
1. We had more fun with the teachers	3
2. Teachers were better than regular teachers	3

Table 23.11 (*Continued*)

Category or Factor	Student Responses	Number of Responses
	3. Teachers were more interested in us	2
	4. Teachers were more interesting	2
	5. Teachers spent more time with us	2
	6. Teachers were more understanding	2
	7. The teachers gave us more help	2
	8. Teachers didn't pick on you	2
	9. Teachers were easier to get along with	1
	10. Teachers were more pleasant	1
	11. Of the attitudes of the teachers	1
	12. Teachers were not as cruel as regular teachers	1
E. Methods		17
	1. We could learn at our own speed and not worry about grades	6
	2. The different way of teaching—helped you figure it out, didn't tell you	4
	3. Teachers encouraged us to say what we thought	3
	4. Helped me understand things better	1
	5. You had a chance to improve yourself	1
	6. We did a lot of work ourselves	1
	7. We didn't have books to write from	1

appear to have been the case according to a comparison of the average scores obtained by a random sample of the drop-outs and stay-ins on the initial inventory. Apparently *those who chose to drop out feel better about their abilities* to a significant degree than do those who remained in the program. The t-ratio obtained follows in Table 23.13.

It is difficult, however, to make any assumptions about these young people who chose not to attend the program because attendance was affected by a variety of things—many of which are unknown. The pupils completing the final instruments report that their classmates did not attend the program for three major reasons:

· Lack of interest and motivation.
· Work and other commitments.
· Personal problems.

Whether the lack of interest was generated by the activities of the summer Institute or by the other demands and desires to use their summer time in other ways cannot be determined. It does point

Table 23.12 Question B-5: One Way I've Changed This Summer is:
(Total responses—86)

Category Student Responses	Number of Responses
A. Self Esteem—Self Enhancement	39
1. I can express myself better in a group—not as shy	20
2. I act better toward others	5
3. I am not lazy anymore	4
4. I feel more sure of myself	3
5. I know how to learn better	3
6. I have learned to think more clearly	1
7. I think things out more	1
8. I have more friends	1
B. Attitudes toward School	23
1. I am more interested in my school work	5
2. "I found that school can be fun and not just a drag"	4
3. I'm more determined to succeed in college and in life	3
4. I understand teachers better	2
5. I get along better with teachers	2
6. I pay attention in class	2
7. I like school more	2
8. I have learned that I need to learn more	1
9. I learned to like teachers	1
10. "I can speak up in class because teachers didn't yell at me"	1
C. Curriculum Gains	20
1. I have gained knowledge	8
2. I know more about math and science	4
3. I know more about English and social studies	3
4. I feel I can do better in math now	2
5. In English, I've learned more	1
6. I learned a lot of French	1
7. I read more	1
D. Assumption of Responsibility	4
1. I learned to be prompt	2
2. I tried to be neater in my work	1
3. By not getting into trouble	1

Table 23.13 Summary of t° Test Between Average Scores of "Drop-Out" and "Stay-In" Students on Cleveland Inventory of Student Self-Attitudes

Sample	No.	Average Score	df	t	Outcome	
Stay-ins	100	47.29	129	2.19	$<.05$	$>.02$
Drop-outs	30	45.06				

Table 23.14 Question B-6: Some of My Classmates Did Not Complete Summer School Because: (Total responses—102)

Category	Student Responses	Number of Responses
A. Lack of Interest—Lack of Motivation		78
	1. They weren't interested enough	20
	2. They didn't like it enough	19
	3. They thought it was boring, no fun, no action	15
	4. They were lazy	11
	5. They had the courses before	5
	6. Their friends didn't come	3
	7. They found they didn't have to come	1
	8. They weren't receiving credit	1
	9. They were more interested in other things	1
	10. They didn't like the method of teaching	1
	11. "They liked the street better"	1
B. Work and Other Commitments		20
	1. They got jobs—had to work	10
	2. They went on vacations with their family	5
	3. They wanted to go swimming or something	3
	4. They had to baby sit	2
C. Personal Problems		4
	1. They didn't like the other students	2
	2. They thought it was too hard	1
	3. They didn't want to participate in class	1

up, however, that schools and teachers need to be concerned with the holding power of their programs and must give directed attention to building interest factors. It no longer appears defensible to operate on a "take-it-or-leave-it" basis. If the schools are to fulfil expectations, they must develop programs that will meet the needs as well as the interests of the young people. Table 23.14 lists the responses of the students to the question: "Some of my classmates did not complete summer school because. . . ."

Teacher Sensitivity and Understanding of Disadvantaged Youth

It would appear from the information collected in this evaluation that the participants have sharpened their sensitivity and understanding of disadvantaged youth during the course of the Institute. Self report information from the Teacher Questionnaire indicates

· More than 87 percent *anticipate that their teaching will improve* because of the Institute.
· 78 percent indicate that they *believe they have acquired a new understanding of disadvantaged youth.*

Analysis of the responses on the Teacher Survey reveals *a positive shift in teacher understanding of disadvantaged youth* based on a comparison of the pre-Institute and post-Institute results. These responses for part I of the survey which called for teacher's appraisals of the possibility of change of certain stereotypes of disadvantaged youth are listed in Table 23.15. These data produce a chi-square of 19.98, which for four degrees of freedom is significant at the $<.001$ level. The participants appear most hopeful that an appropriate school program will produce change in those behavioral characteristics of disadvantaged youth which could be classified as learning problems, such as "readiness for school" and "ability to follow directions." They are least optimistic that an appropriate school program could do much to change habits, for example, "smoking" and "drinking."

Another indication of the shift in teacher attitude can be seen in the comparison of the frequencies obtained in the initial and final testing on part IV of the survey. These data, presented in Table 23.16, produce a chi-square of 23.70. With four degrees of freedom,

Table 23.15 Responses to Part I—Teachers' Survey* (N = 56)

Testing	Easily Changed	Frequently Changed	Possibly Changed	Rarely Changed	Don't Know
Pre	191	791	879	316	63
Post	220	838	906	231	45

* Part I contains 40 items.

this is significant at the <.001 level. On the final administration of the survey, the teachers accepted to a greater extent those statements of educators, sociologists, and psychologists which showed approval of the disadvantaged, such as: "The talent in low-income groups is overlooked most frequently by the school." It appears that they rejected to a greater degree those statements supporting the present status quo in education. An example of such an anti-status quo statement is: "Public education has become one of the most effective techniques for maintaining class differences." The least degree of change was in connection with the acceptance of statements showing a knowledge of the research in teaching the disadvantaged. Inspection of the Institute program shows this area did not receive primary emphasis.

Table 23.16 Responses to Part IV—Teachers' Survey* (N = 56)

Testing	Agree	Agree with Reservations	Disagree with Reservations	Disagree	Cannot Say
Pre	587	642	393	471	147
Post	612	749	387	385	107

* Based on 40 items.

Related to these reports is the participants' ratings of the goals attained by the Institute program. The participants assign the highest degree of success to the achievement of the following program goals:

· To stimulate a questioning attitude regarding one's approach and attitude in the classroom.
· To promote an increased awareness and understanding of self and one's effect on others.
· To stimulate some thought about new ways to use oneself as an instrument in stimulating growth and change in students, in the school system, and in society.
· To illustrate the need to and value of involving students in the learning-teaching process.

The teachers view the Institute as having achieved all of its goals with some degree of success. Table 23.17 presents the average ratings of success assigned by the participants to the Institute goals. (See question 12 of the Teacher Questionnaire.)

Another indication of teacher sensitivity and understanding is reflected in the students' responses to item 5 on the Pupil Questionnaire.

Table 23.17 Summary of Average Ratings Assigned by Participants to Institute Goals

Average Rating*	Institute Goal
1.6	d. To stimulate a questioning attitude regarding one's approach and attitude in the classroom. For example: Am I doing what is best for the kids? Am I as effective as I can be?, etc.
1.9	b. To promote an increased awareness and understanding of self and one's effect on others.
1.9	j. To stimulate some thought about new ways to use oneself as an instrument in stimulating growth and change in students, in the school system, and in society.
1.9	k. To illustrate the need to and value of involving students in the learning-teaching process.
2.1	e. To develop or increase one's sensitivity to and understanding of the needs, pressures, concerns, feelings, etc., of students.
2.2	f. To increase awareness of conditions in our society.
2.2	h. To learn new techniques and methods.
2.3	a. To illustrate a variety of creative approaches in the classroom.
2.3	i. Exposure to new and developing curricula and ideas in math, science, English, and social studies.
2.4	c. To develop more sensitivity to and understanding of peer group culture and its influence on the classroom.
2.5	g. To increase awareness of the nature of learning.

* Based on rating scheme of one to five to show degree of success.

Out of 120 students, 97, or 81 percent, reported that this summer's program *had helped them to feel more sure of themselves as persons.* Twenty-two, or 18 percent, indicated that the program had not made much difference in the way they felt about themselves. It seems plausible to assume that the sensitivity and understanding on the part of the teachers might be related to the increased confidence reported by the students.

Teacher Attitudes toward Self and Others

As has been indicated elsewhere in this report, teachers see their attitudes as having changed as a result of this summer Institute, particularly in the area of sensitivity and understanding of students. They consider that among the most successfully attained goals of the Institute are the *promotion of increased awareness and understanding of self and others* and the *illustration of the need and value of involving students in the learning-teaching process.*

Some evidence of teacher attitudes toward others can be gleaned from the Pupil Questionnaire which indicates that 60.7 percent of the students report that the teachers respected them more than they do in regular school. Responses to this item (question 7 of the Questionnaire) follow.

This summer the teachers respected me

	Percent
a. Much more than they do in regular school	60.7
b. A little more than they do in regular school	0.0
c. About the same as they do in regular school	36.8
d. A little less than they do in regular school	1.7
e. Much less than they do in regular school	.8

Because of this summer's program, 96 pupils (80 percent) indicate that they feel they can be better students than they were before. Twenty-three of the students (17.5 percent) assert that they will be about the same as before. Only one student reports that he will be a worse student than he was before.

The problems perceived by teachers before and after the Institute reflect their perception of their task and their attitude toward themselves. In part II of the Teacher Survey, the participants selected the degree of problem associated with teaching the disadvantaged. This was the only section of the survey which produced no significant chi-square statistic. It would appear that the Institute experience did not change the dimensions which teachers perceived about the problem areas of their work. They believed that such tasks as "keeping pupil interest and "securing parental support of school" are still problems to some degree, although an inspection of the frequencies for this part of the survey indicates a shift toward a feeling of less problem, but not a significant shift. Table 23.18 lists the frequencies for this portion of the survey.

This data produced a chi-square of 3.04. It is not significant with four degrees of freedom.

Although teachers still see problems associated with their task, they believe they are more successful in solving certain of these problems. A second portion of part II obtained their ratings of the degree of success they would estimate for themselves in teaching inner-city

Table 23.18 Responses to Part II—Teachers' Survey* (N = 56)

Testing	Not a Problem	A Slight Problem	A Considerable Problem	A Very Great Problem	Don't Know
Pre	138	354	349	247	32
Post	151	363	341	244	21

* Based on 20 items.

pupils. Comparison of the frequencies from the initial and final testing results in a chi-square statistic of 25.82 which is significant at the <.001 level with four degrees of freedom. They saw their success growing to the greatest degree in such areas as discovering pupil talents, adapting instruction to needs of pupils, and "trying new ideas in instruction." They are also hopeful that they can provide "challenging assignments." They still feel a lesser degree of success in "using data obtained from standardized tests."

Table 23.19 summarizes the frequencies obtained on this section of part II.

Table 23.19 Responses to Part II—Teachers' Survey* (N = 56)

Testing	Very Successful	Good Success	Average Success	Fair Success	Unsuccessful
Pre	158	404	316	185	57
Post	155	483	326	121	35

* Based on 20 items.

Teacher Performance

Information from the Pupil Questionnaire provides feedback on the pupil's appraisal of teacher performance. As has been stated in this report, the appeal of the classes, the subjects, and the teachers seems to be the major incentive for pupils to attend the program. As can be seen from the following, about 74 percent of the responses citing reasons for continuing attendance at the Institute in answer to question 2 of the questionnaire fall into these categories.

After you found out what the school was like, why did you keep on coming?

		Percent
a.	I wanted to be with my friends	2.8
b.	My parents wanted me to come	7.6
c.	The classes were fun	16.0
d.	The subjects were interesting	30.1
e.	I liked the teachers	16.5
f.	The teachers seemed to be interested in me	11.2
g.	I like to finish what I've started	13.7
h.	Other	2.8

Again and again, pupil attitude is shown to consider that the summer experience was more interesting and enjoyable (fun) than regular school. A large majority of the students (82.5 percent) consider that summer school was more fun, whereas 70 percent note that the subjects this summer were more interesting than in regular school. Responses to questions 3 and 4 on the Pupil Questionnaire show

This summer school was

		Percent
a.	More fun than regular school	82.5
b.	About the same as regular school	11.5
c.	Not as much fun as regular school	6.0

The subjects this summer were

a.	More interesting than in regular school	70.0
b.	About the same as in regular school	21.0
c.	Less interesting than in regular school	9.0

Pupils have very definite perceptions of what a good teacher should be. They stress in particular the aspects of the student-teacher relationship wherein the teacher is helpful, understanding, interested in them, and kind. Classroom attitude is of concern to them as well. They see the good teacher as being fair and pleasant, yet having qualities of humor, strictness, and honesty. It would appear that there is little variance between the students' perception of the "ideal" teacher and that of the educators. Many of the qualities are evidently mutually desirable. Table 23.20 lists the pupil responses to question B-3A of the Pupil Questionnaire.

Forty-four of the students responding note that they would like

Table 23.20 Question B-3: A Good Teacher Should Be:
(Total responses = 179)

Category or Factor Student Responses	Number of Responses
A. Student-Teacher Relationships	95
1. Helpful	18
2. Understanding	11
3. Interested in each student	10
4. Kind	10
5. Nice to all kids	8
6. Patient	6
7. Interested in how his students feel	5
8. Friendly	5
9. Respected by the pupils	5
10. Considerate	4
11. Respectful of the pupils	3
12. Be concerned about students	3
13. "Someone you can tell your troubles to"	2
14. Good to the students	1
15. Able to get along with his students	1
16. Respectful	1
17. Polite	1
18. Like all his students	1
B. Classroom Attitude	47
1. Fair to every student	6
2. Fun to work with	4
3. Pleasant	4
4. Take time to help students	4
5. Courteous	3
6. Kind of strict sometimes	3
7. One who wants to help you learn	3
8. Not too strict	2
9. Not too easy or too bad	2
10. Cheerful	2
11. Open-minded	2
12. Open and honest	2
13. Help students to find their own answers	2
14. Have a sense of humor	2
15. One who wants you to learn and not play	1
16. Tolerant	1
17. Sympathetic	1
18. Happy all the time	1
19. Not scream all the time	1
20. Informal	1

Table 23.20 (*Continued*)

Category or Factor	Student Responses	Number of Responses
C. Capable—Subject Matter and Methods		18
	1. Well prepared	5
	2. Interesting	3
	3. One who will teach what the students want to learn	2
	4. Stern but flexible	2
	5. Informative	1
	6. Have interesting projects	1
	7. Be able to communicate with *all* students	1
	8. "One who doesn't try to be hip and use a lot of slang"	1
	9. Able to explain the work	1
	10. Smart	1
D. General		12
	1. In school every day	2
	2. On time	2
	3. Dependable	1
	4. Interested in teaching the best he can	1
	5. Able to accept any challenge he might face	1
	6. Interested in teaching	1
	7. Soft-spoken	1
	8. Paid more	1
	9. Responsible	1
	10. Well groomed	1
E. Teacher-Heroes		9
	1. Like the teachers this summer	4
	2. Like Miss Trout	1
	3. Be an example for students	1
	4. Like Mr. Carlin	1
	5. Like Miss Jackson	1
	6. Like Mr. Vybirol	1

to be teachers. They cite the fact that this would enable them to help others as a major reason for this occupational choice. For the 75 pupils who would not like to be teachers, working conditions pose their major objection to such an occupation. It might be inferred that the teachers have presented a "worthy" model to these youngsters. The pupil responses to question B-4A and B-4B are presented in Table 23.21.

Table 23.21 Question B-4A: I Would Like To Be a Teacher
Because: (Total responses = 44)

Category Student Responses	Number of Responses
A. Helping Others	28
1. I would like to help other children	10
2. I would like to help others learn to help themselves	7
3. I would like to help others as my teachers have helped me	6
4. I would like to help children who need help	3
5. I would like to help others with art	1
6. I would like to share knowledge with others	1
B. Working Conditions	16
1. I like children	5
2. I could learn more every day	2
3. I like to see kids learn	2
4. It would be fun	2
5. I like to talk	1
6. I could do a good job	1
7. I wouldn't have to work in the summer	1
8. I like math very much	1
9. It would be an enriching and rewarding profession	1

Question B-4B: I Would Not Like To Be a Teacher
Because: (Total responses = 75)

A. Working Conditions	34
1. They must take too much abuse from some kids	10
2. I would not like it	10
3. It would be the same routine all week—boring	5
4. It is too hard work	5
5. Not enough money	3
6. I don't like children	1
B. Other Preference	23
1. I want to be/do something else	23
C. Feeling of Inadequacy	18
1. I don't have enough patience to work with some kids	12
2. I'm not good at talking in front of a class	2
3. I'm not smart enough	1
4. I don't have the ability to do it well	1
5. I couldn't study enough to be good	1
6. I don't know anything about it	1

Teacher Knowledge of Methods, Techniques, and Materials

As mentioned previously, the teachers believe that their teaching will improve as a result of the experiences of the Institute. That some of this anticipated improvement is related to increased knowledge of methods, techniques, and materials is suggested by the average ratings of several of the goals listed in item 12 of the Teacher Questionnaire. For example, the teachers feel that the Institute was quite successful in:

· Illustrating the need to and value of involving students in the learning-teaching process.
· Helping teachers learn new techniques and methods.
· Exposing teachers to new and developing curricula and ideas in math, science, English, and social studies.
· Illustrating a variety of creative approaches in the classroom.

Of the aspects of instrument that were demonstrated by the co-ordinating teachers, the participating teachers believe that the most beneficial are: *new materials, ideas, methods, and techniques; inductive method; involving students in the learning process; organization and planning techniques;* and *warmth of teacher personality.* The following list includes those comments made on item 10 of the Teacher Questionnaire. The number at the right indicates the number of teachers who responded in a similar way.

New materials, ideas methods, techniques	18
Inductive method	10
Get students involved	6
Organization and planning	6
Warmth of personality—love of teaching	5
Get students to think	3
Rapport among students	2
Confused, disorderly teaching	2
Development of skill building	2
Role-playing	2
Paperback books	2
None	2
Pathfinders	1
Understanding of disadvantaged pupils	1
Audio-visual aids	1
Classroom exhibits	1
SQ3R	1

Sense of humor	1
Reading as communication	1
Knowledge of subject	1
Group discussion	1
Stress success, word failure	1
Teaching reading in social studies	1
Background of literary experiences	1
Motivation	1

In response to question 14 which asked what they think they might do differently when they return to school, most emphasis was placed on *anticipated changes in methods and attitudes toward others.* Some change in curriculum and materials is also expected by the teachers. Table 23.22 includes the responses to item 14 arranged in four categories.

Student responses to item 6 in the student questionnaire suggest that teaching methods and attitudes in the summer school encouraged class participation to a greater degree than in regular school for 60 percent of the students. Responses to question 6 follow.

I participated in class

	Percent
a. Much more than I do in regular school	30.6
b. A little more than in regular school	28.9
c. About the same as in regular school	29.7
d. A little less than in regular school	9.9
e. Much less than in regular school	0.8

According to the Teacher Survey, the Institute participants shifted their ratings of certain methods, techniques, and materials in terms of effectiveness for inner-city children. Results for part III of the survey produce a chi-square statistic of 61.70 which is significant at the .001 level with four degrees of freedom. The greatest change occurred in the participants' abandoning of the response "Don't Know." Table 23.23 lists the frequencies for this section of the survey.

The participants changed to the greatest degree in their rating of progressive teaching activities such as role-playing, field trips, experimenting with laboratory materials, and individualized projects. Their appraisal of audio-visual aids did not change to any degree and only a slight degree of change in terms of less effectiveness is registered in their rating of evaluation activities.

Table 23.22 Question 14—Teacher-Anticipated Changes upon Returning to School   (Total responses = 46)

Category	Teacher Responses	Number of Responses
A. Methods and Attitudes toward Others		28
	1. Involve students more in the learning process—encourage more participation	7
	2. Be more sympathetic to pupils—more aware of needs and problems	7
	3. Experiment to a greater extent and vary my approaches	6
	4. Involve students in social studies more often	1
	5. Apply subject matter to meet student needs	1
	6. Role-playing	1
	7. Help students discover for themselves	1
	8. Use "Time, Space, and Matter" approach	1
	9. Be more open than before	1
	10. Be more patient with the disadvantages	1
	11. A much better job of teaching in all areas	1
B. Curriculum and Materials		8
	1. Seek out new materials and have students take a greater part in planning	2
	2. Use new materials	2
	3. Put greater importance on reading	2
	4. Increase paperback books dealing with Negro	1
	5. Use more audio-visual aids	1
C. General		8
	1. Very little	3
	2. Not sure	3
	3. Everything	1
	4. My first day technique will be changed	1
D. Academic and Professional		2
	1. Fight harder	1
	2. Participate more actively in scholastic affairs	1

Table 23.23 Responses for Part III—Teachers' Survey* (N = 56)

Testing	Very Effective	Effective	Sometimes Effective	Rarely Effective	Don't Know
Pre	224	684	742	323	267
New	312	714	751	332	131

* Based on 40 items.

Conclusions

The information presented in this section provides strong evidence that the Institute was an outstanding success in the eyes of most of the participating teachers and most of the students in the high school. Whether or not there will be any lasting value or real changes in behavior cannot be determined at this point. However, the perceptions of the teachers and students regarding their gains is encouraging and provides some support for believing that the goals of the Institute were achieved in some degree for the majority of the people involved.

The strong positive statements on the part of teachers and students support the conclusions that the Institute was generally effective and that:

· Teachers have increased their sensitivity and understanding of disadvantaged youth.

· Some change in teacher attitudes toward self and others was facilitated.

· There has been an increase in teacher knowledge of methods, techniques, and materials.

· Teacher performances may change as a result of the summer experiences.

It is obvious that the flavor of the Institute was experimental and that the process of education was the primary focus. There was, from the T-groups to the demonstration classes and seminars groups, a *commitment to involvement.* Teachers and students were encouraged in a variety of ways to involve themselves in a cooperative effort directed toward personal growth and the facilitation of the growth of others. Student comments emphasize over and over again that they enjoyed this experience, that they felt better about themselves and about school as a result of the program. They also seem to be saying: "Why can't regular school be exciting instead of a drag?" "Why can't it be fun instead of boring?" "Why can't it be respectful instead of rejecting?" "Why can't it be freeing instead of controlling?"

Certainly PTI will not provide specific answers to questions like these which, in part, grow out of an overburdened and increasingly complex public school system. Perhaps one thing that laboratory programs like PTI can do is to encourage teachers to continue to involve themselves and their students in a *cooperative* effect directed toward change and growth.

24. Teacher Interviews as an Evaluation Tool

MARSHALL STALLEY

This is a report on my activities to assist in the research, guidance, and evaluation phases of the Institute and to conduct seminar sessions in a series of group meetings among the participating teachers on the subject of the use of the community for supportive services as an extension of the classroom.

The role of evaluation was performed by observing the Institute in its various stages and phases; studying the impact of faculty, co-ordinating teachers, staff, participating teachers, and program; endeavoring to determine results in accomplishing the goals of the Institute; and reporting comments of the participants regarding the program. This was secured through observation of and participation in a variety of meetings, sessions and programs, and through conversations and scheduled interviews with a sample of the participating teachers.

The interviewing of the participating teachers was agreed upon as one means of determining the degree to which the objectives were carried out. A random sample of 12 participating teachers was selected. Interviews were scheduled during the early phase of the Institute, the second week, and during the sixth week, which was the final week of the program.

Based on the announced purposes of the Institute and the objectives as described in the written materials which were distributed to the participants, a list of questions and a guide for the interviewing procedure was prepared. The questions and interview guide consisted of two parts: (1) a section used for the first series of interviews with

Marshall Stalley was responsible at the Princeton-Trenton Institute for helping in the evaluation of the PTI program. He developed a series of teacher interviews which he describes in his article. Mr. Stalley is Assistant Director of the Rutgers University Urban Studies Center and was Visiting Lecturer at the Princeton-Trenton Institute in 1966.

the 12 selected teachers, and (2) that used for the interviews with the same participants five weeks later during the closing week of the Institute. This "before" and "after" list of questions for the interview guide is in the Appendix.

In a general meeting of the participating teachers, an Institute staff member explained the purpose of the interviewing, announced the names of the participants selected on a random sample basis, and informed those selected as to the time and place where the interviewing would be conducted.

The interviews were "on the record" and recorded on tape after the reporter explained the procedure and obtained the consent of the persons to be interviewed. The length of the typical interview was 25 minutes and the range was between 20 and 35 minutes.

Several of the questions which were asked in the first sequence were repeated in the second series of interviews and new questions were added, designed to obtain comments, suggestions, and criticisms regarding the program.

The tape-recorded interviews after being transcribed to a written record of the interviews will then be analyzed with the view of determining the nature of the impact of the Institute program on the participating teachers and the extent to which the goals were achieved.

In addition to the formal interviews, conversations were held with the participants and the entire group was divided into three subgroups, based on school districts, and through a process of guided group discussion, comments were obtained through these group meetings in an effort to obtain evaluation by the teacher-participants.

The formal interviews had the value of receiving directly from the participants before and after opinions and reactions which contributed to the evaluation of the Institute as a whole, self-appraisal of success of self, and comments of use for future institutes and other teacher training programs.

In general, it can be said that the participating students "participated." There was widespread and repeated evidence that the program had involved the teachers. The response and reaction of the participants was consistently forthright, direct, readily offered, whether of a favorable or unfavorable nature. The extent of articulation on the part of the participating teachers may be regarded as evidence that the program reached the persons for whom it was intended and provided on the whole a meaningful and constructive experience toward accomplishing the goals of the Institute, namely, to promote understanding of the environment of disadvantaged youth, offer new methods and techniques, encourage teachers to assist in the training of their colleagues in their school systems, and develop attitudes toward working with disadvantaged youth that will help to promote growth and change.

The degree of involvement in the institute experience might also be regarded as evidence of the desire of teachers to do more than they are now doing to improve their teaching skills. The extent of such involvement was deeper than that which might be expected from a "summer teacher training program."

Generally, the members of the group showed interest in receiving new knowledge, further insights, and additional materials to apply to their roles as teachers. Where there seemed to be "school district commitment" to the idea of teacher training in relation to educationally disadvantaged youth, there seemed to be a more favorable response to the Institute, and where this was lacking a less favorable response.

Although the written reports of the interviews are not at this stage available, it is noted that one question in the first series received a response which was unanimous. The question was: "When you were getting your education (to be a teacher), did you learn any things there that have been useful to you in working with disadvantaged youth?" All who were interviewed responded "No," some a resounding "No," and some a hesitant "No"; no one saw a meaningful and helpful connection between his teacher training and what he was doing now in working with disadvantaged. Presumably, what was learned about disadvantaged youth was either known before receiving his training as a teacher or learned "on the job."

The interviews were designed to reveal teacher concepts and descriptions of "disadvantaged" students. A preliminary appraisal of the data leads to the conclusion that this concept was substantially enhanced. Initially, brief statements were offered to the effect that such students "do not communicate," "do not involve themselves in the classroom," and in the subsequent interviews, more detailed descriptions of the student and his home and community environment were offered.

A recurring theme expressed by the participating teachers was the importance of "follow-up." This is interpreted as meaning that in and of itself, the Institute has limited value. The "pay-off" is the extent to which continuing teacher training programs can be carried on during the regular school year, the degree to which teachers may be relieved of the ordinary pressures and schedules of their teaching assignments to engage in such activities, and the extent to which a school system can come to regard the continuing training of the faculty to become more effective in serving the needs of the disadvantaged as an integral part of its over-all goal and a vital component, not peripheral, to the day-to-day work of the teacher.

The Institute served its objective of providing instruction and experience in the use of new materials as well as proven techniques. Some teachers stated that the idea of obtaining the participation of students and "reaching" them to enhance the learning process was a "new" idea. Methods of teaching various subjects were referred to by some teachers as programs which they had read about in journals, but which they had not seen applied. One teacher observed that he had "learned not to talk too much." He referred to the T-group experience as giving him an entirely new approach to teaching which he planned to apply starting in the fall, an approach whereby he would endeavor to obtain the participation of the students in the learning process, with himself in the background, in contrast to his previous approach of day-after-day lecturing to the students.

On the whole, however, it would appear that the Institute was more successful in promoting understanding of the psychological and socio-economic environment of disadvantaged youth than it was in providing instruction and experience in the use of new materials and techniques. This is attributable in the opinion of this writer to the consistency of the "message" in the written material, the lectures, the seminars, and the general viewpoint of the Institute faculty and staff. The total impact of a variety of forms of in-put, either repeating or supplementing each other, had the effect of re-enforcement and of giving a unity of expression to the nature of the urban poor and the understandings and attitudes which are needed to deal effectively with the educational problem which exists in central-city school systems. In some cases teachers as a result of the Institute experience showed evidence of gaining new insights; in other cases, the consistency of the message seems to give "sanction" which they accepted to the notion that where disadvantaged youth have special problems, new understandings, attitudes, and methods may be needed.

Where the teacher's work load seemed overwhelming, or the personal and professional lives of the teachers showed evidence of frustration or disillusionment, teachers tended to put the finger of responsibility on the school system, frequently described as "the bureaucracy." Until the system improves, they pleaded, there is not much more they can do to improve their teaching of students, advantaged or disadvantaged.

Concerning the goal "encourage these teachers to assist in the training and counseling of their colleagues and newly recruited teachers in their school systems," the teachers interviewed for the most part said they proposed to "try." This was stated with real conviction, however, only when they saw opportunities within their institutional structure for reporting and discussing on a basis more receptive than what was described as "teachers' meetings where the principal sticks to his agenda and does most of the talking." One teacher stated in an interview that he would endeavor to organize a "kind of T-group where teachers can talk about their successes and failures without bragging or being defensive."

It is anticipated that such teacher training of other teachers is more likely to take place where several teachers from the same school district were participants in the Institute and where the superintendent, principals, and administration demonstrate an interest in encouraging such teacher growth and development.

There was no clear and consistent evidence of a deep and continuing commitment on the part of the majority of participating teachers to "teaching of the disadvantaged," although a substantial number indicated they "preferred" working with this group of students. Some replied they wanted to work with "both groups" or students "whoever they are." Most of those interviewed before and after stated they expected to be teaching "five or ten years from now," as the question was expressed. Some added—if they could afford it. Several showed evidence of a strong personal and professional commitment to the teaching of the disadvantaged. Most showed a continuing commitment to education, especially to teaching. There was a marked absence of interest in "administration." Teachers acknowledged that administration was necessary, but exhibited a definite tendency to disassociate themselves from such a potential ladder to promotion. A few teachers expressed the opinion that the differential spread between teacher salaries and the salaries of administrators was too great.

A variety of comments, suggestions, and criticisms were offered during the course of the formal interviewing and the informal conversations and group discussions with teachers. These comments are summarized not in order of importance nor reflecting those statements in support of the Institute. They are reported in the interests of program evaluation and as a guide to the planning of future institutes and programs for the training of teachers of the "disadvantaged."

An analysis of the favorable and unfavorable comments, suggestions for change, etc., will be made after the written report of the interviews is available. Some comments are offered in a preliminary fashion to illustrate opinions and attitudes expressed, as follows:

(1)   The seminars (T-groups) were a new experience. Most comments were highly favorable or highly unfavorable. Few teachers appeared "neutral."

(2) The lecturers were described as "good." Several persons suggested that they should have been scheduled immediately after lunch and not as the last event of the day.

(3) Teachers living beyond the central Jersey area with long commuting trips felt the program should have ended earlier in the afternoon. Some said this would have given more time for "reading and reflection."

(4) The Trenton school children were described as not sufficiently under-achievers and the size of the classroom too small to be typical of central-city classes (15 students as opposed to 30 students in the regular classroom situation).

(5) More emphasis should be placed on the "demonstration of new techniques and methods." In some instances this comment appeared to reflect a desire for magical solutions to difficult problems or the wish for reassurance by definite answers to questions which are not readily answerable.

(6) Arrangements are needed to integrate the training of teachers of the disadvantaged as part and parcel of the on-going school system program and the day-to-day job of the teacher.

(7) Greater attention needs to be given to the recruitment and selection of the students, that is, the students from the Trenton schools.

(8) Incentives and opportunities should be offered to the dedicated and effective teacher of disadvantaged to share his experiences with his colleagues and, in general, more opportunity is needed for teachers to observe each other and share their experiences as teachers.

APPENDIX

Questions for Interview Guide for Teachers
Participating in Princeton NDEA Summer Institute

Before

(Mention or establish teacher's name)
  1. What is the highest degree you have received?
     Year?
     Subject-area (education? or a specific discipline)
     Has teaching been the only job since earned degree?

Or worked at other jobs or taken time out from teaching?
Any further (more recent) education?

2. What grade do you teach at present?
   Have you always taught this grade?
   How long (each)?

3. What subject area do you teach at present?
   Have you always taught this subject area?
   How long (each)?

4. What kinds of students have you had in your classroom, in general? (If not mentioned, ask: Have you dealt with many "disadvantaged" students?)
   What kinds of experiences, both rewarding and frustrating, have you had with disadvantaged students?
   What kind of student would you prefer to teach if you had the choice?

5. Which school system do you teach in at present? (that is, Burlington, Trenton, Newark, other)
   How long there?
   Does your school system (city) have any problems unique to that particular area that another city like (Newark/Trenton) would not have?

6. What were your reasons for signing up to participate in this summer Institute?
   What do you feel you will get out of your participation here?
   Do you expect to get anything more than money and credits?)
   (If not mentioned, say: As you know, this institute is designed to help communicate to teachers some ways of working with disadvantaged youth.)
   What do you feel are the main problems of disadvantaged youth?
   When you were getting your education, did you learn any things there that have been useful to you in working with disadvantaged youth?
   Have you been making any special efforts, yourself, to do anything for disadvantaged students in your classes?
   Is there anything more you could be doing?
   How do you feel about learning new ways of working with disadvantaged youth? (Do you feel there are actually some things that you can learn by being here for this six-week period?)

7. Some people feel that this type of student doesn't have the capacity to do the work required of them, so there's no point in spending more time and money on them. How do you feel about this issue?

8. Some people feel that even if this type of student did get a high school or college education, there wouldn't be any jobs for them (or they would not have the same opportunity of getting jobs).
   How do you feel?

9. Others feel that the students' family problems are so bad that they can't study at home, and can't concentrate in school, so there's no point in trying to work with them. How do you feel about that?

10. What do you think can be done, if anything, to help disadvantaged youth in schools?

11. Here are some things that have been said about disadvantaged youth—please comment briefly, telling me whether you agree or disagree with the description.
    Disadvantaged youth:
    > lack skills
    > lack education
    > lack opportunity
    > lack hope
    > lack ability
    > lack intelligence
    > lack initiative
    > lack motivation

12. Which sort of teaching experience would give you the most satisfaction?
    (a) Teaching a person who has had little previous opportunity to learn but may have potential, or
    (b) teaching a bright, dedicated person who comes from a good cultural background and has good opportunities for college.

13. Is it true that disadvantaged students are dull, do not ask questions, or have much insight into problems?
    If this is so, can anything be done to motivate them?

14. How is the best way to evaluate whether or not the disadvantaged student is learning anything? (if not mentioned, ask: Is IQ the only way to evaluate such a student?)

15. How did other teachers (colleagues) in your school feel about your coming to this institute?

    Do you think they will be interested in hearing about and using any new materials and techniques you may tell them about?

16. What do you expect to be doing, say five or ten years from now?

    Will you still be *teaching?* (or in administration? or in subject-matter field?)

    If still teaching, what sort of teaching environment would you like to see for yourself five to ten years from now? (for example, probe to get at whether really wants to continue to work with "problem" or disadvantaged students, or if wants to move to "better" type of school system, or to college or preschool, or junior college, etc.)

    If not teaching, why do you plan to leave teaching?

After

1. We have talked about some of these questions when we spoke together a few weeks ago, and some of the questions are new. What sorts of students have you worked with, in general, in your teaching experience?

    (The point of this question is not to repeat the same information, but to steer the discussion toward the teacher's description of "disadvantaged students—to help determine if anything has been changed in his/her "understanding of the environment of the youth.")

    What do you feel are the main problems of disadvantaged youth? Do you feel there is anything you could be doing in your own classes to help disadvantaged youth?

2. Some teachers feel this type of student doesn't have the capacity to do the work required of them, so there's no point in spending more time and money on them. How do you feel about this issue?

3. Some (other teachers) feel that even if this type of student did get a high school or college education, there wouldn't be any jobs for them (or they would be prevented from getting jobs). How do you feel?

4. Others feel that the students' family problems are so bad that they can't study at home, and can't concentrate in school, so

there's no point in trying to work with them. How do you feel about that?

5. How is the best way to evaluate whether or not the disadvantaged student is learning anything? (Is IQ the only way to evaluate such a student?)

6. What do you feel you got out of your participation here? (Get anything more than money and credits?)
   Do you think your colleagues (in your school district at home) will be interested in hearing about using any new materials and techniques you may want to tell them about?

7. What would you have liked to have had done differently during this Institute?
   What changes would you make if you were to run (or attend) it next year?

8. What will you probably be doing say five or ten years from now? (If teaching, probe to get specific aspirations re: teaching disadvantaged vs. other students)
   If not teaching, why do you plan to leave teaching?

9. Do you have any other comments or suggestions regarding the Institute?

25. *Appendix   Questionnaire Survey Forms for Evaluation*

Princeton-Trenton Institute

CLEVELAND TEACHER SURVEY*

There are no right or wrong answers to the survey items. We would like your help in collecting information about many of the issues and problems associated with teaching in inner-city schools.

Do not sign your name to any of these papers. Use the permanent number which has been assigned to you to identify your answer sheet. Retain the envelope containing your permanent number for use at a future time.

Please follow the directions which relate to the various sections of this survey.

Kindly give your position on the survey items as they first impress you. Indicate what you believe, rather than what you think you should believe.

---

* Developed by Margaret Fleming, Cleveland Public Schools.

Part I

Directions

Part I contains a list of behavioral characteristics which teachers have attributed to inner-city pupils from time to time. If an appropriate school program were provided, what possibility of change do you see in these characteristics? Record your responses for this section in Part I, items 1–40, of the answer sheet. Please use the following scale:

    a. Easily changed
    b. Frequently changed
    c. Possibly changed
    d. Rarely changed
    e. Don't know

(Please record answers
on answer sheet)

	a	b	c	d	e
1. Use of profanity					
2. Little self-respect					
3. "Chip on shoulder"					
4. Aggressiveness					
5. Smoking					
6. No readiness for school					
7. Lack of suitable models to emulate					
8. Poor grooming					
9. Lack of manners					
10. Impulsiveness					
11. Insolence					
12. Boisterousness					
13. Dishonesty					
14. Dislike of school					
15. Dislike of teachers					
16. Anti-intellectualism					
17. Poor motivation					
18. No well-defined vocational goals					
19. Distrust of authority					
20. Drinking					

	a	b	c	d	e
21. Little participation in school-sponsored activities					
22. "Sloppy work"					
23. Substandard speech habits					
24. Lack of study skills					
25. Do not follow directions					
26. Inadequate listening skills					
27. Are nonreaders					
28. Poor experiential background					
29. Fear of tests					
30. Inability to work within time limits					
31. Rarely complete homework					
32. Cutting classes					
33. Truancy					
34. Low scholastic aptitude					
35. Fear of failure					
36. Inability to handle abstract ideas					
37. Short attention span					
38. Vandalism					
39. Defiance of authority					
40. Extreme clothing styles					

End of Part I. Please continue with Part II.

Part II

Directions

Please locate Part II on your answer sheet. Your responses for Part II should be recorded in items 41–60.

What do you see as problems in the teaching of inner-city youth? Using the following scale, please select the response which matches your opinion.

  a. Not a problem
  b. A slight problem
  c. A considerable problem
  d. A very great problem
  e. Don't know

	a	b	c	d	e
41. Keeping pupil interest					
42. Maintaining class order					
43. Securing parental support of school					
44. Providing challenging assignments					
45. Teacher's experience with inner-city pupils					
46. Ability grouping					
47. Accessibility of resource persons					
48. Discovering pupil talents					
49. Estimating scholastic potential					
50. Teacher's interest in inner-city pupils					
51. Evaluation of pupil progress					
52. Appropriate teaching methods					
53. Appropriate materials					
54. Providing instruction to meet needs					
55. Interpretation of test results					
56. Teacher's understanding of inner-city pupils					
57. Diagnosing pupil needs					
58. Quality of textbooks					
59. Applying findings of experts					
60. Meeting goals of course of study					

Directions

Beginning with item 61 on your answer sheet, please continue with this section of Part II.

The following are certain factors in the teaching situation. In line with your experience in the classroom, what degree of success have you had, or feel you would have, in teaching inner-city pupils?

Using the following scale, please mark the letter of the response which matches your feeling.

a. Very successful
b. Good success
c. Average success
d. Fair success
c. Unsuccessful

	a	b	c	d	e
61. Maintaining pupil interest					
62. Using data obtained from standardized tests					
63. Applying findings of experts to teaching					
64. Securing cooperation of disruptive pupils					
65. Respecting pupils					
66. Discovering pupil talents					
67. Adapting instruction to needs of pupils					
68. Determining needs of pupils					
69. Trying new ideas in instruction					
70. Providing concrete illustrations					
71. Relating instruction to pupil experiences					
72. Securing parental support of school goals					
73. Evaluating pupil progress					
74. Providing experiences in democratic practices for pupils					
75. Counseling pupils on vocational goals					
76. Encouraging pupil identification with suitable adult models					
77. Facilitating pupil discussion					
78. Using role-playing techniques					
79. Providing challenging assignments					
80. Showing pupils how to study					

End of Part II.

Part III

Directions

On Part III of your answer sheet, record your responses for this section in items 81–120.

The following is a list of activities, methods, techniques, and devices used in teaching.

Consider the effectiveness of these procedures for inner-city children.

Please indicate your rating of these procedures using the following scale:

   a. Very effective
   b. Effective
   c. Sometimes effective
   d. Rarely effective
   e. Don't know

	a	b	c	d	e
81. Teacher lecture					
82. Teacher demonstrations					
83. Teacher use of blackboards					
84. Teacher's questioning of class					
85. End of course test					
86. Letter marks (A, B, etc.)					
87. Point systems for pupil progress					
88. Percentage marks (89%, 70%, etc.)					
89. Adjective rating system: good, satisfactory, unsatisfactory					
90. Standardized tests					
91. Class textbook					
92. Paperback books					
93. Blackboard work for pupils					
94. Classroom collections of books					
95. Class officers					
96. Class discussions					
97. Directed study periods					
98. Nondirected study periods					
99. Discussion of personal problems					

	a	b	c	d	e
100. Experimenting with laboratory materials					
101. Field trips					
102. Keeping notebooks					
103. Individualized projects					
104. Making models					
105. Making posters					
106. Movies					
107. Oral reading in class by pupils					
108. Reading newspapers					
109. Reading primary source documents					
110. Pupil panels					
111. Using workbooks in class					
112. Reading paraphrased literary pieces					
113. Role-playing					
114. Viewing, using, and discussing pictures (photographs and paintings)					
115. Using teacher-prepared worksheets					
116. Using programmed materials					
117. Writing poems					
118. Writing autobiographies					
119. Writing creative compositions					
120. Writing book reviews					

End of Part III.

Part IV

Directions

For Part IV, please record your responses on the answer sheet for items 121–160.

The following statements represent opinions rather than facts. As opinions, they are neither right nor wrong. Kindly record on the answer sheet which position you take on these statements as they first impress you. Indicate what you believe, rather than what you think you should believe, using the following scale:

a. I agree with the statement
b. I tend to agree with the statement (with reservations)
c. I tend to disagree (with reservations)
d. I disagree
e. I cannot say (have no feeling one way or another)

	a	b	c	d	e
121. Public education has become one of the most effective techniques for maintaining class differences.					
122. The higher the socio-economic status of the pupils, the higher the educational achievement.					
123. An IQ score indicates the needs of the child in education.					
124. Children from disadvantaged families need a different educational approach than children from middle-class families.					
125. Being a resident of the inner-city is largely a function of discrimination.					
126. Being culturally disadvantaged is often due to a lack of the desire to get ahead.					
127. "Culturally disadvantaged" should be replaced with the term "socially rejected" in the final analysis.					
128. Inner-city children usually find schools unprepared to cope with their problems.					
129. A major reason for low school achievement of inner-city children is a low level of scholastic ability.					

	a	b	c	d	e

130. Low-income groups would improve them- if they were given a chance.

131. Illiteracy is the largest single factor that gets and keeps people on relief.

132. School dropouts are better off out of school where they cannot disrupt classes.

133. The talent in low-income groups is over-looked most frequently by the school.

134. The same range of achievement exists in all socio-economic levels.

135. A score on a scholastic aptitude test indicates a child's readiness to cope with school.

136. Many current educational programs for the disadvantaged will have to overcome the dis-trust of the public

137. It has been demonstrated that the mental style of low-income youngsters strongly re-sembles that of one type of highly creative person.

138. Teachers are unprepared to handle the needs of the inner-city child.

139. The class system in America is an open sys-tem for anyone "who has it in him" to climb the ladder of success.

140. Middle-class values should determine the organization of the classroom and the con-tent of the curriculum because that is what the inner-city pupil must master if he will succeed.

141. There is a need for better measures of a child's experiential, rather than mental, age.

142. The school will succeed if it can utilize the positive values which the inner-city child's environment has developed in him.

143. Lack of experience keeps the inner-city child from maturing in the areas of perception, language, cognition, and interpersonal skills.

144. Schools in the inner-city should have objec-tives different from the usual standards.

	a	b	c	d	e

145. About 50 percent of the junior high school pupils in inner-city areas need massive remedial work if they are to be brought up to grade level.

146. There are learning styles among the low-income groups that represent unique, untapped sources of creativity.

147. There is a need for the school to take over some of the tasks of the home in developing the child's readiness for school.

148. The inner-city child's home is his greatest liability against school success.

149. Just about every type of personality can be found among the culturally disadvantaged.

150. Most teachers cannot value the view of the world accepted by many inner-city families.

151. Dropouts are revolting against a deep and pervasive attack upon their integrity as human beings when they leave school.

152. Children from disadvantaged areas bring into the classroom psychological problems which interfere with the educational process in the classroom.

153. It is unrealistic to pretend that all disadvantaged children will ever reach average levels in school performance.

154. A just criticism of the school is that it is geared to prevent minority group pupils from achieving middle-class levels.

155. Exhorting the stricken to reform themselves is an ancient substitute for constructive social action.

156. Parents in the inner-city tend to be interested in their children as are parents in other areas.

157. American society has established norms which assume that most of the minority group members will not be able to attain majority standards.

	a	b	c	d	e

158. When judgments about pupils' ability determine what is done for them, the results tend to justify the assumptions.

159. Culturally disadvantaged people result from the process that deliberately and chronically victimizes them at the hands of the larger society in general.

160. The retention of inner-city pupils in a grade will never produce the mastery of subject matter for which it is indended.

August 2, 1966

❈ ❈ ❈ ❈ ❈

We would appreciate your reactions to the following questions about this summer's program. Please indicate your choices by placing a check at the item or by writing your brief comments where required.

1. Much of what you heard and saw this summer, in terms of your work as an educator, could be termed
   a. _____Of great use
   b. _____Of much use
   c. _____Of some use
   d. _____Of little use
   e. _____Almost useless

2. Would you recommend this program to your colleagues in your school system who might not yet have taken this type of training?
   a. _____Yes
   b. _____Yes, with reservations
   c. _____No
   d. _____No, with reservations

3. Do you anticipate that your teaching (or counseling, supervising, etc.) will improve because of the Institute?
   a. _____Yes
   b. _____No
   c. How?_____

4. What do you think that you as an individual have contributed to the effectiveness of the Institute?

5. The timing of the Institute for you as an educator was
   a. _____Too late
   b. _____Too early
   c. _____Good, any time
   d. _____Just right
   e. _____None of these

6. Because of this summer's program, have you gained any new understanding of disadvantaged youth?
   a. _____Yes
   b. _____No
   c. Name one example: _____

7. Please *rank* the following activities in terms of how effectively they contributed to your understanding and the growth of your experience as a teacher or supervisor working with the disadvantaged (use 1 for the most effective activity, 2 for the next most effective, then 3, and on through 11, etc.):
   a. _____Demonstration teaching by coordinating teachers
   b. _____Lecture series
   c. _____T-Group sessions (first week)
   d. _____Resource materials
   e. _____Home visits
   f. _____Critique and planning sessions
   g. _____Meeting and knowing various individual pupils
   h. _____Teaching the classes
   i. _____Field trips
   j. _____Seminar group meetings
   k. _____Individual study and research

8. If you were to change some aspects of this program to make it a more suitable one, generally what would you suggest?

9. As a feature of this training program, which of the following represents your opinion of the demonstration classes?
   a. _____Be continued just as they were this summer
   b. _____Eliminate them
   c. _____Be continued, but allow participating teacher to teach more
   d. _____Other: _____

10. The coordinating teachers demonstrated what aspects of instruction which you consider beneficial, if any?
    a. _____
    b. _____

11. Why did you come to this Institute?

12. The following list contains some things that might be considered goals of the Institute. Please indicate, by writing the appropriate number (1,2,3,4, or 5) at the left of each statement, how successful the Institute was in achieving or in helping you achieve each goal. Use this scale:

1. Extremely successful
2. Quite successful
3. A little successful
4. Not successful
5. Extremely unsuccessful

For example, if you feel that the Institute was a little successful in achieving goal (a) for you you should put the number 3 in the space to the left.

a. _____ To illustrate a variety of creative approaches in the classroom.

b. _____ To promote an increased awareness and understanding of self and one's effect on others.

c. _____ To develop more sensitivity to and understanding of peer group culture and its influence on the classroom.

d. _____ To stimulate a questioning attitude regarding one's approach and attitude in the classroom. That is, Am I doing what is best for kids? Am I as effective as I can be, etc.

e. _____ To develop or increase one's sensitivity to and understanding of the needs, pressures, concerns, feelings, etc., of students.

f. _____ To increase awareness of conditions in our society.

g. _____ To increase awareness of the nature of learning.

h. _____ To learn new techniques and methods.

i. _____ Exposure to new and developing curricula and ideas in math, science, English, and social studies.

j. _____ To stimulate some thought about new ways to use oneself as an instrument in stimulating growth and change in students, in the school system, and in society.

k. _____ To illustrate the need to and value of involving students in the learning-teaching process.

13. What is the most significant thing that happened to you during the Institute?

14. As a result of this summer's Institute what do you think you might do differently when you return to your school?

15. Years of teaching experience:_____years
16. College credits:
    a._____Bachelor's degree
    b._____Bachelor's degree and graduate work
    c._____Master's degree
    d._____Master's degree and graduate work
17. Other comments—suggestions or criticisms.

CLEVELAND INVENTORY OF STUDENT SELF-ATTITUDES*

Name:_____   Date:_____

Directions

The following are some statements on which you are asked to rate yourself. For each of the statements circle the number which you think best describes yourself at the present time.

Abilities   My Ability Is at Present

	Very great	Great	Average	Not too great	Some-what small
1. To make up my mind	1	2	3	4	5
2. To be a leader	1	2	3	4	5
3. To work by myself	1	2	3	4	5
4. To solve problems	1	2	3	4	5
5. To speak before the class	1	2	3	4	5
6. To tell my ideas in writing	1	2	3	4	5
7. To do what I think is right	1	2	3	4	5
8. To think clearly	1	2	3	4	5
9. To carry out responsibility	1	2	3	4	5
10. My understanding of social studies	1	2	3	4	5
11. My ability in English	1	2	3	4	5
12. My reading ability	1	2	3	4	5
13. My math ability	1	2	3	4	5
14. My intelligence	1	2	3	4	5
15. My science ability	1	2	3	4	5
16. My ability to get along with others	1	2	3	4	5
17. My self-confidence	1	2	3	4	5
18. My interest in school	1	2	3	4	5
19. My imagination	1	2	3	4	5

* Developed by Margaret Fleming, Cleveland Public Schools.

Directions

Some pairs of words that are used to tell about things follow. Please tell how you feel about these things by placing a check on one of the lines between the words.

For example, if you feel that *homework* is "easy" *all of the time* place a check on the first line after "easy." If you feel that *homework* is "hard" *all of the time,* place a check on the line before "hard."

If you believe that *homework* is "easy" *most of the time or* "hard" *most of the time,* place a check on the second line in from either "easy" or "hard." Choose the third line in if you feel homework is often "easy" or often "hard."

(In the following sample, the pupil placed a check on the middle line between "hard" and "easy" beause he felt that homework was sometimes "easy" and sometimes "hard.")

Put only one check on a line.

Homework

| Easy | ____ | ____ | ____ | ____ | Hard |

School

Good	____	____	____	____	Bad
Fair	____	____	____	____	Unfair
Interesting	____	____	____	____	Drag
Like	____	____	____	____	Hate
Helpful	____	____	____	____	Not helpful
Organized	____	____	____	____	Disorganized
Easy	____	____	____	____	Hard

Teachers

Good	____	____	____	____	Bad
Fair	____	____	____	____	Unfair
Interesting	____	____	____	____	Drag
Like	____	____	____	____	Hate
Helpful	____	____	____	____	Not helpful
Organized	____	____	____	____	Disorganized
Easy	____	____	____	____	Hard

Other Pupils

Good	____	____	____	____	Bad
Fair	____	____	____	____	Unfair
Interesting	____	____	____	____	Drag
Like	____	____	____	____	Hate
Helpful	____	____	____	____	Not helpful
Organized	____	____	____	____	Disorganized
Friendly	____	____	____	____	"Fight"

PRINCETON-TRENTON INSTITUTE

Student Evaluation of Morning Classes

Your answers to the following questions will help us in planning future summer schools. Please be as honest as possible, and do not put your name on the questionnaire.

A. *Circle* the word or phases which describe the way you feel. You may want to circle more than one answer for some questions.

1. Why did you attend this summer school?
   a. I was behind in school and wanted to catch up.
   b. My parents wanted me to come.
   c. My principal urged me to come.
   d. My teacher urged me to come.
   e. I wanted to get a head start in high school.
   f. I came because some of my friends were coming.
   g. I wanted something to do this summer.
   h. Other (please describe) _____

2. After you found out what the school was like, why did you keep on coming?
   a. I wanted to be with my friends.
   b. My parents wanted me to come.
   c. The classes were fun.
   d. The subjects were interesting.
   e. I liked the teachers.
   f. The teachers seemed to be interested in me.
   g. I like to finish what I've started.
   h. Other (please describe) _____

3. This summer school was
   a. More fun than regular school.
   b. About the same as regular school.
   c. Not as much fun as regular school.

4. The subjects this summer were
   a. More interesting than in regular school.
   b. About the same as in regular school.
   c. Less interesting than in regular school.

5. This summer's program has
   a. Helped me to feel more sure of myself as a person.

    b. Has not made much difference in the way I feel about myself.

    c. Has made me feel less sure of myself as a person.

6. I participated in class
   a. Much more than I do in regular school.
   b. A little more than in regular school.
   c. About the same as in regular school.
   d. A little less than in regular school.
   e. Much less than in regular school.

7. This summer the teachers respected me
   a. Much more than they do in regular school.
   b. A little more than they do in regular school.
   c. About the same as they do in regular school.
   d. A little less than they do in regular school.
   e. Much less than they do in regular school.

8. Because of this summer I
   a. Feel that I can be a better student than I was before.
   b. Feel that I will be about the same as before.
   c. Feel that I will be a worse student than I was before.

9. After this summer I think I will take part in classes
   a. More than I used to.
   b. About the same as I used to.
   c. Less than I used to.

10. I feel that I learned
    a. A great deal about what science is this summer.
    b. A little bit about what science is this summer.
    c. Nothing about what science is this summer.

11. I feel that I learned
    a. A great deal about English this summer.
    b. A little bit about English this summer.
    c. Nothing about English this summer.

12. I feel that I learned
    a. A great deal about social studies this summer.
    b. A little bit about social studies this summer.
    c. Nothing about social studies this summer.

13. Because of this summer's work I think that
    a. I will be more interested in learning than I used to be.
    b. I will have the same interest in learning as I used to have.
    c. I will be less interested in learning than I used to be.

14. Because of this summer's work I feel
  a. More sure of myself about speaking up in class.
  b. About the same about speaking up in class.
  c. Less sure of myself about speaking up in class.

B. Please complete the following.

1. The best thing about this summer school was _____

2. This summer was different from regular school because _____

3. A good teacher should be _____

4. Complete either a or b.
  a. I would like to be a teacher because _____

  b. I would not like to be a teacher because _____

5. One way that I have changed this summer is _____

6. Some of my classmates did not complete summer school because

Personal Information

1. Age at last birthday _____.
2. Next year I will be in the _____ grade.
3. Last year I went to _____ school.
4. Place of birth _____.
                        (city)   (state or county)
5. How long have you lived in Trenton? _____
6. Where did you live before? _____
7. School plans: (circle correct letter)
  a. I would like to drop out of school at age 16.
  b. I would like to finish high school.
  c. I would like to go to a trade school.
  d. I would like to go to a college or university.
  e. Other (explain) _____

8. What kind of work do you want to do when you finish school?
9. What kind of work would your parents like you to do? _____
10. Family background: (circle correct letter)
    a. I live with my mother.
    b. I live with my father.
    c. I live with both my mother and my father.
    d. Other (explain) _____
    _____

11. How many brothers and sisters do you have? _____
12. How many people live in your home? _____
13. How many bedrooms are there in your home? _____
14. Do you live in (circle the correct letter)
    a. A separate, detached house?
    b. A row house?
    c. A duplex?
    d. An apartment?
    e. Other (explain) _____
    _____

15. My father was born in _____.
16. My father works as a _____.
17. My mother was born in _____.
18. My mother works as a _____.
19. My father (circle correct letter)
    a. Works for someone else.
    b. Is self-employed.
20. My mother (circle correct letter)
    a. Works for someone else.
    b. Is self-employed.
21. Do you have a part-time job? (circle correct letter)
    a. Yes (if yes, describe)_____
    _____

    b. No.

26. Postscript

A Warning Against Conclusions

The Princeton University-Trenton Schools Institutes were directed to 109 teachers from six school systems. This report is intended as a means of allowing a reader to make up his own mind, based on the detailed accounts of the staff and coordinating teachers. This report, then, is offered as data from which judgment may be drawn about teaching methods and teacher attitudes.

To state specific conclusions or recommendations at this point would be presumptuous and hazardous. It would be presumptuous because the true effects of this summer cannot be fully known for years to come; it would be at least partly misleading. No one person can possibly know all that took place in two projects involving nearly 400 students and teachers.

Yet there is unanimous agreement upon one point: students will respond when they know that their response is valued.

There was in these Institutes a clear thread of inductive teaching—to use a somewhat technical term for a moment—but in the last analysis inductive teaching must always depend upon student response. Student response depends upon classroom climate, upon the "tone" set by the teacher. In this respect as is so often true, the teachers can learn from the students.

Appendix

27. Plan of Operation for NDEA Summer Institute for Teachers of Urban Youth—June 27– August 6, 1966

A. Introduction

The plight of the disadvantaged has been reported widely and documented extensively. The most widespread and dramatic confrontation between disadvantaged youth and social institutions takes place in the schools, which for many such students is a hostile and frustrating environment. Fear, ignorance, and deprivation feed on each other and the indivdual becomes entrapped by lack of skills, lack of education, lack of opportunity, and, finally, lack of hope. For many teachers, assigned to teach in the inner city, the challenge of teaching and the satisfaction of accomplishment are lost in the daily battle to maintain a tenuous and often precarious *status quo*. Lost, too, as a consequence, are their hopes for their students who do so badly and need their help and their hopes.

In the school systems of Trenton, Burlington, and Newark, New Jersey, there are many disadvantaged children who stand in most serious need of special help from their teachers.

Trenton has a population of 114,000 living in an area of 7.2 square miles. The 1960 census figures reveal a Negro population of about 25 percent (there is reason to believe that this figure is higher today—58 percent of Trenton's school children this year being colored), and a family income of $3000 or less for 4600 of the 27,000 families living in Trenton at that time. Poverty and near-poverty were found to be fairly evenly distributed throughout this geographically compact city and thus every one of its 700 public school teachers may be aptly described as a teacher of disadvantaged youth. The degree of educational impoverishment in Trenton is suggested by the finding, again of the 1960 census, that of the 71,000 men and women 25 years or more of age, 17,806 had completed six years of school or less.

The total population of Newark in 1960 was 405,220 and over 19 percent of its families received incomes that year of $3000 or less. In the same year 14.4 percent of Burlington's families were similarly impoverished. Although poverty is not as evenly distributed through these cities as it is in Trenton, those teachers with significant obligations to disadvantaged youth are readily identifiable for purposes of providing special training or support.

As to educational impoverished, in both Burlington and in Newark, as in Trenton, many of the schools' problems are at least the indirect consequence of the cities' large populations of only partially educated adults. In Newark 53,514 adults (25 years old or more) had completed only six years of schooling or less, and in Burlington County over 12 percent of the same age group was similarly deficient in schooling. (1960 census data: no education statistics available for the City of Burlington alone.) The children of these, in most cases, functionally illiterate adults are students in the cities' elementary and secondary schools today. If these children are to achieve through education a place of worth and consequence in our society, their teachers must be prepared in extraordinary ways to support them. Standard educational strategies have proven as ineffective in breaking the vicious cycle of educational deprivation as have conventional economics in breaking the vicious cycle of material deprivation.

In the face of these conditions Princeton University proposes to initiate, in cooperation with the school systems of Burlington, Newark, and Trenton, a six-week summer institute for the teachers of disadvantaged youth.

We are encouraged to make this proposal by several circumstances:

· The proximity to the three cooperating cities of the university's more than adequate educational plant and facilities, unencumbered by any full-scale summer school program.

· The well-established precedents of successful joint endeavor with all three school systems in the Princeton Cooperative Schools Program for disadvantaged youth (funded in December 1963 with a grant from the Rockefeller Foundation) and, even more pertinently, with the Trenton school system in last year's Institute for Teachers of Disadvantaged Youth.

· The useful advisory presence of the Princeton-Trenton Council, a group composed of six Trenton teachers and six Princeton University staff who meet regularly to evaluate the results of last year's Institute and to reinforce its effects.

· The helpful presence on campus of the Princeton Secondary School Science Project, a group of faculty and staff who for the past three years have been developing a new science curriculum for the junior and senior high school. (Materials of this program have been used successfully in both last year's Institute and in the Princeton Cooperative Schools Program for disadvantaged youth. More details of the project's methods and materials will follow.)

· The strong support which all recent university projects related to secondary education have received from President Goheen and many members of the Princeton faculty, a support and interest which have aided the projects noted previously in gathering onto their staffs some of the country's most outstanding teachers.

We propose, therefore, to extend and to build directly upon our experience with last summer's Princeton-Trenton Institute (PTI, as we shall henceforth refer to it) in which 40 Trenton secondary school teachers participated. This Institute was based on the idea that an increase in the competence of a relatively large group of teachers from a single urban school system both in subject matter and in relevant teaching skills can make a significant impact on teaching in that system. We believe that the 1965 Institute was successful, and that it would be desirable to increase both the number of participating teachers and the number of students in our program. As noted before, Princeton University has also established a close working relationship with the school systems of Newark and Burlington and both are eager to participate with Princeton and Trenton in a joint Institute in which approximately 30 participating teachers will be drawn from the Trenton schools, 32 from the Newark schools, and ten from Burlington. Teachers from other communities and Huntingdon in particular have expressed a sincere desire to become involved in our institute. They have convinced us that they can make significant changes within their school system. We may, therefore, select approximately three individuals as alternate participants from communities other than Newark, Trenton, and Burlington.

B. Specific Objectives

In the proposed Institute we shall seek to

(1) Promote understanding on the part of the participating teachers of the psychological and socio-economic environment of disadvantaged youth.

(2) Provide for these teachers instruction and experience in the use of new materials as well as proven techniques through the observation of and interaction with master teachers, visiting lecturers, community resource advisors, plus a comprehensive resource and research center.

(3) Provide an opportunity for the participating teachers to test in actual classroom situations these new materials and teaching techniques for the disadvantaged.

(4) Encourage these teachers to assist in the training and counseling of their colleagues and newly recruited teachers in their school system.

(5) Develop in the teachers attitudes toward working with disadvantaged youth that will help to promote growth and change.

C. Number of Participants

Seventy-two accredited secondary school teachers and supervisors will be chosen for the Institute. Approximately 30 participants will be selected from the Trenton schools, 32 from Newark, and ten from Burlington. The Trenton teachers will include roughly three from each of the five Trenton junior high schools and 15 from Trenton Central High School.

There will be 12 coordinating teachers, or master teachers. It is felt that each participating teacher should be afforded the opportunity to teach one class per week and that the coordinating teacher should be easily accessible for cooperative planning and counseling. Hence the decision to limit each coordinating teacher to involvement with five participating teachers. The remaining 12 participating teachers will be included in the residential Princeton Cooperative Schools Program, in which they will work and live with 40 disadvantaged urban youth. A ratio of four to one is considered most conducive to easy accessibility to the teacher for purposes of advice, counseling, and tutoring. Class schedules of the students dictate the number as well.

D. Criteria for Eligibility of Participants and Pupils

I. Selection of the participating teachers will rest on the following criteria:

Both men and women will be eligible.

All will be certified public school teachers or supervisory personnel on the secondary level.

All participants must deal directly with disadvantaged youth.

The majority of participants will have taught in urban schools for more than two years, but some newly recruited teachers will also be considered.

A majority of the teachers will be selected from one of the following four subject areas: English, social studies, math, and science.

All should show potential for professional leadership in serving disadvantaged youth.

All will expect to remain in the teaching profession for some time to come, especially in disadvantaged areas and in training fellow teachers. Maximum age of teachers will be 55 years.

We are anxious to include some supervisory personnel among the participants in the Institute, since the impact of the new ideas, materials, and methods will depend in part on the degree of enthusiasm with which they are received and passed on by supervisory personnel in the Trenton and other New Jersey school systems.

Final selection of participants will be made by a committee consisting of the Director of the Institute, a representative from each of sponsoring school districts, and one other staff member of the Institute.

II. Each pupil selected next spring for the program will have one or more of the following characteristics:

Be a member of the eighth, ninth, or tenth grade.

Be over the average age-in-grade.

Have a history of promotion on the basis of age rather than of achievement.

Have a well-established pattern of general academic underachievement.

Be below average for his age and class in reading and math.

Have a below-average IQ.

Have a history of adjustment problems and violations of school regulations.

Counselors and teachers in the participating schools will be urged to recommend likely student prospects. Final selection of students will rest with a committee composed of guidance counselors and administrators of the Trenton schools, the Director of the Institute, and the PTI Council.

E. Description of the Program

The basic outline of the program which follows has been worked out in consultation with and with the encouragement of the Boards of Education of the Cities of Trenton, Burlington, and Newark. For convenience it is presented in chronological order.

    I. February–June
        A. Organization of staff.
        B. Selection of participants.
        C. Planning with staff.
        D. General preparations for the Institute.
    II. June 27–August 5—Institute Program
        A. First week, June 27–July 1.

The first week of the Institute will begin with all 72 participating teachers and staff in an orientation meeting on Monday morning, June 27 (see Table I). The aims, purposes, and goals of the Institute will be discussed. The participating teachers will be given an opportunity to meet with the coordinating master teachers with whom they will be working closely. Dr. Margaret Fleming, research evaluator, will also administer a pre-program evaluation of teacher attitudes during the morning session. Post-tests to note change, if any, in teacher attitudes will be given at Central High School in Trenton

Table I Schedule of First Week

Time	Monday 6/27/66	Tuesday 6/28/66	Wednesday 6/29/66	Thursday 6/30/66	Friday 7/1/66
9 A.M. to noon	Orientation and organization. Pre-testing of teacher attitudes	Human Relations Workshop		Home visits for 60 non-residential participants. Conferences with PCSP staff for 12 residential participants	
Noon to 1 P.M.			Lunch		
1 P.M. to 5:30 P.M.	Human Relations Workshop			Same as Thursday morning	Reports on home visits Dismiss at 5 P.M.

from 11:45–12:30 P.M. on Monday, Tuesday, and Wednesday of the last week of the Institute.

A Human Relations Workshop will begin on Monday afternoon at 1 P.M. and will end by 5:30 P.M. Wednesday afternoon. The Workshop will be directed toward the general goal of increasing the teachers' sense of personal adequacy, especially in the area of work with disadvantaged youth.

The core of the Workshop will be the small discussion groups (teams) which will be designed to provide an opportunity for the members to assess their own values, attitudes, self-perceptions, and interpersonal relationships. The 72 participating teachers and the 12 coordinating teachers will be divided into six teams. One of the teams will be led by Dr. Donald Carew of our staff. The other five group leaders will be highly trained psychologists familiar with group techniques, most of whom will be drawn from the Laboratory for Applied Behavioral Science, Graduate Division, Newark State College, Union, New Jersey.

An outline of the Human Relations Workshop activities follows:

Human Relations Workshop Schedule
June 27 to June 29, 1966

Monday

1–1:45	Orientation to Human Relations Workshop—Carew
1:45–3:15	Group discussion No. 1.
3:15–3:30	Break.
3:30–5:30	Group discussion No. 2.

Tuesday

9–10	General session. Lecture on conflict and interpersonal perceptions—Human Relations staff.
10–12	Group discussion No. 3.
12–1	Lunch.
1–2:30	Group discussion No. 4.
2:30–3:30	General session. Lecture on communication and feedback —Human Relations staff.
3:30–5:30	Group discussion No. 5.

Wednesday

9–9:30	General session. Lecture on group growth—Carew.
9:30–11	Group discussion No. 6.
11–12	General session. Lecture on helping relationship.
12–1	Lunch.

1–2	General session. Lecture on peer group culture and its effect on learning—Staff.
2–3	Lecture on techniques for the home visits—Carew, Kontos, and staff.
3:30–4:30	Small group discussion regarding home visits.
4:30–5:30	General discussion on possible problems inherent in the home visit—Carew, Kontos, and staff.

The nonresidential participating teachers will conduct home visits beginning on Thursday morning of the first week and ending by noon the next day. They will meet at Central High School Thursday morning and use the high school as their headquarters. The Human Relations Workshop will have provided the teachers with preparation for these visits. Participating teachers will visit in pairs. Each pair of participating teachers will be given a list of 12 students and will visit the homes of as many of these as time permits. The students to be visited will be those who have enrolled in the section which teachers are to observe and teach.

There are three purposes for these home visits. The first is to allow the participating teacher to gain first-hand experience of the environment of the child, thereby gaining a keener insight into the student problems not apparent in the classroom. The second is to help the participating teacher to develop rapport with the student and his parents in an informal situation which will effect a more immediate communication between teacher and student during a relatively short summer classroom schedule. The third purpose is to reinforce the desire of the students who have enrolled in the Insitute to attend the summer classes. The participating teachers will be supervised on these visits by members of the staff and coordinating teachers.

The 12 residential teachers will meet with members of the PCSP staff for consultation and planning in preparation for their morning program on the Princeton campus while the nonresidential teachers are conducting home visits.

Friday afternoon from 1–2:30 P.M. all participating teachers and staff will return to the Princeton campus and will meet in their Human Relations Workshop groups to discuss briefly the results of their home visits. Dr. Carew will then lecture to the entire group on "Perceptions and the Helping Relationship" from 3–5 P.M.

B. Second through sixth weeks, July 5–August 5.

The remaining five weeks of the Institute program will consist of two parts: a nonresidential program and a residential program. The nonresidential program will include 60 participants involved in a teaching session in Trenton during the mornings and an evaluation-planning-lecture-study program at Princeton during the afternoons. The 12 teachers in the residential program will live on campus, observing and working closely with 40 boys from inner-city schools in a program funded separately by the Rockefeller Foundation. These 12 teachers will take part in afternoon sessions with the 60 nonresidential teachers.

1. *Residential Program*

The Princeton Cooperative Schools Program PCSP seeks to increase the number of qualified college applicants from the ranks of disadvantaged students. The program, which began in January 1964, consists of two phases. During the first phase 40 boys drawn from New Jersey urban high schools, come to Princeton University at the end of their sophomore year for an intensive six-week summer session. During the second phase the PCSP staff, as well as teachers and guidance personnel in their high schools, continue to work with these students throughout the year of college decision.

The PCSP curriculum includes science-mathematics, English language and literature, social studies, and creative arts. A basic finding of the PCSP program is that the effects of the academic work during the summer session do survive the transfer from the Princeton campus to the students' own school and home environment. During the summer session, PCSP seeks to create a climate in which the boys discover what learning is, find out that they have the ability to ask questions, gather data, analyze them, draw conclusions, and take intellectually defensible positions. We believe that this can be done by affecting the attitude of able but uncommitted youngsters toward learning.

During the 1966 summer session the PCSP program wishes to include within its organization 12 high school teachers who would not only act as participant observers in the classrooms, but would be available at other times to work with the boys as tutors. These teachers would be resident on the campus and would live in the same quadrangle as the students. We would like to have six participating teachers in the area of science-mathematics and six in the area of English-social studies. The teachers would not have disciplinary duties, but would serve as models and helpers for students. We expect that their experience in this program will be important to them in a number of ways. They would be both observing teachers practiced in teaching new materials to disadvantaged students and they would have the opportunity of participating in the teaching. They would see the boys not only in the classroom, but also in the more relaxed atmosphere of the dining halls, the dormitory, and the playing fields, and thus have the chance of seeing the students as they really are.

Ideally, *all* members of the Institute would have the opportunity to gain at first hand this understanding of inner-city youth, but the Cooperative Schools Program is unfortunately unable to absorb more than 12 without damage to its own structure and purposes. We do believe, however, that the experience gained by these 12 will be effectively communicated in many of its essentials to the other members of the Institute during the afternoon sessions and will enrich the Institute far beyond the capacity of the most lucid lecturer.

During the mornings the participating teachers would be attending classes and critique plus planning sessions in their subject areas. The afternoons would be spent in part tutoring and counseling individual students or small groups of students, and in part attending the formal program of lectures and seminars to be described, together with the nonresidential teachers.

2. *Nonresidential Program*

The nonresidential program is built on the experiences of last summer's Princeton-Trenton Institute. A morning summer school for 360 students will be established which will be physically structured to resemble large city schools in that periods will be 45 minutes long and 30 students will be assigned to each class. The teaching, however, will *not* be typical. Four subjects: English, social studies, science, and math will be taught by the best teachers we can find nationally. The coordinating teachers, as we call them, have already been recruited (see section F on Institute staff). Each coordinating teacher will be responsible for directing the activities of five participating teachers, and will be demonstrating to their assigned groups of participating teachers their most successful teaching materials and methods. The participating teachers will teach at least one class per week (see Table II for class schedules), where it will be possible for them to try out new techniques and new subject matter with the help and guidance of the coordinating teachers.

The nonresidential morning program is best explained by following the schedule (see Table II) of a coordinating teacher. At 9 A.M. he conducts a class for 30 students, observed by his assigned five participating teachers. At 9:50 A.M. the same class is taught by one participating teacher, observed by the coordinating teacher and the remaining four participants (each of whom will themselves teach this class once per week). A milk break is scheduled for the time

Table II Tentative Morning Class Schedule for Coordinating and Participating Teachers (Weeks 2-6)

C.T.	1	2	3	4	5	6	7	8	9	10	11	12
Grade	8th	8th	8th	8th	9th	9th	9th	9th	10th	10th	10th	10th
Time												
9:00– 9:45	E(C.T.)	S.S.(C.T.)	(C.T.)	S(C.T.)	E(C.T.)	S.S.(C.T.)	–	–	M(C.T.)	S(C.T.)	E(C.T.)	S.S.(C.T.)
9:50–10:35	E(P.T.)	S.S.(P.T.)	(P.T.)	S(P.T.)	E(P.T.)	S.S.(P.T.)	–	–	M(P.T.)	S(P.T.)	E(P.T.)	S.S.(P.T.)
10:35–10:50	– – – – –			Milk Break				– – – – –				
10:50–11:35	E(C.T.)	S.S.(C.T.)	M(C.T.)	S(C.T.)	E(C.T.)	S.S.(C.T.)	M(C.T.)	S(C.T.)	M(C.T.)	S(C.T.)	E(C.T.)	S.S.(C.T.)
11:40–12:25	Time allotted to pupil tutoring or counseling by both coordinating and participating teachers, or to C.T.-P.T. planning and organization of class work.											

Legend
E = English
S.S. = Social Studies
M = Mathematics
S = Science
C.T. = Coordinating Teacher
P.T. = Participating Teacher

303

period from 10:35 to 10:50. At 10:50 the coordinating teacher teaches a different group of 30 students. The five participants may elect to remain with him or to observe a class taught by another coordinating teacher. From 11:40 to 12:25 (or the fourth period) the coordinating teacher and his five participating teachers will be available to students for tutuoring and counseling. If student demands permit, the coordinating teacher may spend this time organizing and planning with the participating teacher scheduled to teach on the following day. All high school activities will be coordinated by Mrs. Charlotte Brooks, who is also supervisor of the English-social studies area of the Institute. She will have an administrative aide, Mr. Roland Maize, at the high school.

The science curriculum will consist of a course entitled "Time, Space, and Matter." This science course, which has been developed by Princeton University, was successfully used in the 1965 PTI with disadvantaged youngsters. The curriculum consists of a series of inter-related sequential investigations, structured toward his discovering, through direct observation and inference, something of the nature and history of the physical world about him. Mr. James Pennington of Homewood, Illinois, and a member of the 1965 PTI faculty will teach one of the sections. Mr. James McCracken of St. Petersburg, Florida, and Mrs. Corolynne Branson of Washington will teach the other two.

The mathematics curriculum will be developed around the "Time, Space, and Matter" course of study. The investigations in the science program will serve as the basis for teaching basic arithmetic skills, and as a point of departure for teaching more sophisticated mathematical principles. Our Associate Director, Mr. Ernest Poll, has been directing a program with this approach to mathematics in the University of Chicago Laboratory School. This class will be taught by Mrs. Lillian Koltnow of Philadelphia, Pennsylvania, and Mr. James L. Wolfe and Mr. Russell Abraham, both of Portland, Oregon.

The English and social studies courses will also concentrate on the discovery method or inductive method which is proving successful in the teaching of disadvantaged youth. The English curriculum will be based on the study of literature, composition, and linguistics. Each of the three master teachers will develop a thematic approach around his or her particular English specialty over a five-week period. Mrs. Lawana Trout, for example, of Central State College, Oklahoma, will organize her course around the social history of language and linguistics. Mrs. Trout developed this course of study during the 1965 PTI session and had a great deal of success with it. We expect that in the other two English classes the method will be inductive and the subject matter will be literature and composition. Mrs. Evelyn Harper of Atchison, Kansas, and Mr. David Sohn of Westport, Connecticut, will teach these two English sections.

The social studies curriculum will be built around the history of the development of the democratic ideal. The method will be inductive. Each of the three coordinating teachers will select a period in American history in which he feels most competent and develop a five-week course of study, drawing on the use of source materials as well as secondary sources. The three master teachers for the social studies program are: Mr. Peter Carlin of Cleveland, Ohio, Mrs. Henrietta Miller of Chicago, Illinois, and Mr. John Gallagher of Huntington, New York.

Each coordinating teacher will be on duty through a 40-hour week. The mix of formal and informal contact teaching hours will be varied according to the needs of each participant in the program. Formal class time with the students will occupy approximately 11 hours of the alloted 40 for both coordinating and participating teachers, with an additional four hours of tutoring and counseling of students.

A unique feature of the Institute will be the establishment of a resource center. The center will be staffed by two curriculum specialists, both members of the staff of last year's Institute. Mr. Howard Cranford of Washington, D.C., for English and social studies, and Mr. Carl Voth of Princeton, New Jersey, for math and science. They will plan field trips, prepare abstracts of important works on the disadvantaged, gather monographs, unpublished materials, articles, and other related educational media for use by the participating teachers. They will also collect and distribute the latest materials emphasizing curriculum revision. The personnel of the resource center will also be responsible for securing and reproducing materials for use in the morning classes at Central High School. The center will serve as the focal point for new and experimental materials and media and as an information retrieval center of professional materials. The center staff will produce, by the end of the Institute, an annotated bibliography of professional materials and a complete collection of curriculum materials developed at the Institute for every participating teacher. The resource center will remain open until 10 P.M. each evening for the convenience of the staff and participants. A graduate student will serve as the librarian during these hours. He will be paid from indirect costs.

After the morning program the staff and participating teachers will return to the Princeton campus by chartered bus. The participating teachers and staff will have lunch together, where, it is hoped, they will carry on a continuing dialogue on problems of the disadvantaged and on the progress of the Institute. The lunch hour should also help to provide a social setting that will enable staff and participants to develop an attitude or cordiality and mutual trust and respect.

A formal afternoon lecture course will be given from 2–3:50 on Mondays, Wednesday, and Fridays and from 2–3 on Tuesdays and Thursdays, beginning with the second week of the Institute (see Table III). This course will deal with the psychological, social, and economic factors affecting learning in the disadvantaged child. It will be taught by a small group of distinguished experts in the field of disadvantaged youth, supplemented by the Institute staff. These experts will serve as visiting lecturers and lecture on their subjects in two- to five-day sequences.

Table III Afternoon Schedule (Weeks 2–6)

Time	Monday	Tuesday	Wednesday	Thursday	Friday
1 P.M. to 2 P.M.			Lunch		
2 P.M. to 3 P.M.			Lecture Series Psychological, socio-economic factors affecting learning in disadvantaged youth		
3 P.M. to 4 P.M.		Individual research and planning		Individual research and planning	
4 P.M. to 5 P.M.	Critique session		Critique session		Critique session

The continuity of the lecture series will be the responsibility of the director and associate director. The course will include discussions of the learning styles of the disadvantaged, self-image of the deprived, diagnosing pupil needs, the role of the school and welfare agencies in the inner-city, making use of the suportive social services, the use of the community as an extension of the classroom, poverty as viewed by the disadvantaged child and his parents, teacher qualities needed for inner-city teaching, and related literature to the field of teaching disadvantaged youth. Some additional lectures will be given in the Trenton community during field trips. We expect to involve two residents of the inner-city as special consultants and resource personnel during the field trips. The two community residents used as special consultants on these field trips will be paid by United Progress, Inc., the Trenton Community Action Program.

James R. Tanner of the Cleveland Public Schools, Dr. Jack Abramowitz of the Farmingdale (New York) Public Schools, Dr. Harvey Pressman of Tufts University, Dr. Marvin Bressler and Dr. Melvin Tuman, both of Princeton University, have consented to participate as visiting lecturers in the Institute for an average of four days each. Mr. Tanner will lecture on the disadvantaged child in the school situation and strategies for meeting the needs of disadvantaged youth. Dr. Abramowitz will lecture on curriculum revision for disadvantaged youth. Dr. Pressman will lecture on learning theory and its application to disadvantaged youth by drawing upon various action programs in operation in their field. Drs. Bressler and Tuman will lecture on the nature of poverty and its effect on children. We will also occasionally secure the services of special consultants if an obvious need arises during the course of the Institute.

The participating teachers will be required to read four books in conjunction with the lecture series: *Education in Depressed Areas*, edited by A. Harry Passow; *Education and Income*, by Patricia Cayo Sexton; *The Culturally Deprived Child*, by Frank Riessman; and *Up the Down Staircase*, by Bel Kaufman. The visiting lecturers and staff will require other reading as the course develops.

Following the lecture series on Monday, Wednesday, and Friday, the nonresidential participating teachers will take part in a critique session from 4-5 P.M. The participating teachers will be divided into six groups. Each group will be composed of ten participating teachers, "their" two coordinating teachers, and one member of the staff for discussion. This is not to imply that the critique sessions will be limited to these topics. It is hoped that the sessions will serve as a forum in which the participating teachers will evaluate their philosophy of education and their performance as teachers of disadvantaged youth. We felt that this personal teacher evaluation did occur in the critique sessions in the 1965 Institute program and are therefore encouraged to believe that the same results will accure to our proposed institute.

The 12 resident teachers involved in the Princeton Cooperative Schools Program will also meet at this time with the Associate Direc-

Table IV Table of Organization

Princeton University
Director of Summer Studies
H. D. Holland

Director
P. Kontos

Associate Director
E. Poll

Administrative Director
of Summer Studies
P. L. Coddington

Supervisor of Guidance,
Research, and Evaluation
D. Carew

Supervisor of English-Social Studies
and Coordinator of High School Demonstration
Program Activities
C. Brooks

Supervisor of Science-Math
C. Keith

Research Associate
M. Fleming

Coordinating Teachers of English (3)
L. Trout
E. Harper
D. Sohn

Coordinating Teachers of
Science (3)
J. Pennington
C. Branson
J. McCracken

Research Associate
M. Stalley

Guidance Associate
L. Barclay

Coordinating Teachers of Social Studies (3)
P. Carlin
J. Gallagher
H. Miller

Coordinating Teachers of
Mathematics (3)
L. Koltnow
R. Abraham
J. Wolfe

Resource Center Specialist
(English-Social Studies)
H. Cranford

Resource Center Specialist
(Science-Mathematics)
C. Voth

Special Personnel: Visiting lecturers (4–5, part time); consulting psychologists—Human Relations Workshop (5, part-time); Trenton community consultants (4, part-time); administrative assistants (2); resource center assistant (1, part-time).

308

tor to discuss their morning activities, the readings, and the afternoon lectures. The Associate Director will also occasionally schedule these teachers into the other critique sessions with the nonresident partici- pating teachers in order to acquaint both groups with other aspects of the PTI program.

F. Evaluation and Post-Institute Activities

The major part of the evaluation will consist of the reports and reactions of all of the staff, participating teachers, and students in- volved. This approach to evaluation for the 1965 Institute resulted in the accompanying report which includes a great deal of information which is extremely useful in assessing the effects of the Institute as of August 6, 1965. This report includes a copy of the questionnaires which were used to solicit the participating teachers' and the students' reactions (Appendix to part five). Similar questionnaires, refined in terms of one year's use, will be used at the end of the summer pro- grams. The evaluation will be the responsibility of Dr. Carew, Dr. Fleming, Mr. Barclay, and Mr. Marshall Stalley.

A need also exists for a continuing reappraisal of the strategies and materials of the program as well as continuing encouragement and support of teachers trying out new and/or unfamiliar methods. The brunt of continuing and supplementing this aspect of the program during the regular school year will rest with the Princeton-Trenton Institute Council which was described in the introduction of this proposal. The PTI Council will be expanded to include Newark and Burlington teachers and as one of its major responsibilities it will develop a series of workshops dealing with problems of teaching disadvantaged youth. These workshops will be held at various Tren- ton, Newark, and Burlington schools and at Princeton University dur- ing the 1966 academic year. The PTI Council will also serve in helping to direct the in-service activities of the PTI participating teachers by engaging them as resource personnel in department meetings in various schools and by directing them for consultation to other teach- ers who might benefit from the PTI summer experience.

G. Physical Facilities

We have been assured the use of the classrooms and other facilities of the Trenton Central High School for morning demonstration classes. Afternoon discussions and seminars will be held on the Princeton University campus in appropriate conference rooms and lounges.

Library privileges will be extended to all participants by the University and other campus facilities will be made available as needs arise.

Although little occasion for recreation is contemplated in the schedule, University tennis courts, swimming pool, and playing fields will be available to the participants, and should it be desirable, arrangements can be made to open these facilities to the students in the demonstration classes.

Adequate dormitory facilities are available for all participating teachers who hope to live on the Princeton campus during the Institute.

H. Nondiscriminatory Provisions

(a) In selecting individuals for attendance at the Institute and in otherwise conducting the Institute, Princeton University will not discriminate because of the sex, race, creed, color, or national origin of the applicant or enrollee.

(b) Princeton University will not require nor recommend submission of a photograph of an applicant prior to the acceptance of said applicant.

(c) Princeton University will include the following statement on all brochures, circulars, announcements, and similar publicity publications announcing the Institute: "In selecting individuals for attendance at the Institute, and in otherwise conducting the Institute, this institution does not discriminate on account of the sex, race, creed, color, or national origin of an applicant."

28. Bibliography of Materials for Pupils and Teachers

HOWARD CRANFORD and CARL VOTH

As a part of the Princeton-Trenton Institute a materials resource room was established at Princeton University. Easily accessible to the Institute members and staff, this room contained a wealth of books, pamphlets, teaching kits and machines, paperbacks, and mimeographed materials.

When the faculty in the spring set up the curriculum areas to be covered, each one indicated the materials and equipment that would be needed in his classroom at the demonstration school, Trenton Central High. He also was asked to suggest materials for the resource room that would benefit the participating teachers. These suggestions were turned over to the two materials coordinators—Carl Voth in the areas of mathematics and science and Howard Cranford in the fields of English and social studies.

The large book companies, reading laboratories, magazine and paperback companies, the Office of Education, the National Councils, and the far-reaching National Education Association were informed of the planned Institute. Directors and area representatives made many valuable suggestions of materials that would be helpful, and a large number also agreed to provide many of the materials free of charge or on a loan basis. The companies were very helpful, and their cooperation and assistance are greatly appreciated.

Howard Cranford and Carl Voth spent the summers of 1965 and 1966 gathering and evaluating materials for two teacher institutes at Princeton University. They began when interest by publishers in this field was low and then suddenly found themselves deluged when educational industries discovered the vast market of urban education. That they were able to function effectively in spite of the wall of paper that was thrown about them is testimony to their effectiveness as materials coordinators. Mr. Cranford is Special Assistant to the Supervisor of English in the District of Columbia Schools, and Mr. Voth is with the Princeton Junior Museum and attends the Princeton Theological Seminary.

A month before the Institute opened, a form letter was used to order materials from companies across the nation. All materials were shipped to the director of the Institute at Princeton University, who directed them to the resource room, a large, air-conditioned, well-situated room perfect for our needs. The tremendous resources of the NEA, Office of Education; NCTE and other national associations were tapped. Mrs. Charlotte Brooks, who headed the English-social studies area of the Institute, provided much valuable material on loan from her English office in Washington. Her valuable suggestions and many contacts among publishers and editors also added greatly to our materials stockpile. Other members of the staff contributed great amounts of valuable mimeographed materials as well as suggestions for additional reference sources.

Thirty feet of shelving, from floor to ceiling, were installed along two walls of the resource room. One section was devoted to professional materials in English and curriculum, another to social studies, and a third to the professional mathematics and science writings. A large area of shelves was taken up with materials on reading. Another section was filled with paperbacks and periodicals. On the lower shelves were a number of reading, composition, and comprehension kits, as well as Scholastic literature units. A section was devoted to the contributions of minority Americans to our society. Certainly, this was a tremendous and valuable stockpile covering a wide educational range.

Two large tables in the center of the resource room were kept filled with displays of materials which could be had for the taking—pamphlets, mimeographed speeches, and articles pertaining to the teaching of disadvantaged children and education in general, and reams of publishers' materials that were very useful. Displays were changed frequently, with a paperback exhibit added. There was never any lack of display materials.

The members of the Institute soon developed the habit of dropping into the resource room after lunch and during any free time in the afternoon to browse or search for materials in their area of teaching or in connection with their study group activities. It is regrettable that, because the schedule was a tight, well-packed one, more time was not available for this purpose. However, much material was taken out. Interest in reading materials was high, as well as in the areas of curriculum and supervision and the education of the disadvantaged. We felt that the participants became acquainted with a great variety of professional materials. Of course, they did not have time to peruse carefully more than a fraction of what was available, but they made note of much that they felt would be of value to them in their particular teaching situations. After the Institute many will continue to read and discover better methods and techniques for making their teaching more effective.

Here then are some representative lists from that resource room.

Bibliography

Representative Curriculum Materials

A list of representative curriculum materials that were found helpful by the staff and participants is included. Although it is not complete, it is at least a list that has been compiled after being scrutinized by several hundred teachers. Undoubtedly other material exists and was unfortunately omitted. It should be noted, however, that the inclusion of this material should not imply endorsement by the authors or editors. It is intended only as a representative sample—a place for an educator new to the field of urban education to begin his own evaluations of curriculum materials.

The materials are classified into four groups: English, social studies, science, and math.

English Curriculum Materials

Armstong, E. G., D. Porter, and H. F. Spitzer, *Word Problems Programmed.* New York: McGraw-Hill Book Company, 1966.

Ballantine, E. et al., *Readings in the Language Arts.* New York: Macmillan Company, 1964.

Bamman, H. and R. Whitehead, *World of Adventure Series.* (Chicago: Benefic Press).
  Flight to the South Pole. 1965.
  The Lost Uranium Mine. 1964.
  Hunting Grizzley Bears. 1963.
  Fire on the Mountain. 1963.
  City Beneath the Sea. 1964.
  The Search for Pirarha. 1964.
  Sacred Well of Sacrifice. 1964.
  Viking Treasure. 1965.

Bond, G. L. and T. Clyma, *Developmental Reading Series.* (Chicago: Lyons and Carnahan).
  A Call to Adventure. 1962.
  Deeds of Men. 1962.
  Days of Adventure. 1962.
  Stories to Remember. 1962.

Brake, R. G., *New Phonics Skill Text Series.* Books A–D. Detroit: Merrill-Palmer Institute, 1964–1965.

Brewton, J. E., B. Lemon, and M. Ernst, *New Horizons Through Reading and Literature.* Books 2 and 3. Summit, Jersey: Laidlaw Brothers, 1962, 1964.

Buchanan, C. D., *Programmed Reading for Adults.* Books 1–4. New York: McGraw-Hill Book Company, 1966.

Burgard, G. et al., *A Programmed Approach to Writing.* Books I and II. Boston: Ginn and Company, 1964.

Burton, A. E. and J. Mersand, *Stories for Teen Agers.* Books 1 and 2. New York: Globe Publishing Company, 1959 and 1966.

Bushman, Laser et al., *Scope Reading Series.* (Elmsford, New York: Harper and Row, Inc.)
Book 1. *People and Places.* 1965.
Book 2. *Your World and Others.* 1965.
Language I. 1965.

Call Them Heroes. Books 1–5. Morristown, New Jersey: Silver Burdette Company, 1963–1965.

Carlson, J. and H. I. Christ, *English on the Job.* Books 1 and 2. New York: Globe Publishing Company, 1961–1962.

Carlson, R. K., *Sparkling Words.*

Christ, H. I., *The Odyssey of Homer.* New York: Globe Publishing Company, 1960.

Colton, R. G., G. M. Davis, and E. Hanshaw, *Living Your English Series.* Books 7–12. Boston: D. C. Heath and Company, 1965.

Diamant, C. B. and F. T. Humphreville, *On the Threshold.* Fair Lawn, New Jersey: Scott, Foresman and Company, 1965.

Ellis, W., *A Teacher's Guide to Selected Literary Works.* New York: Dell Publishing Company, Inc., 1966.

Franklin, B., *Autobiography.* New York: Washington Square Press, Inc., 1966.

Fries, C. C., *Merrill Linguistic Readers Series.* Books I–IV. Summit, New Jersey: Laidlaw Brothers, 1966.

Frost, R., *Robert Frost's Poems.* New York: Washington Square Press, Inc., 1965.

Gainsburg, J. C. and S. I. Spector, *Better Reading.* New York: Globe Publishing Company, 1962.

Gershenfeld, H. and A. E. Burton, *Stories for Teen Agers.* New York: Globe Publishing Company, 1963.

Gordon, E. J. et al., *A Programmed Approach to Writing.* Books I and II. Boston: Ginn and Company, 1964–1965.

Halliburton, W. J. and M. E. Pelkonen, *New Worlds of Literature.* New York: Harcourt, Brace and World, Inc., 1966.

Halvorsen, M. et al., *Phonics We Use.* Books D–G. Chicago: Lyons and Carnahan, 1966.

Harrison, B. C., *Better Spelling Series.* Books I and II. Indianapolis: Bobbs-Merrill Company, Inc., 1962.

Henderson, E. C., *Learning to Write.* New York: Holt, Rinehart and Winston, Inc., 1965.

Herber, H. L., *Learning Your Language Series.* (Chicago: Follett Publishing Company).
Book 1. *Conflict and Courage.* 1964.
Book 2. *Escape to Danger.* 1964.
Book 3. *Folk Tales and Folk Songs.* 1964.

Book 4. *Victory and Defeat.* 1964.
Book 5. *On the Lighter Side.* 1964.
Book 6. *Family and Friends.* 1964.
Hook, J. N., *Writing Creatively.* Boston: D. C. Heath and Company, 1963.
Houghton Mifflin Literature Series, Jewett, A. (ed.). (New York: Houghton Mifflin Company).
　Chase, M. E. et al., *Values in Literature.* 1965.
　Daiches, D. et al., *English Literature.* 1965.
　Schorer, M. et al., *American Literature.* 1965.
　Van Doren, M. et al., *Insight into Literature.* 1965.
Howes, V. M. et al., *Readings in the Language Arts.* New York: Macmillan Company, 1964.
Hurley, W., *Dan Frontier Developmental Reading Series.* (Chicago: Benefic Press).
　Dan Frontier, Sheriff. 1960.
　Dan Frontier and the Wagon Train. 1959.
　Dan Frontier, Trapper. 1962.
　Dan Frontier Goes to Congress. 1964.
Jewett, A., M. Erdman, and P. McKee, *Adventure Bound.* New York: Houghton Mifflin Company, 1965.
———, *Journeys into America.* New York: Houghton Mifflin Company, 1965.
Kottmeyer, W. and K. Ware, *Basic Goals in Spelling.* New York: McGraw-Hill Book Company, 1964.
———, *Conquests in Reading.* New York: McGraw-Hill Book Company, 1962.
———, *The Magic World of Dr. Spello.* New York: McGraw-Hill Book Company, 1963.
Lass, A. (ed.), *A Student's Guide to Fifty American Novels.* New York: Washington Square Press, Inc., 1966.
Lass, A. and E. L. McGill, *Plays from Radio.* New York: Houghton Mifflin Company, 1948.
Learner, L. and M. Moller, *Follett Vocational Reading Series.* (Chicago: Follett Publishing Company).
　The Delso Sisters—Beauticians. 1965.
　John Leveron—Auto Mechanic. 1965.
　Marie Perrone—Practical Nurse. 1965.
　The Millers and Willie B.—Butcher, Baker, Chef. 1965.
Leavitt, H. D. and D. A. Shohn, *Stop, Look and Write.* New York: Bantam Books, Inc., 1964.
Lesser, M. X. and J. N. Morris, *The Friction of Experience.* New York: McGraw-Hill Book Company, 1962.
Lessons for Self-Instruction in Basic Skills Series. (Monterey, California: California Test Bureau).
　Capitalization. 1963–1966.
　Following Directions. 1–4. 1963–1966.
　Punctuation. 1 and 2. 1963–1966.
　Reading Interpretations. Series I and II. 1963–1966.
　Reference Skills. 1–4. 1963–1966.
　Sentence Patterns. 1 and 2. 1963–1966.
　Verbs, Modifiers, and Pronouns. 1963–1966.
　Verbs, Number and Case. 1963–1966.

Lish, G., *English Grammar Series*. Vols. I and II. Palo Alto, California: Behavioral Research Laboratories, 1964.

Loesel, W., *Help Yourself to Read, Write, and Spell*. Books 1 and 2. Boston: Ginn and Company, 1965.

Lynch, J. L. and B. Evans, *High School English Textbooks*. Boston: Little, Brown and Company, 1963.

McCracken, G. and C. C. Walcutt, *Basic Reading Series*. (Philadelphia: J. B Lippincott Company).
  Pre-Primer and Primer. 1963.
  Reader 2-1. 1964.

McKee, P., *Reading*. New York: Houghton Mifflin Company, 1966.

McKee, P., A. McCowan, et al., *Reading for Meaning*. (New York: Houghton Mifflin Company).
  Bright Peaks. 1966.
  High Roads. 1966.
  Sky Line. 1966.

Merriam Webster Pocket Dictionary. New York: Pocket Books, Inc.

Niles, O. S., D. K. Bracken, et al. *Basic Reading Skills Series*. (Fair Lawn, New Jersey: Scott, Foresman and Company).
  Tactics in Reading. Books I and II. 1965.

Nunn, J. A., *Four Complete Teen-Age Novels*. New York: Globe Publishing Company, 1963.

Plays for Reading. (New York: Walker and Company).
  Bierce, A., *Shipwreck*. 1965–1966.
  De Maupassant, G., *The Necklace*. 1965–1966.
  O. Henry, *The Romance of a Busy Broker*. 1965–1966.
  Saki. *The Open Window*. 1965–1966.

Poquet, L., *Study Exercises for Developing Reading Skills*. Books A–D. Summit, New Jersey: Laidlaw Brothers, 1965.

Postman, N., *Postman Language Series*. (New York: Holt, Rinehart and Winston, Inc.).
  Discovering Your Language. 1963–1965.
  Language and Systems. 1963–1965.
  The Language of Discovery. 1963–1965.
  The Uses of Language. 1963–1965.

Potler, R. R., *Myths and Folk Tales Around the World*. New York: Globe Publishing Company, 1963.

Prestwood, E. L., *Practice in English*. New York: Houghton Mifflin Company, 1963.

Readers' Enrichment Series. (New York: Washington Square Press).
  London, J., *White Fang*. 1965.
  Rostand, E., *Cyrano De Bergerac*. 1966.
  Shakespeare, W., *Julius Caesar*. 1965.
  Stevenson, R. L., *Treasure Island*. 1965.

Riverside Literature Series. (New York: Houghton Mifflin Company).
  Annixter, P., *Swiftwater*. 1962.
  Austin, J., *Pride and Prejudice*. 1963.
  Bowen, C. D., *Yankee from Olympus*. 1962.
  Bronte, C., *Jane Eyre*. 1965.
  Bronte, E., *Wuthering Heights*. 1965.

Cather, W., *My Antonia.* 1949.

Coolidge, O., *Greek Myths.* 1964.

Crane, S., *Red Badge of Courage.* 1964.

Dickens, C., *David Copperfield.* 1965.

————, *Great Expectations.* 1962.

————, *Tale of Two Cities.* 1962.

Eliot, G., *Silas Marner.* 1962.

Forbes, E., *Johnny Tremain.* 1960.

Forester, C. S., *Captain Horatio Hornblower.* 1964.

Franklin, B., *Autobiography.* 1966.

Hardy, T., *Return of the Native.* 1964.

Hawthorne, N., *House of Seven Gables.* 1966.

————, *Scarlet Letter.* 1963

Hilton, J., *Goodbye, Mr. Chips.* 1964.

————, *Lost Horizon.* 1962.

Homer, *The Odyssey.* 1965.

London, J., *Call of the Wild.* 1962.

Longfellow, H. W., *Evangeline.* 1962.

Nordhoff, C. and J. N. Hall, *Mutiny on the Bounty.* 1962.

Schaefe, J., *Shane.* 1964.

Shakespeare, W., *Hamlet.* 1965.

————, *Julius Caesar.* 1962.

————, *Macbeth.* 1964.

Stevenson, R. L., *Treasure Island.* 1962.

Tennyson, A., *Idylls of the Kings.* 1963.

Thoreau, H. D., *Walden.* 1964.

Twain, M., *Adventures of Huckleberry Finn.* 1962.

————, *Tom Sawyer.* 1962.

Schleyen, M., *Stories for Today's Youth.* New York: Globe Publishing Company, 1965.

Shaffer, V. and H. Shaw, *Handbook of English.* New York: McGraw-Hill Book Company, 1962.

Shakespeare, W., *Four Tragedies.* Englewood Cliffs, New Jersey: Scholastic Magazines and Book Services, 1964.

Shehan, L. P., *English and You.* New York: Holt, Rinehart and Winston, Inc., 1962.

————, *English Can Be Easy.* New York: Holt, Rinehart and Winston, Inc., 1960.

————, *English for Americans.* New York: Holt, Rinehart and Winston, Inc., 1965.

Smiley, M. B., *Gateway English Series.* (New York: Hunter College).

1. *Creatures in Verse.* 1965.
2. *People in Poetry.* 1966.
3. *Striving.* 1965.
4. *Two Roads to Greatness.*
5. *A Western Sampler.* 1966.

Smith, N. B., *Be A Better Reader Series.* Books 1–6. Englewood Cliffs, New Jersey: Prentice-Hall, Inc., 1960–1963.

Sohn, D. A., *Ten Modern American Short Stories.* New York: Bantam Books, Inc., 1965.

Stone, C. R., A. Burton et al., *New Practice Readers*. Books A–G. New York: McGraw-Hill Book Company, 1960–1962.

Tichner, E., F. Ross, and E. Simpkins, *Success in Language Series A*. (Chicago: Follett Publishing Company).
  Unit 1. *Reflections*. 1964.
  Unit 2. *Lend an Ear*. 1964.
  Unit 3. *As a Matter of Fact*. 1964.
  Unit 4. *The Sounds Around Us*. 1964.
  Unit 5. *Let's Talk It Over*. 1964.
  Unit 6. *Say It on Paper*. 1964.
  Unit 7. *What's Behind the Cover?* 1964.
  Unit 8. *The Job in Your Future*. 1964.

Turner, R. H., *The Turner-Livingstone Reading Series*. (Chicago: Follett Publishing Company).
  1. *The Family You Belong To*. 1962.
  2. *The Friends You Make*. 1962.
  3. *The Jobs You Get*. 1962.
  4. *The Money You Spend*. 1962.
  5. *The Person You Are*. 1962.
  6. *The Town You Live In*. 1962.

Walker, L. C. et al., *A Handbook for Young Writers*. Englewood Cliffs, New Jersey: Prentice-Hall, Inc., 1965.

Wright, L. B., et al. *American Literature Series*. Vol. 3: *The Last Part of the 19th Century*. New York. Washington Square Press, Inc., 1966.

The Springboards Reading Program (New York: Portal Press, Inc.)

Reading for Enjoyment and Comprehension

1. *Luis Makes New Sports Rules*.
2. *Why Luis Hates Hate*.
3. *Luis and Mary O'Toole*.
4. *Luis the Good Citizen*.
5. *Mike Shannon and the Pigeon*.
6. *Mara the Blind Girl*.
7. *Mara Stops a Thief*.
8. *Limpy*.

Grammar Skills

1. *Mike Writes to Johnny About a Fight*.
2. *Helen Writes to Joan About Her Party*.
3. *Nick Writes to Pete About the Football Game*.
4. *Helen Writes to Al in the Army*.

Social Studies Reading

1. *Roger Williams Stops a War*.
2. *Dangerous Mission* (George Washington).
3. *Valley Forge*.

4. *Mountain Men.*
5. *Shall All Men Be Free?* (Emancipation Proclamation).
6. *Susan Anthony Dares to Vote!*
7. *Boss Tweed Steals a City.*
8. *On Top of the World* (Peary and Henson Reach the Pole).
9. *Sunday Morning at Pearl Harbor.*
10. *The Iron Hand of Nazism.*
11. *Dwight D. Eisenhower, American Citizen.*
12. *Harry S. Truman, the Man Who Never Gave Up.*
13. *John F. Kennedy.*
14. *The Tough Little Scientist* (George W. Carver).
15. *Miss Red Cross* (Clara Barton).
16. *They called Him "T. R."*
17. *Doctor Dan.*
18. *Young Abe Lincoln.*
19. *The Man Who Put America on Wheels* (Henry Ford).

World and National Problems

1. *The Iron Hand of Communism.*
2. *My Job Was Taken By a Button.*
3. *Civil Rights.*
4. *Freedom to Worship.*
5. *How We Elect a President.*

Social and Personal Problems

1. *Helen Gives a Party.*
2. *Nick and the Gang.*
3. *The Big Game.*
4. *Helen Wants a Summer Job.*

Social Studies Curriculum Materials

Abramowitz, J., *Study Lessons in Our Nation's History.* Chicago: Follett Publishing Company, 1964.
———, *Study Lessons on Documents of Freedom.* Chicago: Follett Publishing Company, 1964.
———, *Study Lessons on World History.* Chicago: Follett Publishing Company, 1964.
Ames, G. and R. Wyler, *The Earth's Story.* Mankato, Minnesota: Creative Educational Society, Inc., 1965.
Boak, A. E. et al., *The History of Our World.* New York: Houghton Mifflin Company, 1965.
Brown, H. M. and J. F. Guadagnolo, *America Is My Country.* New York: Houghton Mifflin Company, 1961.
Caughey, J. W., J. H. Franklin, and E. R. May, *Land of the Free.* New York: Benziger Brothers, Inc., 1966.
Chu, D. and E. Skinner, *A Glorious Age In Africa.* New York: Doubleday and Company, Inc., 1965.

Davidson, B., *A Guide to African History*. New York: Doubleday and Company, 1965.

Dobler, L., *Arrow Book of the United Nations*. Englewood Cliffs, New Jersey: Scholastic Magazines and Book Services, 1963.

————, *Great Rulers of the African Past*. New York: Doubleday and Company, Inc., 1965.

Dobler, L. and E. A. Toppin, *Pioneers and Patriots*. New York: Doubleday and Company, Inc., 1965.

Feldmann, S., *African Myths and Tales*. New York: Dell Publishing Company, Inc., 1963.

Ginn Social Science Enrichment Series. (Boston: Ginn and Company).

    Farnum, M., *John Hancock*. 1964.

    Jashemski, R., *Letters from Pompeii*. 1963.

    Kenworthy, L., *Three Billion Neighbors*. 1965.

    Stratton, M., *Negroes Who Helped Build America*. 1965.

Hollander, S. S., *Impressions of the United States*. New York: Holt, Rinehart and Winston, Inc., 1964.

Job, K., *Study Lessons in Map Reading*. Chicago: Follett Publishing Company, 1965.

Judd, P., *African Independence*. New York: Dell Publishing Company, Inc., 1963.

Kissen, F., *They Helped Make America*. New York: Houghton Mifflin Company, 1963.

Kottmeyer, W. and K. Ware, *Our Constitution and What It Means*. New York: McGraw-Hill Book Company, 1965.

Lawson, D., *The United States in World War I*. Englewood Cliffs, New Jersey: Scholastic Magazines and Book Services, 1965.

McCarthy, A. and L. Reddick, *Worth Fighting For*. New York: Doubleday and Company, Inc.

McCloskey, P., *The United States Constitution*. Palo Alto, California: Behavioral Research Laboratories, 1964.

Science Curriculum Materials

Barr, G., *Here's Why: Science in Sports*. Englewood Cliffs, New Jersey: Scholastic Magazines and Book Services, 1965.

Beauchamp, W. L., J. C. Mayfield, and P. D. Hurd, *Science Problems*. Fair Lawn, New Jersey: Scott, Foresman and Company.

Beck, J. H., *Understanding the Automobile*. Chicago: Follett Publishing Company, 1965.

Eisman, L. and C. Tanzer, *Biology and Human Progress*. Englewood Cliffs, New Jersey: Prentice-Hall, Inc., 1964.

Fitzpatrick, F. L., *Investigating Living Things*. New York: Harcourt, Brace and World, Inc., 1966.

————, *Living Things*. New York: Harcourt, Brace and World, Inc., 1966.

Herron, W. B. and N. P. Palmer, *Matter, Life, and Energy*. Chicago: Lyons and Carnahan, 1965.

Holton, G. and D. Ruller, *Foundations of Modern Physical Science*. Reading, Massachusetts: Addison-Wesley, Inc., 1959.

Moore, S., *Science Project Handbook*. New York: Ballantine Books, 1964.

Pella, M. O. and A. G. Wood, *Physical Science for Progress*. Englewood Cliffs, New Jersey: Prentice-Hall, Inc., 1964.

Selsam, M. E., *Birth of an Island*. Englewood Cliffs, New Jersey: Scholastic Magazines and Book Services, 1965.

Stollberg, R. and F. F. Hill, *Physics: Fundamentals and Frontiers*. New York: Houghton Mifflin Company, 1965.

Stone, C. K., *Science in Action*. Englewood Cliffs, New Jersey: Prentice-Hall, Inc., 1964.

————, *Science You Can Use*. Englewood Cliffs, New Jersey: Prentice-Hall, Inc., 1964.

Sullivan, M. W., *A Programmed Introduction to the Game of Chess*. Palo Alto, California: Behavioral Research Laboratories, 1963.

————, *Programmed Astronomy*. New York: McGraw-Hill, Inc., 1963.

Thurber, W. A. and R. E. Kilburn, *Exploring Earth Science*. Rockleigh, New Jersey: Allyn and Bacon, Inc., 1965.

————, *Exploring Life Science*. Rockleigh, New Jersey: Allyn and Bacon, Inc., 1966.

————, *Exploring Physical Science*. Rockleigh, New Jersey: Allyn and Bacon, Inc., 1966.

Weisbruck, F. T. et al., *A Laboratory Text for Physical Science*. Boston, Massachusetts: D. C. Heath and Company, 1965.

Science Texts

Creative Science Series. Ress, E. S. (Mankato, Minnesota: Creative Educational Society, Inc.).
  Atoms, Energy and Machines. 1965.
  The Earth's Story. 1965.
  Planets, Stars and Space. 1965.
  The Way of the Weather. 1965.

Exploring Science Series. (Rockleigh, New Jersey: Allyn and Bacon, Inc.). Thurber, W. A. and M. C. Durkee. Books 4–6. 1966.

The Science Bookshelf—each text with a filmstrip. (Chicago: Benefic Press).
  Munch, T., *What Is Light?* 1960.
  ————, *What Is a Rocket?* 1961.
  ————, *What Is a Solar System?* 1961.
  Reuben, G., *What Is a Magnet?* 1961.
  Syrocki, B., *What Is Electricity?* 1960.
  ————, *What Is Weather?* 1960.

Science Skills Text Series. (Columbus, Ohio: Charles E. Merrill Books, Inc.). Neal, C. D. and D. E. Perkins. Books 4–6. 1965–1966.

Mathematics Curriculum Materials

Aiken, D. J. and C. A. Beseman, *Modern Mathematics—Topics and Problems*. New York: McGraw-Hill Book Company, 1964.

Armstrong, E. G., D. Porter, and H. F. Spitzer, *Introduction to Multiplication.* New York: McGraw-Hill Book Company, 1964.

Bartoo, G. C. and J. Osborn, *Foundation Mathematics.* Palo Alto, California: Fearon Publishers, Inc., 1954.

Kahn, C. H. and J. B. Hanna, *Money Makes Sense.* New York: Houghton Mifflin Company, 1960.

————, *Using Dollars and Sense.* New York: Houghton Mifflin Company, 1963.

Nelson, G. P., *General Mathematics for the Shop.* Englewood Cliffs, New Jersey: Prentice-Hall, Inc., 1956.

Peters, E., *Going Places With Mathematics.* Englewood Cliffs, New Jersey: Prentice-Hall, Inc., 1962.

Reckless, M. W., *Understanding Arithmetic.* Englewood Cliffs, New Jersey: Prentice-Hall, Inc., 1961.

Stein, E. I., *Refresher Mathematics.* Rockleigh, New Jersey: Allyn and Bacon, Inc., 1966.

Studebaker, J. W. et al., *Self-Teaching Arithmetic.* (Five Books). Englewood Cliffs, New Jersey: Scholastic Magazines and Book Services, 1962–1965.

Mathematics Texts

Consumer Mathematics Series. Knowles, D. H. (Palo Alto, California: Behavioral Research Laboratories).
    Book 1. *Vocational Opportunities.* 1965–1966.
    Book 2. *The Pay Check.* 1965–1966.
    Book 3. *The Household Budget.* 1965–1966.

The Continental Press Pre-Printed Master Carbon Units. (Elizabethtown, Pennsylvania: Continental Press).
    Learning New Skills in Arithmetic. (Grades 1–6). 1962–1964.
    Reading-Thinking Skills. (Levels 4–6). 1962–1964.

Decimals and Percentage Series. Hauck, W. et al. Books 1 and 2. New York: McGraw-Hill Book Company, 1966.

Discovering Mathematics Series. DeVault, M. and R. Osborn. Books 1–5. Columbus, Ohio: Charles E. Merrill, 1965–1966.

Foundation of Algebra Series. Lancaster, J. and J. Cardwell. Books 1 and 2. Columbus, Ohio: Charles E. Merrill, 1965.

Fractions Series. Books 1, 2, and 3. Columbus, Ohio: Charles E. Merrill, 1966.

Fundamentals of Mathematics Series. Stein, E. I. (Rockleigh, New Jersey: Allyn and Bacon, Inc.)
    First Course in Mathematics. 1966.
    Second Course in Mathematics. 1966.

Introduction to Secondary Mathematics Series. Haeg, V. H. and A. E. Dubley. Vols. I and II. Boston: D. C. Heath and Company, 1964.

Lennes' Essentials of Arithmetic Series. Lennes, N. J. Books 6, 7, and 8. Summit, New Jersey: Laidlaw Brothers, 1964.

Lessons for Self-Instruction in Basic Skills Series. Brueckner, L. J. (Monterey, California: California Test Bureau).
    Addition 1–5. 1963–1965.

Division 1–5. 1963–1965.

Multiplication 1–5. 1963–1965.

Subtraction 1–5. 1963–1965.

Lessons in Self-Instruction in Contemporary Mathematics. (Monterey, California: California Test Bureau).

Bases I and II. Harvey, E. C. 1965.

Modular Arithmetic. Johnson, V. M. 1965.

Properties of Whole Numbers I and II. Harvey, E. C. 1965.

Sets and Set Symbols. Harvey, E. C. 1965.

Modern Mathematics for Achievement Series. Herrick, M. C. (New York: Houghton Mifflin Company).

Book 1. *The Set of Whole Numbers.* 1966.

Book 2. *Combining Whole Numbers.* 1966.

Book 3. *Number Relations.* 1966.

Book 4. *Understanding Subtraction.* 1966.

Book 5. *Properties of Multiplication.* 1966.

Book 6. *Understanding Division.* 1966.

Book 7. *The Set of Positive Rational Numbers.* 1966.

Book 8. *Applying Number Ideas.* 1966.

Modern Mathematics Series. Dolcieni, M. P. (New York: Houghton Mifflin Company).

Modern Algebra Book I. 1965.

Modern Algebra and Trigonometry II. 1965.

Modern Geometry III. 1965.

New Ways in Numbers. Elwell, C. E. Books 7 and 8. Boston: D. C. Heath and Company, 1965.

Programmed Mathematics for Adults. Sullivan, M. D. Books 1–6. New York: McGraw-Hill Book Company, 1965–1966.

Programmed Modern Arithmetic. Fitzgerald, J. F. (ed.). (Boston: D. C. Heath and Company).

Logic. 1965.

Introduction to Set. S-1. 1965.

Set Relations. S-2. 1965.

Set Operations. S-3. 1965.

Programmed Units in Mathematics. Denmark, E. T. (New York: Houghton Mifflin Company).

Basic Mixture Problems. 1966.

Basic Motions Problems. 1966.

Basic Work Problems. 1966.

Seeing Through Mathematics. Van Engen, H. et al. Books 1–3. Fair Lawn, New Jersey: Scott, Foresman and Company, 1962–1964.

Self-Teaching Arithmetic Series. Studebaker, J. W. Books 1–5. Englewood Cliffs, New Jersey: Scholastic Magazines and Book Services, 1962–1965.

Miscellaneous Curriculum Materials

Anton, S., *Charley, the T.V. Repairman.* New York: McGraw-Hill Book Company, 1965.

Miscellaneous Texts

Accent/Personality Series. Dare, B. F. and E. J. Wolfe. (Chicago: Follett Publishing Company).
Taking Stock. 1965–1966.
You and Heredity and Environment. 1965–1966.
You and They. 1965–1966.
You and Your Needs. 1965–1966.
Curriculum Development Series. Fay, L. C. (Chicago: Lyons and Carnahan).
Better Than Gold. 1966.
Three Green Men and Other Stories. 1966.
Holt Adult Education Series. (Basic, Intermediate, Advanced). (New York: Holt, Rinehart and Winston, Inc.).
Brice, E. W., *Arithmetic.* 1963.
Cooper, W. M. and V. C. Ewing, *How to Get Along on the Job.* 1966.
Crabtree, A. P., *You and the Law.* 1964.
Crothers, G. D., *American History.* 1964.
Fairchild, J. E., *Principles of Geography for Adults.* 1964.
Goss, J. P., *The Thomases Live Here.* 1965.
Grossnickel, F. E., *Fundamental Mathematics for Adults.* 1964.
Harbeck, R. M., and L. K. Johnson, *Earth and Space Science.* 1965.
———, *Physical Science.* 1965.
Henderson, E. C. and T. L. Henderson, *Learning to Read and Write.* 1965.
Israel, S., *Introduction to Geography.* 1964.
Morris, P. D., *Life With the Lucketts.* 1965.
Pomeroy, J. H., *Science.* 1964.
Starks, J., *Measure, Cut, and Sew.* 1966.
Toyer, A., *Get Your Money's Worth.* 1965.
Weinhold, C. E., *English.* 1962.

Materials for Teachers of Urban Youth

A representative list of books for the professional educator follows. Although it is by no means a definitive bibliography on urban education it does represent a group of books that participants in the Princeton-Trenton Institute found particularly helpful.

Allen, V. F., *On Teaching English to Speakers of Other Languages.* Champaign, Illinois: National Council of Teachers of English, 1965.
Anderson, P. S., V. D. Anderson, F. Ballantine, and V. M. Howes, *Readings in the Language Arts.* New York: Macmillan Company, 1964.
Ashley, A. and J. Malmstrom, *Dialects, U.S.A.* Champaign, Illinois: National Council of Teachers of English, 1963.
Ashton-Warner, S., *Teacher.* New York: Bantam Books, Inc., 1964.
Bair, M. and R. G. Woodward, *Team Teaching in Action.* New York: Houghton Mifflin Company, 1964.
Baldwin, J., *The Fire Next Time.* New York: Dell Publishing Company, 1964.

Baldwin, J., *Nobody Knows My Name*. New York: Dell Publishing Company, 1960.

Bang, M. A. and L. V. Johnson, *Classroom Group Behavior*. New York: Macmillan Company, 1964.

Bard, H., W. D. Moreland, and T. N. Cline, *Citizenship and Government*. New York: Holt, Rinehart and Winston, Inc., 1966.

Baumgartner, J. C. and T. P. Blaich, *The Challenge of Democracy*. New York: McGraw-Hill Book Company, 1966.

Bears, Y., *Introduction to the Theory of Errors*. Reading, Massachusetts: Addison-Wesley, 1957.

Bell, N. T., R. W. Burkhardt, and V. B. Lawhead, *Introduction to College Life*. New York: Houghton Mifflin Company, 1966.

Birch, J. W., *Retrieving the Retarded Reader*. Illinois: Public School Publishing Company, 1955.

————, *Improving Children's Speech*. Illinois: Public School Publishing Company, 1958. (Found in Education Index, June 1957–June 1959).

Birch, J. W. and E. M. McWilliams, *Challenging Gifted Children*. Illinois: Public School Publishing Company, 1955.

Birch, J. W. and G. D. Stevens, *Reaching the Mentally Retarded*. Illinois: Public School Publishing Company, 1955.

Birch, J. W. and E. H. Stullken, *Solving Problems of Problem Children*. Illinois: Public School Publishing Company, 1956.

Bloom, B. S., *Stability and Change in Human Characteristics*. New York: John Wiley and Sons, Inc., 1964.

Bloom, B. S., A. Davis, and R. Hess, *Compensatory Education for Cultural Deprivation*. New York: Holt, Rinehart and Winston, Inc., 1965.

Bloom, B. S., *Taxonomy of Educational Objectives*. New York: David McKay Company, Inc., 1966.

Bloomfield, L., *Language*. New York: Holt, Rinehart and Winston, Inc., 1964.

Bloomgarden, C. R., E. D. Furedi, L. W. Randolph, and E. D. Ruth, *Learning to Teach in Urban Schools*. New York: Teachers College Press, 1965.

Bommarito, B. and A. Kerber, *The Schools and the Urban Crisis*. New York: Holt, Rinehart and Winston, Inc., 1965.

Borgh, E. M., *Grammatical Patterns and Composition*.

Bostwick, G., *Lessons for Self-Instruction in Basic Skills*. Monterey, California: California Testing Bureau, 1963–1966.

Brembeck, C. S., *Social Foundations of Education*. New York: John Wiley and Sons, Inc., 1966.

Bruner, J. S., *The Process of Education*. New York: Random House, 1960.

Buchanan, C. D., *Programmed Reading for Adults*. New York: McGraw-Hill Book Company, 1966.

Butman, A., D. Reis, and D. Sohn, *Paperbacks in the Schools*. New York: Bantam Books, Inc., 1963.

Cain, A. H., *Young People and Drinking*. New York: Dell Publishing Company, 1964.

Carlson, R. K., *Sparkling Words*.

Clark, K. B., *Dark Ghetto*. Elmsford, New York: Harper and Row Inc., 1965.

Clegg, A. B., *The Excitement of Writing*. London: Chatto & Winders, 1964.

Cole, L., *Handwriting for Left-handed Children*. Indianapolis: Bobbs-Merrill Company, 1955.

Combs, A. W., *The Professional Education of Teachers.* Rockleigh, New Jersey: Allyn and Bacon, Inc., 1965.

Combs, A. W. and J. B. Snygg, *Individual Behavior.* Elmsford, New York: Harper and Row, Inc., 1959.

Conant, J. B., *The Education of American Teachers.* New York: McGraw-Hill Book Company, 1963.

Conant, J. B., *Slums and Suburbs.* New York: McGraw-Hill Book Company, 1961.

Cottle, W. C., *School Interest Inventory.* New York: Houghton Mifflin Company, 1966.

Crosby, M., *Reading Ladders for Human Relations.*

Crow, L. D., W. I. Murray, and H. H. Smyth, *Educating the Culturally Disadvantaged Child.* New York: David McKay Company, Inc., 1966.

Deighton, L. C., *Vocabulary Development in the Classroom.* New York: Teachers College Press, 1965.

DeLancey, R. W., *Linguistics and Teaching.*

Emery, R. W., *Variant Spellings in Modern American Dictionaries.* Champaign, Illinois: National Council of Teachers of English, 1961.

Emery, R. C. and M. B. Houshower, *High-Interest-Easy Reading for Junior and Senior High School Reluctant Readers.* Champaign, Illinois: National Council of Teachers of English, 1965.

Epstein, S. and B. Epstein, *What's Behind the World?* Englewood Cliffs, New Jersey: Scholastic Magazines and Book Services, 1965.

Erickson, E. N., *Youth: Change and Challenge.* New York: Basic Books, 1963.

Essian-Udomp E. V., *Black Nationalism.* New York: Dell Publishing Company, 1965.

Evans, B. and J. L. Lynch, *High School English Textbooks: A Critical Examination.* Boston: Little, Brown and Company, 1963.

Fader, D. and M. H. Shaevitz, *Hooked on Books.* New York: Berkley Publishing Corporation, 1966.

Featherstone, W. B., *Teaching the Slow Learner.* New York: Teachers College Press, 1951.

Ferman, L. A. and J. L. Kornbleh, *Poverty in America.* Ann Arbor, Michigan: University of Michigan, 1965.

Fox, R. and R. Lippett, *Diagnosing Classroom Learning Environments.* Chicago: Science Research Associates, 1966.

———, *Problem Solving to Improve Classroom Learning.* Chicago: Science Research Associates, 1966.

———, *Role-Playing Methods in the Classroom.* Chicago: Science Research Associates, 1966.

Fraenkel, G., *What Is Language.* Boston: Ginn and Company, 1965.

Fraser, D. M., H. N. Rivlin, and M. Stein, *The First Years in College.* New York: Houghton Mifflin Company, 1965.

Freeman, J., *Literature and Locality.* London: Cassell & Co., Ltd., 1963.

Friedenberg, E., *The Vanishing Adolescent.* New York: Dell Publishing Company, 1966.

Fries, C. C., *Linguistics.* New York: Holt, Rinehart and Winston, Inc., 1964.

Frost, J. L. and G. R. Hawkes, *The Disadvantaged Child.* New York: Houghton Mifflin Company, 1966.

Fuchs, E., *Pickets at the Gates.* New York: Macmillan Company, 1966.

Gibson, J. S., *Ideology and World Affairs.* Houghton Mifflin Company, 1964.

Glaus, M., *From Thoughts to Words.* Champaign, Illinois: National Council of Teachers of English, 1965.

Gleason, H. A., *An Introduction to Descriptive Linguistics.* New York: Holt, Rinehart and Winston, Inc., 1965.

Goldstein, P., *How to Do an Experiment.* New York: Harcourt, Brace and World, 1957.

Goodman, P., *Growing Up Absurd.* New York: Random House, 1960.

Gross, R., *The Teacher and the Taught.* New York: Dell Publishing Company, 1963.

Hall, R. A. J., *Sound and Spelling in English.* Philadelphia: Chilton, 1961.

Hansen, C. F., D. L. Johnson, L. C. Walker, and O. E. Webb, *A Handbook for Young Writers.* Englewood Cliffs, New Jersey: Prentice-Hall, 1965.

Hansen, D. A. and J. E. Gerstl, *On Education—Sociological Perspectives.* John Wiley and Sons, Inc., 1967.

Hayes, A. S., *Recommendations of the Work Conference on Literacy.* Washington, D.C.: Center for Applied Linguistics, 1965.

Herriott, R. E. and N. H. St. John, *Social Class and the Urban School,* John Wiley and Sons, Inc., 1966.

Holt, J., *How Children Fail.* New York: Dell Publishing Company, 1964.

Hunt, K. W., *Grammatical Structures Written at Three Grade Levels.* Champaign, Illinois: National Council of Teachers of English, 1965.

Jennings, F. C., *This Is Reading.* New York: Dell Publishing Company, 1965.

Keats, J., *The Sheepskin Psychosis.* New York: Dell Publishing Company, 1965.

Kelley, E. C., *Education for What Is Real.* New York: Harper and Row, Inc., 1947.

———, *In Defense of Youth.* Englewood Cliffs, New Jersey: Prentice-Hall, 1963.

Kenworthy, L. S., *Three Billion Neighbors.* Boston: Ginn and Company, 1965.

Koernar, J. D., *The Case for Basic Education.* Boston: Little, Brown and Company, 1959.

Landes, R., *Culture in American Education.* New York: John Wiley and Sons, Inc., 1965.

Lane, H. A., *On Teaching Human Beings.* Chicago: Follett Publishing Company, 1964.

Lanning, F. W. and W. A. Many, *Basic Education for the Disadvantaged Adult.* New York: Houghton Mifflin Company, 1966.

Lifton, W. M., *Working With Groups.* New York: John Wiley and Sons, Inc., 1966.

Loban, W. D., *The Language of Elementary Children.* Champaign, Illinois: National Council of Teachers of English, 1963.

———, *Problems in Oral English.* Champaign, Illinois: National Council of Teachers of English, 1966.

Loretan, J. O. and S. Umans, *Teaching the Disadvantaged.* New York: Teachers College Press, 1966.

Malm, M., *Psychology for Living.* New York: McGraw-Hill Book Company, 1964.

Maslow, A. H., *Toward a Psychology of Being.* Princeton, New Jersey: Van Nostrand Press, 1962.

Melman, S., *Our Depleted Society*. New York: Dell Publishing Company, 1965.

Miller, M. V. and E. Gilmore, *Revolution at Berkeley*. New York: Dell Publishing Company, 1965.

Milstein, E., *Language Arts Can Be Creative*. Washington, D.C.: National Education Association, 1959.

Mok, P. P., *Pushbutton Parents and the Schools*. New York: Dell Publishing Company, 1964.

Nash, L. K., *The Atomic-Molecular Theory*. Cambridge, Massachusetts: Harvard University Press, 1965.

Neill, A. S., *Summerhill*. New York: Hart Publishing, 1964.

Newsome, V. L., *Structural Grammar in the Classroom.*

Ogburn, W. F., *Social Change*. New York: Dell Publishing Company, 1966.

Otto, W., and R. A. McMenemy, *Corrective and Remedial Teaching*. New York: Houghton Mifflin Company, 1966.

Passow, A. H., *Education in Depressed Areas*. New York: Teachers College Press, 1966.

Pedersen, D. O., *The Disadvantaged Student: A Conflict of Cultures in the School.*

Prascott, D. A., *The Child in the Educative Process*. New York: McGraw-Hill Book Company, 1957.

Rasmussen, M., *Reading in the Kindergarten?*

Riessman, F., *The Culturally Deprived Child*. Elmsford, New York: Harper and Row, Inc., 1962.

Rogers, C. R., *On Becoming a Person*. New York: Houghton Mifflin Company, 1959.

Russell, D. H. and E. F. Russell, *Listening Aids Through the Grades*. New York: Teachers College Press, 1959.

Sauer, E. H., *English in the Secondary School*. New York: Holt, Rinehart and Winston, Inc., 1965.

Sexton, P. C., *Education and Income*. New York: The Viking Press, Inc., 1965.

Sherif, C. W. and M. Sherif, *Problems of Youth*. Chicago: Aldine Publishing Company, 1965.

Smith, D. V., *Fifty Years of Children's Books*. Champaign, Illinois: National Council of Teachers of English, 1963.

Squire, J. A., *The Responses of Adolescents While Reading Four Short Stories*. Champaign, Illinois: National Council of Teachers of English, 1964.

Stanford, N., *Self and Society*. New York: Atherton Press, 1966.

Stewart, W. A., *Non-Standard Speech and the Teaching of English*. Washington, D.C.: Center for Applied Linguistics, 1964.

Stewart, L. H. and C. F. Warnath, *The Counselor and Society*. New York: Houghton Mifflin Company, 1965.

Stryker, D., *Educating the Teachers of English*. Champaign, Illinois: National Council of Teachers of English, 1965.

Thomas, O., *Transformational Grammar and the Teacher of English*. New York: Holt, Rinehart and Winston, Inc., 1966.

Thomas, R. M., *Social Differences in the Classroom*. New York: David McKay Company, Inc., 1965.

Torrance, E. and R. Strom, *Mental Health and Achievement*. New York: John Wiley and Sons, Inc., 1965.

Tunley, R., *Kids, Crime and Chaos*. New York: Dell Publishing Company, 1966.

Turner, R. H., *A Letter to Teachers of America's Cultural Victims*. Chicago: Follett Publishing Company, 1964.

Usdam, M. and F. Bertolaet, *Teachers for the Disadvantaged*. Chicago: Follett Publishing Company, 1966.

Walcutt, C. C., *Tomorrow's Illiterates*. Boston: Little, Brown and Company, 1961.

Webster, S. W., *Educating the Disadvantaged Learner*. San Francisco: Chandler Publishing Company, 1966.

————, *Knowing the Disadvantaged*. San Francisco: Chandler Publishing Company, 1966.

————, *Understanding the Problems of the Disadvantaged Learner*. San Francisco: Chandler Publishing Company, 1966.

Westby-Gibson, D., *Social Perspectives on Education*. New York: John Wiley and Sons, Inc., 1965.

Wetmore, T. W., *Linguistics in the Classroom*. Champaign, Illinois: National Council of Teachers of English, 1963.

Springboards Program

One of the most successful published programs of reading material for disadvantaged youth is the *Springboards Program* published by Portal Press. *Springboards* is a series of reading designed to get the reader who has not been achieving into the regular curriculum. They are self-contained motivating lessons and can be used in a great variety of ways. Several of the coordinating teachers made use of them over the past two summers at Princeton University. How they were used has been mentioned previously in several essays in the English and social studies section. Because of the unique qualities of *Springboards* we have reproduced an entire *Springboard* as an example of new curricular materials.

FEAR

AIM
To become more balanced in dealing with our helpful and harmful fears.

WHERE DO FEARS COME FROM?
It is generally agreed that all babies when born, have only **two** or three fears, if any at all, such as (a) fear of a loud noise, (b) fear of falling, (c) and a possible fear of its safety or bodily harm.

Most of our fears are learned from the examples of older people, older children and sometimes from parents. Many times fear comes from ignorance, or not knowing what to do.

SOME CAUSES OF FEAR
If we do not have such things as the following we might develop fear; by gaining these things we eliminate many fears.

1. We like to feel secure and safe;
2. We want our parents to be proud of us and to love us; we want others to like us;
3. We want to amount to something and do something worthwhile;
4. We want to be a success;
5. We want to be at least "a little somebody";
6. We want to feel that we belong and are accepted by our family or group;
7. We want to be counted by our group; to be at least a little important;
8. We don't want to be "made fun of," belittled, or laughed at or considered stupid;
9. We want to feel that we are "needed";
10. We want to be able to master life's problems.

FOUR WAYS OF ACTING — WITH FEAR
When we feel that we lack, or do not have some of these ten things, we sometimes over-do or over-act in order to make a better impression on others to gain more recognition, or to make a "better showing" to get more attention, and so feel more secure. However, we might feel like showing off, acting tough, or putting off and running away from facing our problem. But, since most all pupils have a few fears, some pupils face their problems "face on" and **do** something about it. They try and try to get their work done, by working a little harder, a little longer and so learn to master some of their fears. With each victory, they gain more power and courage to face the next problem .

PHYSICAL EFFECTS OF FEAR
Fear, to primitive man, was one of his great blessings in helping him to save his life. For one thing, fear gave him "super-speed" to run away from danger or "super-strength" to fight for his life;

or made him "super-stiff" (scared stiff) so that he was not easily noticed.

People may react to fear in these ways:

1. They may draw back or jump
2. They may hide (even a little child when afraid to look at something, will hide his face behind his hands—then later peek through the opened fingers of his hand)
3. They may tremble with fear
4. They may become alert; hearing sharpens, eyes open wide, fixed stare, even mouth opens wide
5. Their mouth may become dry
6. Their lips may tremble
7. Their heart may beat faster
8. They may breathe faster
9. They may have a cold sweat; shake inside
10. They may have a "sick feeling in the stomach"

FEAR—OF THINGS THAT YOU CAN AND CANNOT CONTROL

Which do some people usually fear more, the known or the unknown; real or imaginary danger; the past, present, or future? It might be interesting for you to check up on how many things came true that you had feared or worried about in the past.

Many a pupil can be a success in many things even if he fails in a few things, or even if he failed in some subject last term. Very few people have been successful in one thing without failing in some other things.

If one learns a lesson from a mistake, then his "mistake can be a stepping stone instead of a stumbling block." There are some things we can't do much about. We can't change the past; so there is no use worrying "over spilled milk." But we can do something about what we are doing TODAY!

FEARS OF SOME STUDENTS

Many students have said that they have had fears while in school. Here are four of the fears that were listed more than others:

1. Fear of being laughed at by the class
2. Fear of not passing
3. Fear of detention
4. Fear of some teachers

Some pupils might fear certain teachers because they do not understand the teacher or his ways.

(a) Find out how to get along with the teacher. How do the other pupils do it? Do you think you could get along better with the teacher if you **really** wanted to?

(b) Whom can you change more easily, yourself or your teacher in making a better adjustment? He has many pupils to get along with at one time and you have only one teacher at a time.

(c) If you do not understand what the teacher says, or if it is not clear as to what is required in the assignment then which is a better thing to do: to ask the teacher what you don't understand (he will make it clear) or to sit there in silent fear while trying to prepare your lesson, confused and not knowing what is wanted? If YOU show interest like that it can't help but bring about a better understanding, and so lessen your fears.

FEAR OF MAKING A MISTAKE AND BEING LAUGHED AT

Try your best to make at **least** one **correct** statement when you begin your recitation. Be sure that you recite, even if you do make a mistake and even if some pupils laugh. If they laugh then you laugh too. Be **determined** to recite and you will soon notice that you will make fewer and fewer mistakes and that you will gain in confidence and poise. Many pupils have hoped and even prayed that the teacher wouldn't call on them on some days. This situation is a warning that it is **necessary** to prepare your lesson thoroughly for the next day.

FEAR OF NOT PASSING AND OF TESTS

Here are some good suggestions from pupils who have overcome some of their fear of failing.

1. Be INTERESTED in your subject.
2. Clearly understand each day's assignment.
3. Study your lesson to learn something, not merely to pass.
4. If you feel that you might fail, have a talk with your teacher at once.
5. Recite the best you can **each** time the teacher calls on you. But be sure to recite, even if you don't do so well at times. Practice will give you more experience and this will help you gain more confidence in expressing yourself.
6. Remember that the teacher can't understand how much you know if you don't tell him.
7. Have in your mind several of the **main** points or **important** ideas of each lesson.
8. If you study with someone else in your class be sure that you get your work done WITH him and not FROM him. Bring in your homework ON TIME.
9. Make up your mind at the beginning of the term that you are going to **work,** to learn, and to pass, not just merely get by "by the skin of your teeth."
10. Set a REGULAR TIME for doing your assignment and homework and let nothing interfere with that time. Don't trade your homework time, for doing something else of less value.
11. Watch the teacher carefully in class recitations and when making lesson assignments. See what he emphasizes most.

Here is a rule that might help you pass—"Understand the assignment CLEARLY, and do your work THOROUGHLY."

IGNORANCE AND FEAR — FAITH

How many people do you think would fail in school if they were in "dead earnest" to succeed and determined to do their best?

As our knowledge and understanding decrease our ignorance and fears, they also increase our feeling of security, self-confidence, self-assurance and self-reliance to face our problems tomorrow.

One way to get rid of many feelings of being inferior is to COOPERATE more with our class or at home, by taking more active part in doing things. Then, trying to CONTRIBUTE some of the ability we have, to improve conditions in the class and at home. In this way we can gain more **real** recognition, satisfaction, and confidence in our ability and so increase our courage and faith to face the future.

All that anyone can do, is to do his best. Who can do more? He who does his best cannot be considered a failure, can he?

WHEN OUR WAY IS CLEAR

After struggling intelligently to understand our fears we gain real joy when we feel and see that "our way looks clear **ahead**." Then, the greater the obstacle to overcome the greater will be the glory in mastering it.

Many people fear the wrong things. WE SHOULD KNOW THE CAUSE OF OUR FEAR AND MASTER FEARS WITH REASON AND PRACTICE! Faith at its best gives us super mental and super spiritual strength to meet our emergencies.

> Today well lived
> Makes every Yesterday a Dream of HAPPINESS
> And every Tomorrow a Vision of HOPE
> Look well, therefore to this Day!
> Such is the Salutation of the Dawn.
> —From THE SANSCRIT

QUESTIONS

1. Explain how fear is in many ways a protection and blessing to us in saving us from some real or actual danger. (Read about adrenal glands in connection with fear.)
2. Explain how people develop some of the fears they have. Give examples.
3. How would you help younger pupils to overcome some of these fears?
   a. Fear of failing
   b. Fear of being laughed at in class
   c. Fear of detention, some teachers, parents, or people with authority
   d. Fear of being alone, of high places, of darkness
4. Name some fears that you had when you were younger, which you have conquered by now. Explain how you did it, if you can.
5. How do fear and faith differ in the ways we face the unknown future problems?

HUMAN ENGINEERING

AIM — The importance of personal responsibility in being a Human Engineer.

Human engineering means the great adventure of building our life. All of us are human engineers because all of us have a life to build. Some of us are good engineers and others are poor ones. Some people like Washington, Lincoln, Edison and Madame Curie build of their lives strong, beautiful and useful structures that people admire and respect.

Here are four questions; answer them carefully.

1. Would you rather build your own life or have someone else build it for you?
2. Why would you rather build it yourself?
3. Who will have to be responsible for the kind of life you are building now and the life you are going to build?
4. BIG QUESTION—Will you be willing to take that responsibility? (Think this over carefully.) Will you be willing to take that responsibility if you fail? If you succeed? What three things are you willing to be responsible for NOW?

One of the big things that a human engineer learns is to have a deep feeling of personal responsibility. He is willing to take responsibility for what he does, whether he succeeds or fails, although he might get help from wherever it is available. Some people are ready and willing to say, "I did it," when everything goes along well but when things don't go along so well it is so easy to blame someone or something else. For example:

1. Grade 95%—"I did it"—Who deserved it?
2. Grade 60%—"The teacher did it"— Who deserved it?

One thing that a human engineer does is not to make so many excuses and alibis for his own mistakes, but he is willing to "face-up" to his own mistakes and correct them so as not to make the same mistake again.

Human engineering is the great adventure of living one day at a time, and making the most of our lives with the abilities we have.

Here are six steps: steps that have helped many people to be human engineers:

NEED — We can make the world or someone need us. When are we happier, when we feel that we are needed or when not needed? When we are needed we feel that we do count and amount to something. Our parents need us, the school needs us, and regardless of how little we can do now or later, our community needs us. How terrible we would feel if no one needed us. True?

What are people going to need **you** for? Perhaps you can answer that better than anyone else. But, one thing is rather certain and that is that you are needed for the things that you can do best, where you have some ability. It doesn't make much difference what kind of a job it is, for all jobs are important if they are helpful jobs. There are no two people exactly alike so each one of us can do something just a little different from anyone else. What are three or four jobs that you can do pretty well already?

PLAN — One of the first things done to build the building which you are in, was the making of the plan, a plan thought out by the architect. Plans will help you to build the kind of a life you want. You might say, "I am young, and cannot plan my whole life." When you know just what you would like to do, you could make a general plan, at least. This would help you to make some definite plan for the next five or ten years, or for one term of school, or at least for one day.

Your day's work can be planned so that you will be able to accomplish more and have time for play. If you planned one day ahead how much time would you allow for working, sleeping, eating, doing homework, playing, and listening to the radio? Are you better off in life with a plan or without one? (Think this over carefully.) What would you think of your father if he tried to build a house without a plan, or what would you think of your mother if she tried to make a dress without some pattern? "PLAN YOUR WORK AND WORK YOUR PLAN."

FOUNDATION — Is the foundation in a building very important or is it just thrown together? Well! it all depends what kind of a building it is, doesn't it?

Each day is a foundation for the next day. So each day is important by itself, just as each stone in a foundation or wall is a foundation for the next stone. A building cannot stand very well if it is built on a weak foundation. Neither can a good life stand up so well under all problems and difficulties, if it is built on a weak foundation.

The bricks of our own foundation for life might be compared to our habits. Perhaps you already have checked up what kind of habits you want. It would be interesting for you to check over such a list with your parents. They might suggest some other very useful habits which you can build into the foundation of your life now.

Life is an exciting adventure isn't it? With a good foundation you can look forward to more successful living, for you will be better able to meet whatever problems you will have to face. Here are four great cornerstones of a Human Engineer's life:

1. A GROWING MIND—growing in understanding.
2. TRAINED TONGUE—wounding less and less and expressing yourself better.
3. BIG HEART—beats with kindness in COOPERATION.
4. SKILLED HANDS—able to CONTRIBUTE to the good of the world.

Do you know what a keystone is—in an arch? If you do, then what would this important keystone be in building your own life?

GOAL—A goal simply means **what** you want to do, or **what** you want to be in life, or living with some purpose in mind. In order to reach some future big goal, we will have to reach some smaller present goals. Some people have worked their entire lifetime to reach their biggest goal. Without a goal we are somewhat like the boy who when asked where he was going, replied, "I don't know but I hope that I will get there." Or like Alice in Wonderland, when she met the Cheshire cat at the fork in the road, and wanted to know which road to take; but since she did not know where she wanted to go, she was told to take either road.

NOW—Some pupils have a definite goal in mind for learning as much as they can this term and passing; for this term is also a foundation for the next term. Not only do they have a goal but also plan to do each day's work and assignments on time, now; to take part in sports, club activities, or doing some extra work around the school. Two future goals that you could have now are: (1) what kind of trade or work would I like to follow when I am through school, or (2) what kind of a person do I want to be or what kind of a life do I want to build? Suppose you know what you would like to be doing ten years from now, then would it be better to plan now, or wait for nine years before making a plan to reach your goal?

IMPROVE—Shall we change our goal and plan after we have once made them? Here are three answers: "yes—no—maybe." "Maybe" seems to be the right answer, but to change our plans and goals **only** if we can IMPROVE them. Many people have had to change their plans and goals, and it is very interesting and exciting to improve our plans and goals from time to time. We might not be able to reach all of our goals, but we can improve our plan so that we can at least reach some of them. Many people have failed until they changed and improved their plans. Many believe that it is better to have a goal and try to reach it, even if they might fail, for at least they have had a lot of fun trying. There is an old saying, "It is better to have tried and failed, than never to have tried at all."

HUMAN ENGINEERING IS A GREAT ADVENTURE—The responsibility for the way we live is chiefly ours in failure or success, although we can get help from wherever it is available.

Human Engineers study the laws of life and how to live better and make use of these laws in their own daily living. They leave very little, if anything, to chance or guesswork. They must know how to think, read, study, and actually do things, as well as to have a clean, clear mind. We do not inherit habits; we develop them. You can choose and develop the habits you want in building the beautiful castle or the tumble-down shack that you must always call "ME." You cannot depend on someone else to build your whole life; YOU and YOU alone will build it.

QUESTIONS

1. Describe a person who you think is a good Human Engineer and tell why you think so.
2. How differently will these two people live; the one who feels responsible for the kind of life he lives, or the one who does not feel responsible?
3. What are some of the things for which you are willing to be responsible for now? At home? At school?
4. Are you better off in life with having a plan or taking life as it comes without a plan? Examples.
5. What difference would it make in a person if he felt that he was needed or if he felt that he was not needed? Examples.
6. Why do we say that no one else can build our whole life as well as we can?
7. Tell of some pupil who you think is a good Human Engineer, and just what makes him a good Human Engineer.
8. Write a small list of things that you believe will make a strong foundation for your life.
9. Here are some of the differences of two ways of living. The castle life and tumble-down shack life represent two different ways for living, but remember that they do not mean rich and poor people, nor do they mean living in a castle or a shack.

Castle Life	Tumble-Down Shack Life
a. Builds up	a. Tears down
b. Has a good foundation	b. Has a poor foundation
c. Sets a goal—makes a plan	c. Sets no goal—makes no plan
d. Cares how he lives	d. Does not care how he lives
e. Works hard	e. Loafs hard
f. Is a good citizen	f. Is a poor citizen

Clarify these problems.

A. Which one would most of us like to be—the shack person or the castle person? That was easy wasn't it?
B. Which one of these two will have more happiness and less sorrow all through life? Why do you think so?
C. If the castle person worked all his life, coming a little closer each day to reach a goal, but did not quite reach it, then which one would have more happiness and less sorrow all through life? Explain your view.
D. If both of these persons receive $2,500 every year as a gift from someone regardless of what they did, then which one do you think would have more happiness and less sorrow all through life?

PATHFINDER CLUBS—CLEVELAND PUBLIC SCHOOLS

MY JOB WAS TAKEN BY A BUTTON!

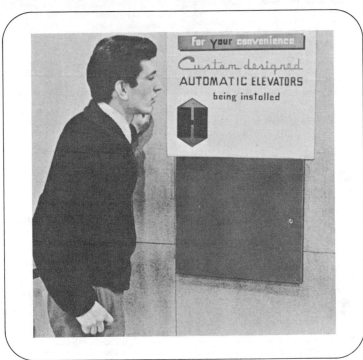

Marvin Allen Lee is a young man, twenty-two years old. He is well-liked by the people he has worked for and the people he has worked with. He always came to his job on time, worked hard, and never left until after quitting time.

Six months ago Marvin lost his job as an elevator man in a large office building in Chicago. You see, the building doesn't need men to run the elevators anymore. Now a passenger gets on the elevator, presses a button, and whizzes up to the floor he wants.

"My job was taken by a button," said Marvin bitterly. He wondered how he was going to make a living. Marvin did not go to school very long. He did not learn any real skill. The only jobs he ever had were those that could be learned in a very short time.

Marvin went home and told his wife his bad news. "What are we going to do now?" she asked, worried. Two young children were playing on the floor, and she was expecting another soon.

"I don't know," said Marvin, looking out of the window at the city. "I tell you this, though. I'm not going to let myself get beaten."

The next day he went to the State Employment Agency. He explained his problem to an interviewer there.

"You've a good record, Marvin," the man said. "Your employers liked you. I think we can do something for you."

Machines and People

Marvin was replaced by automation. That means a machine now does the work he did. This was not the first time Marvin had trouble with automation. Marvin's father was a coal miner in West Virginia. When Marvin was ten years old, a machine was put into the mine. It did the work of Marvin's father and twenty-four other men—and it did the work quicker and better. Marvin's father was thrown out of work and hasn't had a steady job since.

Marvin and his brothers and sisters left school to go to work and help support the family. Five years ago Marvin married and went to Chicago. He wanted to get away from a place where a machine could take away a man's job. Marvin loved his home. His family had lived in the same place for a long time, and he was the first Lee to leave in one hundred years. He missed the hills and the hunting in the fall and the smell of spring in the country. However, he was sure he had a better chance in Chicago.

Now Marvin has discovered that a machine can throw him out of work in a city, too.

What's Going to Be Done About It?

A lot of people have been thinking hard about automation. Some labor union leaders think there ought to be fewer working hours a week than there are now. Instead of a man working thirty-seven to forty hours a week, they say that perhaps he ought to work only thirty hours a week for the same pay. Someone else would have to fill out the missing hours. If this happened, then for every three or four men now working, another man could be hired. In this way many people now out of work would have jobs.

No one knows for sure, but it is thought by many experts that 40,000 people lose their jobs every week because of automation. That's over two million a year! These people can get other jobs if they learn other skills. This is what is called "retraining." Many thousands of unemployed men and women are being retrained today.

Hardest on Youth

Automation is hardest on people who do not have skills. A girl who is a good typist is not likely to lose her job because of automation, but a man who is good at digging ditches can lose his job because a machine can do the work faster and better. Yet, there are over 50,000 jobs in New York City alone that are not filled because people cannot be found for them. These jobs require skills that can be learned in school or in a retraining program.

Automation is hard on young people who have left school before graduation and do not have any skills. Secretary of Labor W. Willard Wirtz thinks that two million youths between the ages of sixteen and nineteen should be taken out of their jobs and sent back to school. Otherwise, he is afraid they will be "automated" out of the jobs they now have—as Marvin was. He feels there ought to be two more years of high school education so boys and girls can learn more technical skills and particular service trades.

Many educators believe that reading is at the heart of the problem. Usually, to learn skills a person must be able to read fairly well. Yet four out of every ten children entering the sixth grade in our nation will not finish school. Most of these students do not read well, but they could learn to read better by remaining in school and taking remedial reading courses. No one is ever too old to learn to read. Andrew Johnson, who became President of the United States after Abraham Lincoln was killed, learned to read and write after he was eighteen years old. Frederick Douglass, the great Negro writer, learned to read when he was more than twelve years old.

Automation Is a Good Thing, Too

We are all lucky to have automation. Machines can make work easier for people. When a farmer thousands of years ago found it was easier to get a horse to pull a plow than to push it himself, he had made the horse an "automated" machine. Today, the horse has been automated out of a job himself. Around 1900, there were fifty million horses in the United States. Almost all of these were used on farms. That was one horse for every two people in our country. Today huge machines have taken the place of horses on farms. They have also taken the place of men. Not too many years ago more people worked on farms than in any other kind of job. Today, it does not take many people to produce food to feed all our people—and many other people in the world. This has happened mainly because of the machine.

Automation has made life a lot easier for most people. Marvin Allen Lee knows this, and he is not as bitter as he was. He went back to school to learn new skills. He has been taking a reading course, too, because he knows he'll need to read to keep up with new things in his work.

Marvin has caught on so quickly to operating a huge lathe, that he has already been promised a job when he finishes his course next month. "You know," he happily told his wife, "it's a lot more fun running a machine than being run out of a job by one!"

Inside photo—(Scott Paper's foam process courtesy of Crane Co.)

WHAT DO YOU KNOW?

In the space at the right, put the letter for the answer you think is correct.

1. Marvin lost his job because (a) Marvin could not read; (b) automatic elevators were put in the building; (c) he never came to work on time.   _____

2. Marvin came to Chicago because (a) he wanted to be in a place where a machine could not replace a man in a job; (b) he wanted to come to school because in West Virginia he had to work to help the family; (c) he had been trained to be an elevator operator, and a city was the place to get a job as one.   _____

3. Marvin's father (a) lost his job in a mine because a machine took his place; (b) lost his job as a farmer because of horses; (c) wanted Marvin to go to Chicago.   _____

4. Some labor union leaders believe (a) men should work longer and then new machines would not be needed; (b) horses should be put back on the farms so more men would work there; (c) men ought to work fewer hours so more people could be hired.   _____

5. Automation means (a) the replacing of men by machines; (b) retraining people who have lost their jobs; (c) working less hours for the same pay.   _____

6. Automation is hardest on (a) teen-agers who have finished school; (b) people who do not have skills; (c) people who have passed the age of forty.   _____

7. Secretary of Labor Wirtz believes (a) there should be more dropouts; (b) many youths should go back to school; (c) people must work longer and harder.   _____

8. Many educators think (a) dropouts shouldn't have been in school at all; (b) reading is necessary to learn new skills; (c) most students should leave school after they finish the eighth grade.   _____

9. Automation makes life (a) easier for most people; (b) easy for young people to find work; (c) harder for people who have skills.   _____

10. Marvin is not so bitter as he was because (a) he went back to West Virginia; (b) he got another job as an elevator operator; (c) he is being retrained for another kind of work.   _____

Score ten points for each correct answer.

SPRINGBOARDS STAFF: *Editor-in-Chief:* Abraham Kavadlo, Teacher, Manhattan Vocational High School, and Lecturer, Hunter College, New York City. *Editorial Consultant:* Peter G. Kontos, Director, Summer Institute for Secondary School Teachers of Disadvantaged Youth, Princeton University, and formerly Curriculum Coordinator for Senior High Schools, Cleveland, Ohio. *Lesson Plan Consultant:* John P. Gallagher, Assistant Principal, Reading Specialist, South Huntington, New York.

Photo Credits: Wallace C. Vogt
     Scott Paper's form process courtesy of Crane Co.

Portal Press Inc., 369 Lexington Avenue, New York, N. Y. 10017

B44270

Publishers and Producers of Educational Materials*

The names and addresses of publishers and audio-visual manufacturers who submitted material for examination by the staff of the Princeton-Trenton Institute follow. This list is included here in the hope that educators will find such a list convenient.

Addison-Wesley, Inc., Reading, Massachusetts.

Allyn and Bacon, Inc., Rockleigh, New Jersey.

Ballantine Books, 101 Fifth Avenue, New York, New York.

Bantam Books, Inc., 271 Madison Avenue, New York, New York 10016.

Behavioral Research Laboratories, Box 577, Palo Alto, California.

Bell and Howell Company, 1700 Shaw Avenue, Cleveland, Ohio 44112.

Benefic Press, 1900 North Narragansett Avenue, Chicago, Illinois 60639.

Benziger Brothers, Inc., 7 East 51st Street, New York, New York.

Berkley Publishing Corporation, 15 East 26th Street, New York, New York 10010.

Bobbs-Merrill Company, Inc., Box 558, Indianapolis, Indiana 46206.

Brandon Films, Inc., 200 West 57th Street, New York, New York 10019.

California Test Bureau, Del Monte Research Park, Monterey, California 93940.

Chandler Publishing Company, 124 Spear Street, San Francisco, California 94105.

Channing L. Bete Company, Inc., Greenfield, Massachusetts 01301.

Classroom Materials, Inc., 93 Myrtle Drive, Great Neck, New York.

College Entrance Examination Board, 475 Riverside Drive, New York, New York 10027.

Collier-Macmillan Publishing Company, 60 5th Avenue, New York, New York 10011.

Commission on English, 687 Boylston Street, Boston, Massachusetts 02116.

Contemporary Films, 267 West 25th Street, New York, New York 10001.

Continental Press, Inc., Elizabethtown, Pennsylvania 17022.

Coronet Instructional Films, 65 East South Water Street, Chicago, Illinois 60601.

---

* Compiled by Howard Cranford and Carl Voth.

Creative Educational Society, Inc., 530 North Front, Mankato, Minnesota 56002.

Thomas Y. Crowell Company, 201 Park Avenue, New York, New York 10003.

Dell Publishing Company, Inc., 750 3rd Avenue, New York, New York, 10017.

Denoyer-Geppert Company, 5235 Ravenswood Avenue, Chicago, Illinois 60640.

Doubleday and Company, Inc., Garden City, Lond Island, New York 11531.

Educational Audio Visual, Inc., Pleasantville, New York 10570.

E.M.C. Corporation, 180 East 6th Street, St. Paul, Minnesota 55101.

Encyclopedia Britannica Films, Inc., 1150 Wilmette Avenue, Wilmette, Illinois 60091.

English Institute Materials Center, 4 Washington Place, New York, New York 10003.

Fearon Publishers, Inc., 2165 Park Boulevard, Palo Alto, California 94306.

Field Enterprises Educational Corporation, Merchandise Mart Plaza, Chicago, Illinois 60654.

Films, Inc., 1150 Wilmette Avenue, Wilmette, Illinois 60091.

Flip 'n' Spell, Box 492, East Lansing, Michigan 48823.

Follett Publishing Company, 1010 West Washington Boulevard, Chicago, Illinois 60607.

Ginn and Company, Statler Boulevard, Boston, Massachusetts 02117.

Globe Publishing Company, New York, New York 10010.

Harper and Row, Inc., Elmsford, New York.

Harcourt, Brace and World, Inc., 757 3rd Avenue, New York, New York 10017.

D. C. Heath and Company, 285 Columbus Avenue, Boston, Massachusetts 02116.

Highlights for Children, 2300 West 5th Avenue, Columbus, Ohio 43216.

Holt, Rinehart and Winston, Inc., 383 Madison Avenue, New York, New York 10017.

Houghton Mifflin Company, 53 West 43rd Street, New York, New York 10036.

Hunter College, City College of New York, 695 Park Avenue, New York, New York 10021.

Indicks, Arlington, Virginia.

Indiana University, Bloomington, Indiana 47405.

Initial Testing Alphabet Publications, Inc., 20 East 46th Street, New York, New York.

Laidlaw Brothers, 36 Chatham Road, Summit, New Jersey 07901.

Lantern, (Published by Pocket Books Inc.), 1 West 39th Street, New York, New York.

J. B. Lippincott Company, East Washington Square, Philadelphia, Pennsylvania.

Little, Brown and Company, Boston, Massachusetts.

Lyons and Carnahan, 407 East 25th Street, Chicago, Illinois 60616.

3M Corporation, 2501 Hudson Road, St. Paul, Minnesota 55119.

Macmillan Company, 60 5th Avenue, New York, New York 10011.

McGraw-Hill Book Company, 330 West 42nd Street, New York, New York 10036.

Meredith Publishing Company, 407 East 27th Street, Chicago, Illinois 60616.

Charles E. Merrill Books, Inc., 1300 Alum Creek Drive, Columbus, Ohio 43216.

Merrill-Palmer Institute, North East Ferry Street, Detroit, Michigan, 48202.

Modern Sound Pictures, Inc., 1410 Howard Street, Omaha, Nebraska 68102.

Modern Talking Pictures, 1234 Spruce Street, Philadelphia, Pennsylvania.

National Conference of Christians and Jews, 43 West 57th Street, New York, New York.

National Council of Teachers of English, 508 South 6th Street, Champaign, Illinois 61822.

National Council for the Social Studies, 1201 16th Street, N.W., Washington, D.C.

National Education Association, 1201 16th Street, N.W., Washington, D.C.

National Film Board of Canada, 680 5th Avenue, New York, New York 10019.

National Science Teachers Association, 1201 16th Street, N.W., Washington, D.C.

New American Library, 1301 Avenue of the Americas, New York, New York.

A. J. Nystrom and Company, 3333 Elston Avenue, Chicago, Illinois 60618.

Open Court Publishing Company, Box 399, LaSalle, Illinois 61301.

F. A. Owen Publishing Company, Instructor Park, Danville, New York 14437.

Pocket Books, Inc., 630 Fifth Avenue, New York, New York 10020.

Popular Library, 355 Lexington Avenue, New York, New York.

Portal Press, Inc., 605 Third Ave., New York, New York 10016.

Prentice-Hall, Inc., Englewood Cliffs, New Jersey 07632.

Princeton University Press, Princeton, New Jersey 08540.

Rand-McNally and Company, Box 7600, Chicago, Illinois 60680.

Reader's Digest Services, Inc., Pleasantville, New York 10570.

Regents Publishing Company, Inc., 200 Park Avenue South, New York, New York 10003.

Scarecrow Press, Inc., 257 Park Avenue South, New York, New York 10003.

Scholastic Magazines and Book Services, 902 Sylvan Avenue, Englewood Cliffs, New Jersey 07632.

Science Research Associates, Inc., 259 East Erie Street, Chicago, Illinois 60611.

Scott, Foresman and Company, 19-00 Pollitt Drive, Fair Lawn, New Jersey 07401.

Shorewood Reproductions, Inc., 724 Fifth Avenue, New York, New York 10019.

Silver Burdette Company, Morristown, New Jersey 07960.

Simon and Schuster, Inc., 630 Fifth Avenue, New York 10020.

Smithsonian Institution, Washington, D.C. 20560.

Teachers College Press, Teachers College, Columbia University, New York, New York.

University of Colorado, Bureau of Audio-Visual Instruction, Stadium Building Boulder, Colorado 80304.

Van Valkenburgh, Nooger and Neville, Inc., 15 Maiden Lane, New York, New York 10038.

Walker and Company, 720 Fifth Avenue, New York, New York 10019.

Washington Square Press, Inc., 630 Fifth Avenue, New York, New York 10020.

Western Publishing Educational Services, 1220 Mound Avenue, Racine, Wisconsin.

John Wiley and Sons, Inc., 605 Third Avenue, New York, New York 10016.

Xerox Corporation, The Widener Building, 1339 Chestnut Street, Philadelphia, Pennsylvania 19107.